A
SHORT HISTORY OF
GERMANY
1815–1945

A
SHORT HISTORY OF
GERMANY
1815–1945

BY

E. J. PASSANT

Sometime Fellow of Sidney Sussex College, Cambridge

ECONOMIC SECTIONS BY

W. O. HENDERSON

AND WITH CONTRIBUTIONS BY

C. J. CHILD AND D. C. WATT

CAMBRIDGE UNIVERSITY PRESS

CAMBRIDGE

LONDON   NEW YORK   NEW ROCHELLE

MELBOURNE   SYDNEY

Published by the Press Syndicate of the University of Cambridge
The Pitt Building, Trumpington Street, Cambridge CB2 1RP
32 East 57th Street, New York, NY 10022 USA
296 Beaconsfield Parade, Middle Park, Melbourne 3206, Australia

ISBN 0 521 05915 1 hard covers
ISBN 0 521 09173 x paperback

First edition 1959
Reprinted 1960
First paperback edition 1962
Reprinted 1966 1969 1971 1976 1977 1978 1979 1982

Printed in Great Britain at the
University Press, Cambridge

PREFACE

THE main substance of this book was prepared during the Second World War in the series of Geographical Handbooks, produced by the Naval Intelligence Division of the Admiralty, whose purpose was 'to supply...material for the discussion of naval, military and political problems, as distinct from the examination of the problems themselves'. The works in this series were originally classified as Restricted but this classification has been removed, and the present book is issued with the consent of the Admiralty and of H.M. Stationery Office.

The material here presented has been revised in the light shed by many of the new works upon German history which have appeared since the end of the war and of the *Documents on German Foreign Policy, 1918–1945* still in process of publication by H.M. Stationery Office. Reference to the authorities used will be found in the bibliographical note at the end of the book, as well as in footnotes to the text.

It is hoped that a succinct account of German history in the century and a quarter since 1815 may prove of value to the general reader as well as to university students and to the higher forms of schools. In the interests of brevity no attempt has been made to deal with the cultural and artistic developments which took place during the period.

The introduction was written by my friend and former colleague in the Foreign Office Research Department, Mr Clifton J. Child, to whom I am also much indebted for his generous and expert assistance in the work of revision both of the text and of the bibliographies. In order to complete the story of the National-Socialist phase of German history a chapter on the war period (1939–45) by Mr Donald Watt, Lecturer in Modern History at the London School of Economics, has been added to the material printed in the Naval Handbook. The economic sections of chapters I and II were published in the original Handbook and were written by Mr W. O. Henderson, now of the University of Manchester.

E. J. P.

CONTENTS

LIST OF MAPS

INTRODUCTION

THE ANARCHY OF THE HOLY ROMAN EMPIRE

UNTIL the nineteenth century the Germans made less progress towards national unity than the other peoples of Western Europe. The Reformation, which in England ultimately helped to knit the nation more closely together, tore Germany violently asunder. The Peace of Augsburg (1555), which ended the first phase of the religious wars, perpetuated the division by allowing each ruler to decide whether Catholicism or Lutheranism was to prevail in his dominions. The Peace of Westphalia (1648), which concluded the second phase—the Thirty Years War— nearly a century later, furthered the process of disintegration by weakening the only surviving symbol of unity—the Holy Roman Empire. It undermined the Imperial authority by recognizing the sovereignty of the member states, which were now permitted to conclude treaties with foreign Powers, and it accepted the territorial fragmentation of the Empire which had been going on since the Middle Ages. In the century and a half which followed the peace settlement Germany remained a mosaic of more than 1800 political entities, ranging in size and influence from the seventy-seven major secular principalities down to the fifty-one Imperial cities, forty-five Imperial villages and 1475 territories ruled by Imperial knights.

The Empire, though still the only constitutional bond between the principalities, was now to prove an obstacle to unity. Its very debility invited self-aggrandisement on the part of the princes. Yet, weak as it was, it was morally obliged to try to protect its smaller members—i.e. the Imperial knights and cities, the last repositories of a true *Reichspatriotismus*—and, in so doing, it discouraged consolidation by the strong at the expense of the weak. But neither the strong nor the weak could look to the Empire—a 'monstrosity', as Samuel von Pufendorf, the seventeenth century jurist and historiographer, called it—for leadership. The Hapsburgs—who, except for three years during the reign of Maria Theresa, wore the Imperial Crown continuously from 1438 to 1806—were now more concerned with their own Austrian domains than with the broader interests of the Empire: their example could therefore but encourage the particularist tendencies of the smaller German courts. Moreover, the Hapsburgs were Catholics, and this, with the presence of a Catholic majority in the Imperial Diet at Regensburg, made the Empire, in Prussian and Hanoverian eyes, at best a device for maintaining the hegemony of the Catholic South at the expense of the Protestant North, and at worst a threat to the religious freedom which they had won with the Reformation.

THE CULTURAL REVIVAL OF THE
EIGHTEENTH CENTURY

The anarchy of the declining Empire and the 'Sultanism' (as Fichte called it) of the German princes led the intellectuals in general to regard politics, and even political writing based upon 'mere actualities', as something distasteful, and caused many, under the impact first of Voltaire and later of the French Revolution, to turn to cosmopolitanism. Nevertheless, much as it might ignore or even repudiate all forms of national feeling, the great literary and intellectual revival of the 'Enlightenment' (*Aufklärung*) and of the ensuing *Sturm und Drang* and Romantic periods, which, taken together, roughly span the years of Goethe's lifetime (1749–1832), contributed decisively to the creation of a German *Kulturnation*, which, as Friedrich Meinecke has pointed out,[1] was an important step in the evolution of the modern national state. The *Sturm und Drang* itself (extending approximately from the appearance of Goethe's *Götz von Berlichingen* in 1773 to that of Schiller's *Die Räuber* in 1781) gave Germany her first national theatre—although some were not disposed to recognize it as such. Indeed, those who did most to exalt the German name in Europe, and thereby to arouse a national pride in the German cultural achievement which later influenced both the political Romantics in the struggle against Napoleon and the nineteenth century liberals who sought to give the

[1] Friedrich Meinecke, *Weltburgertum und Nationalstaat*, pp. 23 ff.

2

country a political organization worthy of its literary heritage, were often the least ready to acknowledge the patriotic motive. Above all, this was true of Lessing, who, having advanced his country to a position of honour in literary criticism, dismissed 'love of Fatherland' as a 'heroic failing' of which he was glad to be free; but it could also be said of Kant who, having placed Germany in the front rank of European thought, devoted his best political writing to the advocacy of an international order transcending national bounds.

THE RISE OF PRUSSIA

If political nationalism as a later age came to know it had yet to be born in eighteenth-century Germany, the struggle for pre-eminence amongst the German states had already begun. To be sure, there were by now only two Powers—Austria and Prussia —capable of playing a decisive role in German affairs. The ambition which (in his own words) whispered to Frederick the Great's listening ear in 1740 locked them in deadly conflict throughout the middle years of the century. The prize which beckoned was not, it is true, the right to claim national leadership so much as the opportunity to acquire more territory. But the strength which Prussia derived from the development of her military resources (she had few others) for territorial aggrandisement was to give her an advantage in the later struggle for political pre-eminence.

Prussia owed the position which she attained in the eighteenth century mainly to two rulers of exceptional ability: the Elector Frederick William (1640–88), known to his contemporaries and to posterity as the Great Elector, and her third king of the Hohenzollern line, Frederick the Great (1740–86). The Great Elector rescued Brandenburg from the debility and ignominy into which it had fallen during the Thirty Years War, making it, by the time of his death, the strongest Protestant state within the Empire. True to the tolerant traditions of his House, he strove, with ultimate success, to secure for the Calvinists the political and religious privileges which the Peace of Augsburg

3

(1555) had given to the Lutherans. As a warrior his outstanding achievement was to free East Prussia—which lay outside the Empire, and where his successor crowned himself king in 1701—from Polish suzerainty. As an administrator he gave his loosely-knit domains a centralized bureaucracy; he rebuilt the city of Berlin, making it a real capital and enabling it, during the later period of his life, to quadruple its population. He encouraged agriculture and industry and stimulated commerce. Above all, he gave Prussia a permanent, well-drilled army, competently administered by a war machine working with the same precision as the civil administration.

In the period between the death of the Great Elector and the accession of Frederick the Great Prussia continued to make military and administrative progress. Frederick I (1688–1713) gave her a crown as a stronger bond between her scattered provinces. His son, the competent, if somewhat boorish and austere, Frederick William I (1713–1740), bequeathed her a centralized financial system and internal administration, a code of civil and administrative law, a generally sound economy in which new industries flourished, and a standing army of about 90,000 based upon a form of conscription in which every military district was required to furnish a quota of men in proportion to its population.

In the civil administration Frederick the Great accepted the framework of government which he inherited from his father, making only the changes which time and the large accessions of territory of his reign (Silesia, 1742; East Friesland, 1744; West Prussia and Ermeland, 1772) necessitated. His great passion was the army, which he raised to a permanent force of 150,000 men and which, absorbing as it did 8·5 out of a revenue of 11 million thalers, inspired Mirabeau's observation that Prussia was not a country which had an army, but an army which had a country. But the achievement of Frederick, the ablest of the Hohenzollerns and the most successful exponent of a *Realpolitik* before Bismarck, was to use his superb military machine to raise Prussia—a country with no natural frontiers—to the rank of a first-rate European power. Unlike his father and grandfather, who had remained loyal to the House of Austria, he was ready to exploit any Hapsburg difficulty—such as the absence of a male heir to inherit the Imperial Crown in 1740—to extend Prussia's influence and increase her dominions. He could, if it suited him, collaborate with the Court of Vienna, as he did in the first partition of Poland (1772). But, as the Hapsburgs could never forgive the rape of Silesia, the collaboration never went very deep, and it did little, in fact, to shorten the long shadow of Austro-Prussian rivalry which his reign as a whole helped to cast over German history for the next hundred years. The experiment of the League of Princes (*Fürstenbund*) with which he became preoccupied in the last months of his life (July 1785–August 1786) suggests that, had he lived a little longer, he might have challenged the Hapsburgs not only for immediate military supremacy, but for the permanent political leadership of Germany also.

THE COLLAPSE OF THE OLD ORDER IN GERMANY

Frederick had not been dead a decade when the collapse of the old order in France—hailed with great rejoicing by writers and thinkers in Germany—produced its first sweeping changes to the east of the Rhine, as well as to the west. Indeed, it was too much to expect that the political mosaic of the Holy Roman Empire would be able to survive the military onslaughts to which the intervention of the German princes in the Revolutionary War exposed it.

The organic changes which the French Revolution and the advent of Napoleon produced in Germany may be briefly summarized. The War of the First Coalition, which Prussia entered in 1792 and from which she withdrew by the separate and cynical peace of Basle in 1795, brought the French into possession of Prussian territories (Mörs, Cleves and Upper Guelders) west of the Rhine, with a promise of compensation for their former owner east of the river. Two years later, with the conclusion of peace between France and Austria at Campo Formio, it led to the surrender by the Hapsburgs of their Rhenish possessions, along with the Austrian Netherlands and Milan (for which, in return, they received Venetia, Istria and Dalmatia), and to their concurrence in the annexation by France of all German territory west of the Rhine. The war of the Second Coalition, leading to the defeat of Austria at Marengo and Hohenlinden (1800) and her acceptance of the treaty of Lunéville (1801), brought in its wake the sweeping changes of the *Reichsdeputationshauptschluss*—sometimes referred to as the 'Act of Mediatization'—of February 1803, by which the German Diet, at the dictation of Napoleon, secularized the ecclesiastical principalities and 'mediatized' the Imperial cities, suppressing in all some 112 of the smaller entities in favour of the larger states like Bavaria, Baden and Württemberg. The War of the Third Coalition (organized by Pitt in 1805) led, after the defeat of Austria at Austerlitz in December 1805, to the separation of the west German states from the Holy Roman Empire, to the constitution under French tutelage of the Confederation of the Rhine (17 July 1806), which brought the number of the German states down to forty, and to the long-overdue demise of the Holy Roman Empire itself three weeks later.[1] Finally, the defeat of Prussia at Jena on 14 October 1806, followed by the crushing Treaty of Tilsit (July 1807), reduced the Hohenzollern possessions to about half their previous size by annexing to the new Kingdom of Westphalia the Prussian territories to the west of the Elbe and by giving to the new Grand Duchy of Warsaw all that Prussia had acquired by the second and third partitions of Poland of 1793 and 1795.

THE REAWAKENING OF PRUSSIA, 1807–14

Her prostration by Napoleon proved, in the event, to be Prussia's opportunity. The limitation of her army to 42,000 men gave Scharnhorst and Gneisenau their chance to improve its weapons and training, to shed its old and incompetent officers, and to create a military reserve by calling the able-bodied male popu-

[1] It should be noted that, when he resigned the imperial dignity as Emperor of the former Empire, Francis II retained the title of Emperor of Austria.

lation to the colours for short periods of service. The partial collapse of the old administrative system—and it was only partial, for the recovery of the next few years was to prove the resilience of the system which the Great Elector had created and which his successors had perfected—made imperative the reforms which, after August 1807, Stein undertook as First Minister. These, in turn, greatly strengthened the Prussian fabric in those places where Frederick's wars had left it threadbare. The Emancipating Edict of 9 October 1807, by abolishing serfdom in principle, prepared the way for social reconstruction, and the Municipal Act which followed laid the foundations of a modern system of local government.

The years 1806–15 witnessed the beginnings of a genuine popular awakening, and the reforms instituted by Stein and his fellow-ministers, unlike the changes brought about by the Great Elector and Frederick, enjoyed the support of a movement which embraced the intellectuals and the middle class, even if it did not reach down to the peasants and artisans and failed to find favour with some of the nobility whose privileges it threatened. Stein himself, in fact, wrote: 'We started from the fundamental idea of raising a moral, religious, patriotic spirit in the nation.' In this he received the assistance of a remarkable coterie of non-Prussian scholars, who had been drawn to Berlin by the Hohenzollern policy of toleration—among them the philosopher, Johann Gottlieb Fichte, who in 1799 had sought refuge in Prussia when the Weimar authorities accused him of atheism. Between 13 December 1807 and 20 March 1808 Fichte delivered his famous *Reden an die deutsche Nation* (Addresses to the German Nation), in which, speaking 'to Germans only, and of Germans only', he pointed to a 'system of national education' as the way out of Prussia's difficulties. His ideas profoundly influenced the Minister of Instruction, Wilhelm von Humboldt, the author of many enlightened reforms, and he himself was privileged to take part in the founding of the National University of Berlin in 1809–10.

Thanks, in part at least, to the ferment among the intellectuals, the war of liberation, which the disastrous French retreat from

Moscow in 1812 made possible, became the nearest thing to a 'people's war' (*Volkskrieg*) which Germany had so far witnessed —so much so, in fact, that Hitler tried in vain to recapture its spirit in 1944–5. Scharnhorst's Landwehr Law took as its premise the idea of a nation in arms, and the King's appeal to his people (*Aufruf an mein Volk*) of 17 March 1813 demanded the sacrifices which a popular war necessitated. In such a war Prussia, truncated though she was, stood out as the natural leader. Although Frederick William III himself vacillated—in February 1812 he actually signed a treaty with Napoleon granting the Grande Armée a passage through his dominions—Stein, summoned to the court of the Tsar from exile, and Yorck, the commander of the Prussian auxiliaries accompanying the French armies to Moscow, forced his hand. On 28 February 1813 the treaty of Kalisch brought Prussia into the war. Six months later Austria joined the allies. Finally, the defeat of Napoleon at Leipzig in October left his protégés, the minor German states, ready to turn against him, and before the end of the year the allies had crossed the Rhine into France. By March 1814 they had entered Paris itself, and within a fortnight Napoleon had abdicated (11th April). Napoleon's attempt at recovery in March 1815 was defeated at the battle of Waterloo (18 June 1815).

THE SETTLEMENT OF 1814–15

The Congress of Vienna made no attempt to restore the chaotic territorial conditions that had existed in the 18th century, and the result of its work was to leave only thirty-nine states in Germany. But the chief importance of the settlement was its effect upon Austria and Prussia, the two rivals for the leadership of Germany as a whole.

Austria secured for her Emperor the permanent Presidency of the new German Confederation, formed to replace the old Holy Roman Empire. But the Emperor of Austria, stripped of the semi-mystical prestige of the Holy Roman Empire, was too clearly seen to be concerned with maintaining the integrity of his mainly non-German possessions to be accepted easily as the defender of 'Deutschtum'. Though, in the Vienna settlement, he recovered his Italian possessions and added Lombardy to them in return for giving up all claim to the southern Netherlands, the Emperor of Austria, with his small German base in the Ostmark, ruled over more Czechs, Hungarians, Poles, Serbs, Croats and Italians than over Germans and was, by the nature of his cosmopolitan Empire, ill-suited to take the lead of a reviving German nationalism.

Whilst Austria emerged from the Vienna settlement less rather than more German in character, her rival Prussia strengthened her claims to German leadership by her new acquisitions. The loss of the more easterly parts of her Polish territories to Russia was far more than compensated for by securing for herself the purely German Rhineland and Westphalia, rich in mineral resources as well as important for their control of the Rhine and for the culture and intelligence of their people. Prussia's western German territories were, indeed, still separated from each other, but this merely gave her the more reason to seek their integral union with the main block of Prussia itself. In the age of nationalism into which Europe was about to plunge, the German character of Prussia as a whole gave her a great advantage over her Austrian ally in the struggle for leadership in Germany. To this advantage the Prussian state could add the exceptional energy and industry of its people, the mineral wealth of the Ruhr soon to be developed, a civil service both efficient and incorrupt, and an army which had proved its worth under Frederick the Great. In the course of the nineteenth century these assets were to prove decisive in Prussia's bid for leadership of the German nation.

CHAPTER I

AUSTRIAN DOMINANCE AND DEFEAT: CREATION OF THE GERMAN EMPIRE, 1815–1871

1. GERMANY IN 1815

POLITICAL DISUNITY AND SOCIAL CONSERVATISM

IN 1815, notwithstanding the national revival of the past eight years, the term 'Germany', like the word 'Italy', was still hardly more than a 'geographical expression'. The great reduction effected by Napoleon in the number of petty states still left the German people parcelled out amongst thirty-nine competing sovereignties. Moreover, the territorial princes were only the more anxious to preserve the independence of their states because of the reduction in their number. Those princes who, like the rulers of Bavaria, Württemberg and Baden, had received accessions of territory or dignity during the Napoleonic period, when the rulers of Bavaria and Württemberg became kings, were determined to preserve and, if possible, extend their advantages; those who returned from exile, or had lost territory (Saxony), were equally determined to reassert their old rights and to preserve every privilege which remained to them.

The two German Great Powers, Austria and Prussia, were rivals both inside and outside the German lands, and neither would subordinate itself to the leadership of the other in the interests of German national unity. To the emperor of Austria the primacy of Austria in German affairs was axiomatic in view of the long centuries in which the Hapsburg House had ruled as Holy Roman Emperors. Prussia was an upstart state, which had made its fortune at the expense of its neighbours, more especially of Austria herself by Frederick the Great's rape of Silesia. To the Prussian kings and their advisers the subordination of Prussia to Austria was equally unthinkable, for it would undo the patient work and hard-won gains of all the Prussian rulers since the

Great Elector. The cause of German nationalism would move neither ruler to sacrifices at the expense of Austrian or of Prussian power.

Both the German Great Powers, too, were not merely German and, in the case of Austria, not even mainly German (Map 1).

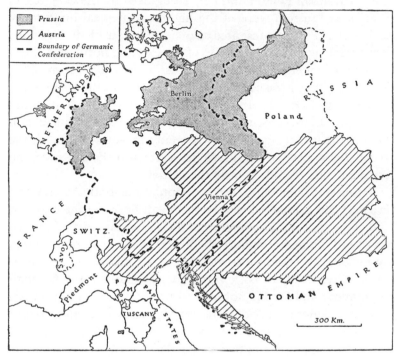

Map 1. Austria and Prussia in 1815

Austria had become steadily more multi-national and, after 1815, the non-German nationalities—Magyar and Czech, Slovak and Pole, Serb, Slovene and Italian—outnumbered the Germans of the old Ostmark. To a state so composed the doctrine of nationality, in the political sense of a right to national self-government, meant utter dissolution. By her very make-up Austria must oppose nationalism at all costs, and German nationalism as much as any other. Metternich described German unity as 'an infamous object' at which to aim.

To Prussia also the doctrine of nationalism presented grave difficulty. It is true that, in 1815, the new territories acquired by Prussia were mainly German in character—Lower Saxony, Swedish Pomerania, the important territories east and west of the Rhine. But, in the east, the territories incorporated since the partitions of Poland and now recognized by the Congress of Vienna as Prussian were of the highest strategical importance to Prussia. They represented the culmination of the age-long Prussian struggle with the Slavs of the east and north-east. They joined the 'colonial' land of East Prussia to the main body of the monarchy, they gave command of the mouth of the Vistula and of the port of Danzig, and they were inhabited predominantly by Poles. If to recognize the doctrine of nationality and to assume the leadership of it in Germany meant even the risk of losing these newly-won lands to a revived Polish state, no Prussian ruler would espouse the cause.

Because of their non-German populations both Austria and Prussia were compelled to rely on the authority of the dynasty, and of the state, as the principle of their internal unity. Personal loyalty to the monarch and obedience to the law administered by his officials could be demanded of all subjects of whatever nationality. And, in both states, it was easy for the German population, and for the nobles and upper classes in particular, who provided the army officers and higher civil servants, to give such loyalty. For, in Prussia's eastern provinces, the system made the Prussians masters of the Poles and, throughout the Austrian Empire, it placed the German-Austrians in a position of advantage over the non-German national groups.

The national differences within the two German Great Powers also made their governments hostile to any representative democratic system, which would provide the non-German populations with the means of expressing and furthering their national aims. But even the rulers of the wholly German states, such as Bavaria, Saxony or Mecklenburg, were equally opposed to the liberal-national idea, both because its realization would involve the reduction of their authority and power, even if it did not lead to their elimination, and because, as in Austria and Prussia also, the principle of monarchical authority was based upon and sustained by a deeply conservative social order. Ever since 1648 the courts of the multitudinous German princes had formed the centres of social, as of political life. Nobility of birth meant even more, and was more rigidly insisted on, as Mme de Staël noted, in the German lands than in pre-revolutionary France and far more than in England. The nobles regarded intermarriage with commoners as *mésalliance* and clung to the privileges they had inherited from the past. Their social and political importance was challenged before 1815 by the reforms of Stein and Hardenberg, by the centralizing tendencies of the state, particularly in Prussia, and by the growth of the class of higher officials needed for its service, though many of these were also nobles. But the officer class in the armed forces remained almost wholly noble; they still sought to fill the chief places in their prince's councils; and their social pre-eminence was admitted by the classes below them.

No group, indeed, played a more important part in nineteenth-century Germany than the Prussian Junkers, the masters of the once Slav estates to the east of the Elbe, who provided the backbone of the Prussian civil service as well as of the officer corps.[1] They were Prussian, as opposed to German nationalists, since they believed that the existing Prussian state, monarchical and undemocratic, would best serve their agrarian interests, and they hated Stein as much for his belief in German unity as for his agrarian reforms. It was their 'Junkerparlament' of 1848 which played an important part in suppressing the revolution of that year in Prussia (see p. 32), and at that time Bismarck, who boasted 'I am a Junker and want to profit by it', enjoyed their confidence. But the dominance of personal interest in their political behaviour is shown by the fact that, whilst they were ready to support state ownership of the railways since this was

[1] Cf. A. J. P. Taylor, *The Course of German History* (London, Hamish Hamilton, 1945) pp. 28–30, 40–2, 99–102, 164–6, 168–70; also Erich Eyck, *Bismarck and the German Empire* (London, Allen and Unwin, 1950), pp. 11–13. The term 'Junker', as 'Jungherr', was originally applied to the sons of the trans-Elbian nobility, and it followed them when they became cadets ('Fahnenjunker') in the army. In the nineteenth century the liberals identified it with landed conservatism ('Junkertum') in general.

the only way to develop them in the eastern provinces, they resisted Bismarck bitterly over the liberalization of the *Kreisordnung* passed in 1872 and not even loyalty to the Crown could prevent them breaking with Wilhelm II over his 'new course' (see pp. 118–20).

The middle class was beginning to develop both in numbers and in wealth. But as yet it was, in the main, bound by interest and sentiment alike to the existing order and found its centre in the court. The town population had become sharply stratified, and, even in the Free Imperial Cities, power in local government had passed into the hands of wealthy, hereditary oligarchies. In Prussia and many of the smaller states the rights of local self-government won in earlier times had been replaced in fact, if not in form, by the power of the ruler; and they were only partially restored by the Municipal Act of 1808. The degree of dependence of the population of a capital city on the court can be illustrated by an analysis of the population of Berlin in 1785.[1] Out of a total population of 141,000, well over a third (57,000) depended directly on the court, and there were only 10,000 citizens with full rights. Multiply this situation by the number of courts in Germany and it will be seen how strong a vested interest in their own preservation had been created by the princes of Germany.

In the countryside, too, where three-quarters of the German population still lived in 1815, society was, over wide areas, in the feudal stage. The Prussian decree of 1807 for the emancipation of the peasantry lost much of its force by later 'interpretative' ordinances, and what freedom the peasants obtained they had, quite literally, to buy at heavy cost to themselves. In Austria and Bavaria serfdom was not 'abolished' till 1848, and even then the process of emancipation was far from complete. Seignorial jurisdiction lasted on in the eastern provinces of Prussia until after 1918, and, although there was greater freedom amongst the peasantry of the Rhineland, the society of the German countryside was, on the whole, still more static and

---

[1] Cf. W. H. Bruford, *Germany in the Eighteenth Century* (Cambridge, 1935), p. 98.

stratified than that of the towns. In it, too, the influence of the courts and the nobility was predominant.

Thus the German movement of ideas towards nationalism and liberalism, which had appeared during the War of Liberation in Prussia, lost much of its impetus once the foreign invader had been expelled. To the main body of the nobility and even to many of the middle class, nationalism, with its threat to the local court and to the traditional ordering of society and with its levelling implications as deriving from the French Revolution, became as repugnant as to the sovereign prince himself. There were, in 1815, it may be said, many Austrians, Prussians, Bavarians and so on. But there were relatively few Germans, outside the universities and the literary salons, willing to subordinate their local loyalties to the ideal of national unity. And if there were few nationally-minded Germans there were still fewer democrats. The existing order had been largely created by, and revolved round, the sovereign prince. Lutheranism and Catholicism alike preached the duty of submission to his authority. The ravages of the Napoleonic wars had stirred a fairly widespread demand for a strong and united nation capable of resisting any future invader. But in 1815, and for long years after, the majority of Germans clung to the existing authorities to give them peace and security, and trusted to the wisdom of their princes to organize and harmonize the interests of the individual states so as to provide for the defence both of the Germany which was vague to them, and of their 'narrower fatherlands', which they knew and loved.

THE GERMAN CONFEDERATION

It is not surprising, therefore, that the organization constructed for 'Germany' in 1815 made little provision for united national action. Various drafts were discussed in Vienna, and the influence of Hardenberg, the Prussian Foreign Minister, was at the outset directed towards securing a constitution which would satisfy some at least of the aspirations of German nationalism, and even of German liberalism. But the influence of Metternich was too strong for him. The Federal Act of 1815 did, indeed, pledge the German rulers to grant their subjects constitutions but, since the time limit of a year included in the original draft was cut out during the discussions, the final Act gave the German people what Görres rightly described as no more than 'an unlimited right of expectation'.

For the rest, the constitution created by the Federal Act was only too reminiscent of that of the old Empire. Austria was awarded the permanent Presidency of the new Confederation; the only organ of government was a Federal Diet in permanent session at Frankfurt-am-Main. The Diet had an inner Council (*Engerer Rat*) of seventeen delegates, with one representative for each of the eleven major states and the other six votes apportioned to combinations of the remainder, and a general assembly or *plenum* of sixty-nine members in which every state had at least one vote, whilst the larger states received four, three or two votes each. In the inner Council a majority vote sufficed, but in the *plenum* a two-thirds majority was necessary and even this was stated in the Federal Act to be insufficient when 'fundamental laws, organic institutions, individual rights or religious affairs' were in question. Since each representative was bound by the instructions of his government it is small wonder that the

Notes to Maps 2 and 3

Based on a contemporary map, *The German Confederated States* (London, 1839). The lower map is an enlargement of the area within the square on the upper map; the two illustrate the territorial complexity in Germany during this period. The states are numbered as follows: (1) Austrian Empire; (2) Kingdom of Prussia; (3) Kingdom of Bavaria; (4) Kingdom of Saxony; (5) Kingdom of Hanover; (6) Kingdom of Württemberg; (7) Grand Duchy of Baden; (8) Electorate of Hesse-Cassel; (9) Grand Duchy of Hesse-Darmstadt; (10) Duchies of Holstein and Lauenburg (to Kingdom of Denmark); (11) Grand Duchy of Luxembourg (to Kingdom of the Netherlands); (12) Duchy of Brunswick; (13) Grand Duchy of Mecklenburg (Schwerin and Strelitz); (14) Duchy and Principality of Nassau, Usingen and Nassau-Weilburg; (15) Grand Duchy of Saxe-Weimar; (16) Duchy of Saxe-Gotha; (17) Duchy of Saxe-Coburg; (18) Duchy of Saxe-Meinungen; (19) Duchy of Saxe-Hildburghausen; (20) Grand Duchy of Oldenburg; (21) Principalities of Anhalt (Dessau, Bernburg, and Kothen); (22) Principality of Schwarzburg; (23) Principality of Hohenzollern; (24) Principality of Lichtenstein; (25) Principality of Waldeck; (26) Principality of Reuss; (27) Principality of Lippe (Schaumburg and Detmold); (28) Principality of Hesse-Homburg; (29) Principality of Layen; the Free Towns of Bremen (30), Frankfurt-am-Main (31), Hamburg (32), and Lübeck (33).

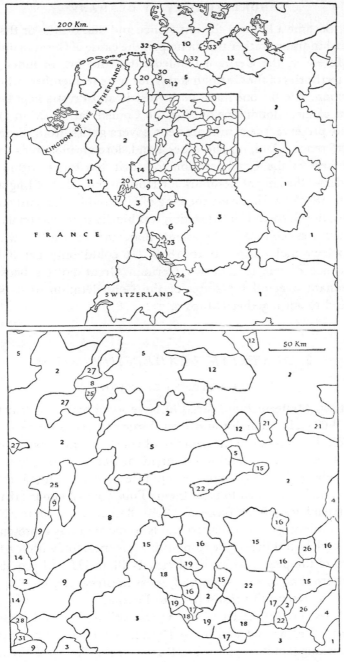

Maps 2, 3. The lesser German states, 1815 (for notes see opposite)

Diet became a byword for impotence and dilatoriness or that it was a hindrance rather than a help to the cause of German unity.

Moreover, the German Confederation neither included all the territories of the German states nor were its members wholly German. On the one hand both Austria and Prussia kept large parts of their dominions outside the Confederation (Map 1) so as to preserve their independent sovereignties from Federal interference. And, on the other hand, foreign monarchs were members of the Confederation for their territories within its borders—the king of Denmark for Holstein, the king of England (until 1837) for Hanover, the king of Holland for Luxembourg. Thus, the German Confederation was hardly more national and hardly less politically impotent than the institution which Napoleon had destroyed in 1806. It could only act if the influence of one of the two German Great Powers became dominant over all the states of the Confederation or if both agreed to act together (Maps 2, 3).

2. AUSTRIAN LEADERSHIP, 1815-58

THE FIRST REACTION

In 1815 Metternich appeared to have some reason to fear the possibility of nationalist and liberal movements in the German states. In addition to the promise of constitutional government contained in the Federal Act, individual German rulers had not only given their own subjects separate promises but, in some cases, had proceeded to fulfil them. Thus Saxe-Weimar (1816), Württemberg (1819), Bavaria (1818), Baden (1818) all received constitutions granting limited rights to more or less representative bodies, but in no case responsible government, within a few years of the peace, whilst Frederick William III had promised on more than one occasion and, most impressively, in 1814, to grant representative institutions to Prussia.

Moreover, Alexander of Russia was still under the influence of liberal ideas and had himself granted a constitution to the Polish kingdom incorporated in Russia by the Treaty of Vienna.

Since Russia was unquestionably the strongest military power on the continent in the years immediately after 1815, the attitude of the Czar was of the highest importance. The extremely limited provision for united action by all the German states made by the Federal Act aroused protests from such writers as Görres,[1] editor of the *Rheinische Merkur*, who published a work on *The Future German Constitution* in 1816, and the desire for greater national unity was felt ardently by some of the younger generation, who formed the student class at the universities. In 1815 some of the students of Jena founded an association of university students called the *Burschenschaft*, of which the aims were both patriotic and, at first, liberal. In 1817 the Wartburg Festival, held as a celebration of the tercentenary of the Reformation and of the victory over Napoleon at Leipzig (1813), led to the formation of the *Allgemeine Deutsche Burschenschaft* (General German Students Association). By breaking away from the older student associations based on local loyalties, and by seeking to organize a national movement, the students of the *Burschenschaft* gave sufficient offence to Metternich. But, at the Wartburg, they added to this by burning emblems of the reaction, amongst others a book on German history by Kotzebue,[2] who had at various times been in Russian employ. When, in 1819, this was followed by the murder of Kotzebue by a member of the *Burschenschaft*, Karl Sand, Metternich was given the opportunity for which he had been waiting to organize reaction. Even Hardenberg exclaimed that a Prussian constitution was now out of the question, and Metternich hastened to take advantage of the situation.

By 1819 Alexander's liberalism had already begun to wane, and the murder of Kotzebue assisted his conversion to reaction. Metternich was able, therefore, to bring his great powers of

[1] Joseph von Görres (1776–1848), admirer of the French Revolution, founded *Der Rheinische Merkur* in 1814. He later became an ultramontane and was given the chair of history at Munich by King Ludwig of Bavaria.

[2] August Friedrich Ferdinand von Kotzebue (1761–1819), German dramatist, who returned to Germany as a Russian agent in 1817, after serving the Czar as a judge, director of the German theatre in St Petersburg and finally councillor of state in the Department of Foreign Affairs. In his *Literarisches Wochenblatt*, published at Weimar, he waged a campaign against the German liberals.

persuasion to bear on Frederick William III of Prussia without fear of counter-influence from Alexander. He found his task sufficiently easy. Frederick William already repented of his promise to his subjects, and was increasingly dominated not only by his own naturally repressive temperament, but by the influence of ultra-conservative feudalists at the Prussian court. In March 1818 the Prussian king had announced in a Cabinet Order that the time for further constitutional reform had not yet come. Now, after meeting Metternich at Teplitz in July 1819, he instructed his Chancellor Hardenberg to concert with the Austrian minister the necessary measures for preventing the spread of revolutionary doctrines and practices in Germany. Acting together at a conference held at Carlsbad (August 1819), under Metternich's leadership, the two Powers next secured the assent of the larger German states to a series of repressive decrees embodying their aims and, with the assistance of this wider circle of allies, they obtained the unanimous assent of the Federal Diet to the publication of these decrees under the authority of the Confederation.

The Carlsbad decrees sealed the ascendancy of Austria and of reaction in Germany for the next thirty years. Not until the 'year of Revolutions' (1848) was the influence of either seriously shaken, and, even though Metternich fell in 1848, a further period of reaction (1850–8) under Austrian leadership was still to follow. During those thirty years the states of Germany all became, if they had not been so before, police states. The press and education were rigidly controlled. Professors, however patriotic, who dared to demand national unity were ejected from their chairs. The *Burschenschaft* ceased to have serious political importance and soon became little more than a replica of the drinking and duelling clubs (*Korps*) which superseded the older *Landmannschaften* during the early nineteenth century. The hopes of national unity and popular representation in a central national assembly lingered on in a few thoughtful minds and revived again after 1840. But the very ease with which the Carlsbad decrees were accepted and enforced, even in the 'liberal' states of south Germany, shows how weak was the desire for liberty in German breasts, how strong the principle of monarchical authority.

By associating himself with the Emperor Francis and Metternich, Frederick William of Prussia made it clear to his subjects that he had no intention of introducing liberal institutions or parliamentary government into the Prussian monarchy. The Provincial Estates, at last summoned in 1823 mainly at the request of an 'old estates' party anxious to preserve ancient social privileges, were heavily weighted on the side of the nobility; the urban representatives were drawn only from urban landowners, and the peasantry was in a hopeless minority. These assemblies had no legislative power, though they could tender advice to the provincial governor and through him to the king, who was free to accept or reject at his own pleasure. But their main functions were strictly limited to local affairs and no central assembly for the whole of Prussia was called into being. For this the Prussian people had to wait till 1847. Not only was there no constitutional development worth the name, but, until Frederick William III's death in 1840, Prussia almost ceased to count as a Great Power, so subservient was her policy to that of Austria. The period of so-called Dualism in German affairs is more properly described as that of Austrian leadership

THE REVOLUTIONS OF 1830 AND THE SECOND REACTION

In 1830 revolutions broke out in France and Poland; there were also risings in Italy, in the Papal States and in Modena and Parma. In every case these movements were inspired by nationalism and liberalism working together.

These events had their influence in Germany. In Hesse-Cassel and Brunswick relatively liberal constitutions were obtained in 1831 and 1832, and the accession of William IV in England was followed in Hanover by the adoption of a very conservative constitution drafted by the historian Dahlmann.[1] But the rulers

---

[1] Friedrich Christoph Dahlmann (1785–1860), German historian and politician, was one of the instigators of the campaign against Denmark in the Elbe duchies (Schleswig-Holstein). In 1829 he was appointed to the chair of history at Göttingen, moving to Bonn in 1842. In 1849 he was one of the deputation which offered the hereditary Imperial Crown to Frederick William IV in Berlin.

of Hesse-Cassel and Brunswick were so scandalously selfish, corrupt and greedy that even Metternich and the German Diet could not decently disapprove of some restrictions being imposed on their power over their luckless subjects, whilst the developments in Hanover, still ruled by the king of England, were a natural corollary of the passage of the Reform Bill of 1832 in England.

Metternich's policy was unshaken, indeed it was reinforced, by the revolutions of 1830. In Italy Austrian troops intervened to restore the pope's control over the Papal States and to repress the movements in Modena and Parma. In the east, Prussia mobilized part of her army to patrol the Prussia-Russian frontier in Poland, rejected an appeal from the Polish insurgents for assistance, and interned the Polish troops which crossed into Prussian territory after defeat at Russian hands. Moreover, in 1833 Russia, Prussia and Austria signed the Treaty of Münchengrätz by which Russia and Austria guaranteed each other's Polish possessions. The danger of liberal-national revolution cemented the ties between the autocratic Powers and, until the year of revolutions (1848), all three Powers presented a united front against the spread of liberal ideas or institutions within their dominions.

Similarly, within the German Confederation, the events of 1830 and the succeeding years were used by Austria and Prussia to strengthen the machinery of repression. In 1831 the *Burschenschaft* revived their political activities and in 1832 held a Festival at Hambach in the Bavarian Palatinate. With the black-red-gold banner of the *Burschenschaft* flying—the flag which became the symbol of German liberal-national movements and was adopted by the Weimar Republic in 1919— a meeting was held at which speeches in favour of free institutions and international fraternity were delivered. Polish and French revolutionaries of 1830 took part. In itself the demonstration might appear to any strong government harmless enough, but it represented to Austria and Prussia the revolutionary spirit and both governments decided on further repressive action.

Metternich and Ancillon,[1] the Prussian Foreign Minister, with the support of their monarchs, drew up six Articles which greatly enlarged the control of the Federal Diet over the internal affairs of the German states and pledged their rulers to make no concessions to liberalism. The kings of Bavaria and Württemberg were induced to support the six Articles and they were passed by the Federal Diet at Frankfurt. In addition, other repressive measures were enacted which forbade public meetings and revolutionary badges, placed suspicious political characters under surveillance, renewed the edicts controlling the universities and the press, and assured help to sovereigns threatened with revolutionary movements. The Federal Diet, which in 1815 Metternich had feared as a possible instrument of German nationalism and liberalism under Prussian leadership, had by now, owing to the alliance of the rulers of Austria and Prussia, become the instrument by which these two Powers enforced their anti-national and anti-liberal policy upon the German nation. In doing so it lost its last claim to the respect or affection of all Germans who hoped for national unity and free institutions. So long as Prussia acted as Austria's faithful ally in the policy of repression, no way, except that of organized popular revolt, lay open for the realization of these aspirations.

For sixteen years more (1832–48) Metternich was able to keep his system in being, and on the surface the German states during the thirties appeared to be becoming less, rather than more, liberal. In Hesse-Cassel the new constitution was rendered ineffective by the Prince Regent and his much-hated minister, Hassenpflug.[2] In 1837 the accession of Queen Victoria in England brought her uncle, Ernest Augustus, duke of Cumberland, to the throne of Hanover, and he at once declared the constitution of 1833 null and void since he had been no party

---

[1] Johann Peter Friedrich Ancillon (1766–1837), former tutor to Frederick William IV (as Crown Prince), who became Metternich's henchman at the Prussian Court, where he exercised a strong conservative influence. In 1832 he succeeded Count Bernstorf as Prussian Minister for Foreign Affairs.

[2] Hans Daniel Ludwig Friedrich Hassenpflug (1794–1862) devoted the greater part of his career to the struggle against constitutionalism in his native Hesse. After the Federal 'intervention' in Hesse of 1848 he became Minister of Finance. He was related, by his first marriage, to the brothers Grimm.

to it. The historian Dahlmann and six of his colleagues of the University of Göttingen protested against this edict and were expelled from their professorships for doing so. In Bavaria, too, King Lewis passed over into the reactionary camp, and his minister, Abel,[1] enforced the policy of repression with severity. Only in Baden, Württemberg and Saxony did a certain limited liberalism maintain itself in the years 1830–40.

THE MOVEMENTS FOR NATIONAL UNITY, 1840–8

But from 1840 onwards a change set in. On 7 June of that year Frederick William III died and was succeeded by his erratic son, Frederick William IV, to whom the last German Kaiser bore so strong a resemblance. The death of the old king, out of respect for whom many demands had been suppressed, created an atmosphere of expectancy throughout Prussia. At last, it was thought, the Prussian government would take a line more liberal, more national, more independent of Austria. These hopes were raised still further by the new king's actions. Arndt, who both in prose and verse had proclaimed the need for national unity, was restored to his professorship at Bonn; Dahlmann was soon appointed to a chair there and the brothers Grimm, who had been expelled with him from Göttingen, were called to posts in Berlin. Boyen,[2] veteran of the War of Liberation, was reappointed Minister of War, an office which he had been compelled to give up at the time of the Carlsbad decrees. It was small wonder that the liberal-national forces in Prussia believed that a new era had begun.

At the same time German nationalism received a double stimulus. Difficulties with France led to threats in the French press and Chamber against the Rhineland and called forth, in

[1] Karl von Abel (1788–1859) became Bavarian Minister of the Interior in 1837 and pursued an ultramontane policy. In 1847 he was dismissed, with other ministers, for opposing the naturalization of the king's mistress, Lola Montez.

[2] Hermann von Boyen (1771–1848) had, as Director General of the War Department, helped to carry out Scharnhorst's military reforms, and was the founder of the Landwehr. Driven into retirement by the reaction in 1819, he served again as War Minister from 1841 to 1847 and was made a field-marshal shortly before his death.

reply, the two famous songs, of Becker ('Sie sollen ihn nicht haben, den freien deutschen Rhein') and of Schneckenburger ('Die Wacht am Rhein'). The crisis in relation to France soon passed, but the enthusiasm for national unity went on growing and soon received new impetus from the opening of the problem of the relationship of the duchies of Schleswig and Holstein to the Danish Crown.

The Schleswig-Holstein problem. In 1839 Christian VIII succeeded to the Danish throne, and it was known that a strong party in Denmark would press the new king to change the personal union of the two duchies with Denmark into complete unification within the Danish state. Holstein was a member of the German Confederation, though Schleswig was not. The population of Holstein was almost wholly and that of Schleswig was preponderantly German in speech, character and outlook, and there was a strong desire in the duchies both to insist on their indivisibility from each other and to extend the connection of Holstein with the German Confederation to Schleswig also. Both in the duchies themselves and throughout north Germany agitation against the plans of the Danes grew from 1839 onwards. The situation became critical only at the death of Christian VIII in January 1848 and must be discussed more fully later. But the sense of the impotence and sluggishness of the Federal Diet in dealing with the possible, and even probable, loss of two 'German' provinces to a foreign Power contributed largely to the spread of the movement for national unity between 1840 and 1848. In 1846 the Federal Diet passed a resolution calling on the Danish king to pay due regard to the rights of the Confederation and of the Holstein estates, but it also requested the German states to restrain the patriotic enthusiasm of their subjects. Even this qualified protest was only made four years after the Danish king had issued an 'open letter' claiming that Schleswig was governed by the same rule of succession as the rest of the Danish kingdom. And, in view of the lukewarm attitude of Austria to the problem and of the military impotence of the Confederation, there seemed little likelihood that either would intervene effectively if the Danish king, who enjoyed the support of Russia and France, proceeded to assimilate the duchies to the rest of the Danish monarchy. 'Schleswig-Holstein became, for long years together,' writes Erich Marcks, 'the symbol of all German wrongs, the bleeding wound, whose pain gave the nation no rest, the sharpest sting in all spiritual resistance, in all new will to unity.'

The chief internal force making for national unity at this time was the growth of an educated middle class engaged in the free professions and in industry and commerce, to whom the divisions of Germany, both political and social, were at once a logical absurdity and a serious hindrance to their activities. The rise of the Zollverein (Customs Union) (see pp. 63–72) under Prussian leadership, from 1834 onwards, contributed to the desire for still closer national unity. The very incompleteness of the Zollverein and the problem of Austria's relation to it, were all stimulants to thought on the ultimate form of German national unity. And in 1841 Fredrich List's *National System of Political Economy* appeared, which advocated the national state as the natural unit of economic production and the imposition of high tariffs to foster German industries.

The particularist selfishness of the German rulers, and not least of those of Austria and Prussia, together with the influence of England, led the nationalist German middle class to combine their demands for national unity with that for free representative institutions, for a German 'Parliament'. Only a nation-wide movement resulting in an assembly representative of the whole people could, they felt, overcome the reluctance of the rulers of the German states to make any sacrifice of their individual sovereignties.

As early as 1839 meetings began to be held for the discussion of common problems by representatives from different German states; in the autumn of 1847 a meeting of radical politicians from different states met at Offenburg, and one of more moderate liberals at Heppenheim, and formulated programmes. A journal, the *Deutsche Zeitung*, was published at Heidelberg to express the views of these more moderate liberals, and the origins of the later National-Liberal Party are to be found here.

The liberal-national tide was rising. The dams and dykes erected by Metternich were threatened with the flood, and neither Austria nor Metternich himself was in a condition to prepare against it. Since the death of the Emperor Francis in 1835, the feebleness of his successor (Ferdinand) allowed bitter rivalry to develop between Metternich and the other Austrian ministers with the result that Austria almost ceased to have any coherent government at all—merely a series of state departments. In this condition of affairs, and with nationalist movements rising in the non-German dominions of the Hapsburgs, it was impossible for Austria to undertake the task of uniting Germany, or to be regarded by German liberal-nationalists as the basis of the united Germany for which they longed. Yet no German nationalist, especially if he were a Catholic, could with equanimity adopt a solution of the problem of German unity from which the Germans of Austria would be excluded. It was practical necessity at the expense of national sentiment which alone led some Germans to regard a 'Little German' (*Kleindeutsch*) solution, with Austria excluded, as more practicable than the 'Great German' (*Grossdeutsch*) solution which the heterogeneous character of the Hapsburg dominions rendered impossible.

Prussia and the National Movement. Between 1830 and 1848, therefore, the minds of Germans who desired unity had been turning towards Prussia as their natural leader. Though Prussia's policy had been not less selfish or politically reactionary than that of Austria, the Prussian state was far more German than its southern rival. Prussia stood guard on the Vistula and Niemen against the Slav, on the Rhine against the French. Her government, if autocratic, was at least efficient, and her bureaucrats, however much disliked, commanded respect by their thoroughness and freedom from corruption. It was in Prussian territory —particularly in Silesia and the Rhineland—that some of the greatest industrial developments were taking place, as it was Prussia, and especially her civil service, which created and maintained the Zollverein. Now, after 1840, the new king's actions seemed to promise a liberalizing policy and the fulfilment

27   2-2

of his father's promise to give Prussia a constitution. If only these hopes proved well-founded a liberal Prussia might, with the support of the nation, create a united liberal Germany, even in the teeth of the opposition of Metternich and the German princes.

Events soon showed the vanity of these hopes. Frederick William IV's views on government were those of an unhistorical mystical feudalism. He believed profoundly in Divine Right, and his vision of a united Germany was that of a revived Holy Roman Empire, in which the emperor of Austria would enjoy the honorific primacy whilst the king of Prussia would act as his deputy. Upon the details of the organization of a united Germany, Frederick William IV was far from clear, but he was as definite in his opposition to any attempt to exclude Austria from the Confederation as in his determination to make no concessions to the principle of popular sovereignty.

Yet the demand for a constitution for the whole monarchy was strong enough in Prussia to induce Frederick William, in 1842, to summon committees of the provincial estates to meet in Berlin, only to find that this measure was far from satisfying their demands. In 1847, therefore, against the advice of both Metternich and of his brother and heir, William, prince of Prussia, the future first German emperor, he issued a Cabinet Order summoning a Combined Diet, comprising the members of the Provincial Estates, to meet in Berlin in April. Frederick William opened the meeting of this body himself, and in order to make his intentions perfectly clear declared: 'Never will I allow a written document to come between God in Heaven and this land in the character of a Second Providence, to govern us with its formalities and take the place of ancient loyalty.' The powers granted to the Combined Diet were extremely restricted and, when its sittings ended in June 1847, the general feeling throughout Prussia was that the king's schemes were wholly inadequate to meet the constitutional needs of the country. On the eve of the great year of revolutions, which swept Europe as well as Germany, Prussia was far from having adopted the principles of constitutional government which might make her leader of the liberal-national movement in Germany.

THE REVOLUTIONS OF 1848 AND THE THIRD REACTION

The widespread nature of the dissatisfaction felt with the existing governmental systems of the German states individually, and of the Confederation as a whole, manifested itself with startling suddenness all over the Germanies in the spring of 1848. On 22 February a revolution broke out in Paris, and within a few weeks revolutions had occurred in almost all the German states. On 13 March Metternich resigned and had to leave Vienna secretly for England, whilst his successors promised Austria a democratic constitution; on 18 March Frederick William IV promised his people both a liberal constitution and the reform of the Confederation under Prussian leadership; and, during March and April, Baden and Württemberg, Bavaria and Saxony, Hanover and the Hesses and the Hanse towns introduced sweeping changes in a liberal direction into their constitutional life. Moreover, the Federal Council blessed the idea of reform of the Confederation itself, and the governments of Austria and Prussia as well as of the lesser states allowed their citizens both to take part in the preliminary meetings of German liberals at Frankfurt (the *Vorparlament*), at which the steps for reform of the Confederation were discussed, and also to elect representatives to the National Assembly of the German people which met at Frankfurt in May. For a few brief months it appeared as though the liberal-national millennium had arrived, and that Germany was to endow itself, almost without bloodshed, with national union and responsible government on a democratic basis both in the central government of a truly Federal state and in the state governments as well. Yet by 1850 the concessions made by the German sovereigns to their subjects had been almost everywhere withdrawn. The movement for national unity had broken down and the National Assembly had been dissolved. The divisions amongst the reformers and their political inexperience were in part responsible for this. But fundamentally it was the strength of those conservative forces described above, together with the rivalry of Austria and Prussia, which brought the hopes of German liberalism to nothing.

Revolution and reaction in Austria. In the Austrian Empire several revolutions broke out simultaneously. The Italian provinces under Austrian rule were swept directly into the Italian national movement and, when the king of Sardinia adopted their cause, the Hapsburg Empire was faced not only by rebellious subjects but by a foreign Power. The fact that Radetzky and many of the best Austrian troops were occupied in Italy until the Austrian victory at Novara in March 1849 explains much of what happened at Vienna during 1848. There, after the initial concessions made by the Imperial government in March, a constitution for the whole monarchy was issued on the emperor's authority in April which granted a two-chamber Parliament to which the ministers were to be responsible. Under pressure from the revolutionaries both the proposed Parliament (Reichstag) and the electoral law were, in May, revised in a democratic sense and, on 17 May, the emperor and his family fled to Innsbruck. For some months a committee of students and National Guards was virtually the only government in Vienna until the Reichstag met on 22 July and began deliberations on the constitution. But the outbreak of revolts in Hungary and Bohemia and the divisions between the subject races of the empire allowed the Imperial government to reassert its control.

After suppressing a revolt in Prague (June 1848), Windischgrätz[1] was appointed commander of all the Imperial troops outside Italy, moved his army on Vienna and, by 31 October, had occupied the city and arrested the democratic leaders, of whom twenty-four were executed. Windischgrätz's brother-in-law, Prince Felix Schwarzenberg,[2] a strong supporter of autocracy, now became Prime Minister. The Reichstag, after being removed to the small town of Kremsier in Moravia, was allowed to continue its debates for some time. But, on 2 December 1848, the Emperor Ferdinand abdicated and was succeeded by the

---

[1] Alfred, Prince Windischgrätz (1787–1862), had distinguished himself in the War of Liberation. In 1849 he was in command of the campaign against the Hungarians, but, having quarrelled with his brother-in-law, Schwarzenberg, he was recalled.

[2] Felix, Prince zu Schwarzenberg (1800–52), had served Metternich at various European courts between 1824 and 1848. He was appointed Prime Minister in November 1848 at the instance of his brother-in-law, Windischgrätz.

young Francis Joseph, aged 18; on 7 March 1849 the Reichstag at Kremsier was dismissed and Schwarzenberg issued a constitution, on the new emperor's authority alone, for the whole Monarchy. On 23 March 1849 the Italian rebels and their Sardinian allies were decisively beaten at Novara and, before the end of August, the Hungarian national movement led by Kossuth had been crushed by the combined action of Austrian and Russian armies. Once order had been restored the Imperial constitution was treated as abortive and was abolished by decree in December 1851. Meanwhile Schwarzenberg devoted all his energies to the congenial task of re-establishing the old order in the German Confederation and in its component states.

Revolution and reaction in Prussia. In Prussia the concessions of the king to the populace of Berlin (March 1848), his homage to the bodies of the Berliners shot by his troops, his theatrical procession through the streets swathed in the national flag—the black-red-gold—and his speeches in which he declared that he wanted 'German freedom and German unity' and that 'Prussia merges (*geht auf*) into Germany', had given evidence of his adhesion, at least for the moment, to the cause of national unity. But Frederick William's emotions were unreliable and his will uncertain, whilst the Prussian military caste was determined to preserve their state both from a democratic system and from dissolution in a democratic Germany. The fate of Prussia and of Germany depended on the strength, unity and rapidity of action of the liberal forces in the Prussian National Assembly and in the German National Assembly at Frankfurt. Unhappily, the liberals were disunited both in Berlin and at Frankfurt, and in neither assembly was swift action taken. Both settled down to prolonged constitutional discussions and, during the months that these continued, the opportunity of the liberal-national movement passed.

In Prussia, though a National Assembly, elected on the basis of manhood suffrage, met on 22 May, and a liberal ministry, in which two Rhineland industrialists were the chief figures, took office, the prolonged debates on the future constitution gave the Prussian conservative forces time to organize themselves. In

August a meeting of Prussian conservatives, mainly nobles and landowners—the so-called *Junkerparlament*—at which Bismarck was present, formed a league 'for King and Country' whose object was to demand the dissolution of the Prussian National Assembly, if necessary by force of arms. By October, whilst the Assembly continued its constitutional debates, the king and his conservative advisers, supported by the army, were ready to act.

On 31 October the king dismissed his liberal ministers and replaced them by a wholly conservative Cabinet, with Otto von Manteuffel[1] as Minister of the Interior and later (November 1850) as Foreign Minister and finally (December 1850) Prime Minister. On 9 November the Assembly was informed that it was to be removed to Brandenburg. Next day General Wrangel occupied Berlin and dissolved the Civic Guard, and when the rump of the Assembly met at Brandenburg it was faced on 5 December with a decree for its own dissolution and a constitution of a very limited character granted (*octroyée*) by the king. Even this constitution was not conservative enough for the king, and in May 1849 the basis of election was changed by the introduction of the famous Prussian Three-Class system of voting (*Drei-Klassen Wahlrecht*),[2] which remained in force in Prussia until the last days of 1918. Frederick William IV was only persuaded with difficulty by his ministers to take the oath to the constitution, and in the three years from 1849 to 1852, during which reaction was in full flood, the constitution was still further modified in a conservative sense.

The Frankfurt National Assembly. The effort of the liberal-national movement to secure unity for Germany as a whole on a constitutional basis was made by the National Assembly which met at Frankfurt on 18 May 1848. Its task was complicated by

---

[1] Otto Theodor von Manteuffel (1805–82) had opposed constitutional reform at the Combined Diet of 1847. He was dismissed in November 1858, when the Prince of Prussia (later Emperor William I) became regent.

[2] This system provided for indirect elections to the lower house of the Prussian Landtag—i.e. the body of voters chose electors, who in turn chose the representatives. But the voters were first divided into three classes, according to the amount they paid in direct taxation. Although Classes I and II, consisting of those who paid most, were numerically much smaller than Class III, they each chose a third of the electors to which their electoral district was entitled.

the political divisions amongst its members, who comprised extreme conservatives and extreme republicans, with every intermediate shade of opinion; but, above all, by the difficulties arising from the rivalry of the two great German Powers—Austria and Prussia. Since the Assembly had no direct control of any armed forces, its decisions depended for their execution on the willingness of the governments of Austria and Prussia—and to a lesser extent of the smaller states—to carry them out. During the summer of 1848, whilst Austria was crippled and Prussia was giving limited support to the national idea, an illusory progress towards a solution of the problem of unity was made. But by the time the Assembly had made up its mind about the form this unity should take, the reaction had set in both in Austria and Prussia and the opportunity had passed.

As soon as the National Assembly met at Frankfurt it was at once faced with the problem of creating a central government. On 27 June the Assembly decided to ignore the governments of the states and to elect a Regent (*Reichsverweser*) who should appoint a Ministry responsible to the Assembly. On 29 June the Archduke John of Austria was chosen Regent and, during July, the Ministry was appointed. But it was significant and un-promising at the outset that, although the *Reichsverweser* was recognized by the German governments, the king of Prussia refused to allow his troops to swear allegiance to him.

Throughout the remainder of 1848 the National Assembly devoted itself to constitutional discussions, mainly on the funda-damental rights (*Grundrechte*) of the German people, a set of propositions asserting what we have come to regard as the commonplaces of political liberty. Finally proclaimed as law on 27 December 1848, they were embodied in the draft constitution. Under its provisions there would have been an hereditary emperor; a Reichstag of two Houses—one representing the states, one the nation as a whole; a responsible Ministry; and complete control by the Federal authority of foreign affairs, army, the decision on war and peace, with a taxing power adequate to the needs of the Federal government. The success of the proposed constitution rested on its acceptance by both

Austria and Prussia but, before it had been adopted, events in Schleswig-Holstein showed how little reliance could be placed on the Prussian king's devotion to the cause of national unity.

The reopening of the Schleswig-Holstein Question. In January 1848 Frederick VII succeeded to the Danish throne and on 28 January promulgated a general constitution bequeathed to him by the late king for the Danish monarchy. Under this instrument the two duchies, whilst retaining their estates for purely local purposes, would be incorporated into the Danish monarchy for general purposes of taxation and legislation, whilst Holstein would be detached from the German Confederation. Protests were at once made in Schleswig and Holstein, followed by preparations for armed resistance. The next heir to the duchies in the male line, Duke Christian August of Augustenburg, obtained from Frederick William IV, on 27 March, recognition both of the independence and indivisibility of the duchies and of the principle that the succession to them was in the male line. The Danes now sought to limit their plans of incorporation to Schleswig and promised a separate constitution for Holstein, as a member of the German Confederation. Not only Prussia, but the *Vorparlament* at Frankfurt, and under its influence the Federal Diet also, espoused the cause of the duchies and, during April and May, Prussian and Federal forces, under the Prussian General Wrangel, drove the Danes from the duchies and entered Jutland. At this point, however, the opposition of the Czar and of Great Britain to the extension of German power in the Baltic and North Sea led the Prussian government to draw back. After prolonged negotiations a truce was signed at Malmö on 26 August, which was accepted only with the greatest reluctance by the National Assembly at Frankfurt, and almost equally reluctantly by the Danes. Its importance in the history of Germany lies in the fact that it was very widely regarded by German patriots at the time as a betrayal of the national cause by Prussia.

The refusal of Frederick William IV to become Emperor. Further light on the attitude of Prussia and its king to that cause was provided in March 1849. The National Assembly at length made up its mind in that month to pass the draft constitution and to proceed with the organization of a united Germany. This involved a final choice between *Grossdeutsch* and *Kleindeutsch* ideas, since an hereditary emperor must be chosen for the new Federal state. The selection of Frederick William IV as emperor by 290 votes, with 248 abstentions, on 28 March marked the victory of the *Kleindeutsch* idea by a narrow margin, and a deputation, led by the respected President of the Assembly, Eduard Simson, a Königsberg Professor of Jewish origin,[1] set off to offer the crown to the king of Prussia. But, since the March days in Berlin, Frederick William had reverted to his fixed political views. He genuinely believed that Austria should retain an honorary primacy in Germany; he would not accept what he called a 'crown of shame'—one that emanated from the people; he must be selected by his fellow-rulers; and the military leadership, which he desired for Prussia, must be established with their consent. Holding these views he gave an answer so hedged with qualifications that the delegation rightly regarded it as equivalent to a refusal. The Austrian government at once withdrew its members from the National Assembly (5 April). The kings of Bavaria, Württemberg, Saxony and Hanover gave the new constitution no recognition. In May both Prussia and Saxony also withdrew their deputies from Frankfurt, and a body of the most active constitutionalists, led by Dahlmann, followed suit. The breakdown of the movement for unity was greeted with passionate resentment by the democrats of the Left and attempts at armed revolution broke out in May 1849 in Saxony, Baden and the Bavarian Palatinate. Despite the fact that there were disturbances in Prussia also, Prussian troops quelled the revolts and brought to an end the struggle for the constitution. The cleavage between the Prussian monarchy and the popular movement for unity and freedom was complete.

The Prussian scheme for unity. Yet Frederick William, if he would accept nothing from below, still wished to do something for the national cause—and that of Prussia—from above. His

---

[1] It was Simson who also headed the Reichstag deputation to Versailles in 1871 when King William of Prussia was proclaimed German Emperor.

scheme was to effect a Union with the other purely German states, of which Prussia should be the head, and a perpetual alliance with the whole Austrian monarchy to meet the Hapsburg claims. It was the solution of 1870, but it had been rejected in advance by Schwarzenberg when in March 1849 he proposed the admission of the whole of the Austrian dominions into the Confederation. It should have been apparent both to the Prussian king and to his adviser, Radowitz,[1] that Austria, now rapidly recovering from the national revolts in Hungary and Italy, would oppose an uncompromising resistance to any scheme which robbed her both of her place and of her preeminence in a German Reich.

In pursuit of their policy Frederick William and Radowitz, in May 1849, invited the other states to send plenipotentiaries to a conference at Berlin and succeeded in inducing the kings of Hanover and Saxony to give a conditional acceptance to a draft German constitution more conservative in character than that of Frankfurt, but recognizing the headship of Prussia in the proposed Federation. Since, however, the Austrian representative withdrew after the first day and the Bavarian remained without instructions, the significance of the qualified adhesion of Hanover and Saxony was greatly reduced and they also withdrew when it was decided by the Council of the Union to hold elections in January 1850 for a house of representatives. By the time these elections had taken place and the resulting parliament had met at Erfurt in March and passed a constitution in April, Frederick William, who did not even declare his acceptance of the constitution, had himself lost confidence in the Union—a fact which he made clear at a conference of the princes still members of it in Berlin on 9 May, when he left their continued adherence to it to their free choice.

Whilst the Prussian king thus vacillated, Schwarzenberg, having successfully completed the counter-revolution in the Hapsburg dominions, was taking resolute steps to restore the Austrian

---

[1] Joseph Maria von Radowitz (1797–1853), former Prussian military delegate at the Federal Diet, had been an intimate friend of Frederick William IV when the latter was Crown Prince. He served as Prussian Minister for Foreign Affairs from September to November 1850 and later as a Director of Military Education.

hegemony in Germany. This meant, among other things, reviving the old Confederation, if possible with all the Austrian possessions included within it. Six months earlier (30 September 1849) he had secured Prussian agreement to the *Interim* by which Austria and Prussia took over jointly the authority of the Confederation until 1 May 1850. In February 1850 he gave general approval to a scheme of constitutional reform put forward by the kings of Bavaria, Württemberg, Saxony and Hanover—the last two both seceders from the Prussian Union—and a few days before the *Interim* expired he issued an invitation from Austria, as president of the former Confederation, to the states which had been members of it to meet at Frankfurt on 10 May to revive its authority and to discuss the revision of its constitution. At that meeting, and despite the absence of Prussia and some of her allies in the Union, Schwarzenberg proceeded to reconstitute the *plenum* of the old Diet. Austria's action was a direct challenge to Prussia and the question arose whether they would carry the divergence between their rival schemes for the future of Germany to the point of war.

Olmütz and the re-establishment of the Confederation. The decision of this struggle for supremacy in Germany between Austria and Prussia came in the autumn of 1850. Schwarzenberg's position was strengthened, as that of Frederick William was weakened, by the knowledge that the Czar, whom both he and Prince William of Prussia visited at the end of May 1850 at Warsaw, was opposed to Prussian policy both in Denmark and in the affairs of Germany. When, therefore, an opportunity occurred for testing Prussian firmness in support of the Union as against the revived Confederation Schwarzenberg was ready to act.

It was Hesse-Cassel, a former member of the Prussian Union, which provided the test case. When the Diet of his state refused to vote taxation without being allowed to see the details of revenue and expenditure, the Elector declared them guilty of rebellion under a Federal law of 1832, which had been abolished in 1848. Since the State officials and the officers of the army also refused to break their oath to the State Constitution, the Elector declared a state of siege, removed himself to Frankfurt and called upon the resuscitated Federal Diet to carry out a Federal execution in his state. When Schwarzenberg and the Diet responded to the Elector's appeal, Prussia was placed in a position of acute difficulty. For not only had Hesse-Cassel been a member of the semi-defunct Prussian Union, but the state was also crossed by two military roads which Prussia alone had the right to use for the passage of troops. Was Prussia tamely to acquiesce in the Federal execution or to challenge it and risk war with Austria?

At first it seemed that Prussia would stand firm. When Bavarian troops occupied Hanau, Prussian troops occupied Fulda and Cassel. But, though mobilization was ordered, the Prussian government had, in fact, decided to give way, for they knew that Austria was supported by the Czar. A meeting was arranged at Olmütz on 28 November between Schwarzenberg and Manteuffel, who had now replaced Radowitz, and, on the next day, the two ministers signed the Punctation of Olmütz, by which Prussia accepted the substance of the Austrian demands. The Federal execution in Hesse was to go forward; the Prussian Union was to be dissolved; the Schleswig-Holstein issue was to be settled by joint Austro-Prussian action; a conference of governments was to discuss the future organization of Germany. When the Conference met, the Federal Diet was formally re-established (16 May 1851) under the forms prescribed by the Federal Acts of 1815 and 1820.

The Schleswig-Holstein 'settlement'. The humiliation of Prussia at Olmütz and the re-establishment of Austrian influence in the Federal Diet involved the disappointment of German national sentiment in the Schleswig-Holstein question. Despite the Truce of Malmö, there was still hope, in the early part of 1849, that the cause of the duchies and of Germany might prevail and, when the Danes denounced the Malmö truce in February, and hostilities were resumed in April, a Federal army of Prussians, Saxons and Bavarians under a Prussian general, von Prittwitz, at first scored striking successes and was able to advance into Jutland. But Frederick William IV was now more anxious to conciliate Russia and Austria than to defend the national cause, and he had little sympathy with a revolt of subjects against their ruler.

On 10 July 1849, therefore, another truce was signed between Prussia and Denmark followed, a year later, by a peace treaty (2 July 1850) which, whilst formally reserving the rights of the two Powers, effectively left the duchies at the mercy of the Danish king. Though the provisional government of the duchies carried on the struggle until January 1851 they then evacuated Schleswig, resigned their powers into the hands of an Austro-Prussian Commission of pacification, and left Holstein from January 1851 until February 1852 in the hands of an Austrian force with a Prussian division attached to it. Schwarzenberg, in accordance with his conservative policy, had no intention of taking up the cause of German nationalism in the duchies and, in May 1852, an agreement (known as the London Protocol) was reached amongst the Great Powers—Austria, Prussia, Russia and Great Britain—by which the integrity of the Danish monarchy was recognized as well as the right of succession to the duchies of the next heir to the Danish Crown. On their side, the Danes recognized that Schleswig and Holstein were united only by a personal union with Denmark and that the duchies should have special rights of self-government through their Provincial Estates in all 'affairs not common to the monarchy as a whole'. The settlement was to prove neither satisfactory nor final. Though Duke Christian August of Augustenburg had handed over to the Danish king his large estates in the duchies in return for a money payment, he was not called upon to renounce his 'right' to the succession because the Danish Government maintained that such a 'right' had never existed. Nor did his acceptance of the settlement bind his heirs. And though the Danes had declared, before the London Protocol was signed, that special treatment would be accorded to the duchies—and particularly to Schleswig—no machinery was provided to enforce this promise. Moreover, the London Protocol was signed by Austria and Prussia as independent Great Powers, not as representatives of the German Confederation. The Federal Diet was presented with the *fait accompli*. But the German nation and its sentiments were completely ignored by its rulers both before and after the event. The fate of the Germans in Schleswig and Holstein was

39

decided according to the immediate interests of the Austrian and Prussian governments, who both regarded the principle of nationality as revolutionary.

The revolutions of 1848 and German nationalism. The signature of the London Protocol, which had been immediately preceded by the death of Schwarzenberg (7 April 1852), seemed to stamp the combined movements of liberalism and nationalism in the Germanies, begun in 1848, with complete failure. So far as liberal institutions were concerned the central representation of Germany was still confined to the governments through the inadequate machinery of the Federal Diet. And, in the individual states, the Austrian constitution had already been abolished; the Prussian constitution was of so conservative a character as to appear incapable of providing adequate representation of liberal opinion; and most of the gains made by the liberals in the smaller states were lost again by 1852. In no single German state had the principle of a government responsible to the elected Chamber been established as a result of the revolutions of 1848.

Nor did it appear that the cause of national unity had been in any way advanced. The rivalry between Austria and Prussia, which prevented national union, had been openly displayed, but the victory of multi-national Austria seemed to postpone indefinitely the dream of a united German state. Nor had the rulers of the smaller states shown any greater willingness than those of Austria and Prussia to sacrifice their power and privileges to the national cause. There were other discouraging lessons for the liberal-nationalists. The divisions in their own ranks had contributed largely to their failure. Still more, it had been made abundantly plain that, so long as the German rulers could rely on the loyalty of their armed forces, and so long as none but a handful of ardent radicals were ready to oppose them in the field, a unified liberal-national Germany would never be attained. Nothing but a great national uprising, prepared if necessary to fight and depose the existing rulers of Germany, and armed with the means to do so, could hope for success. But the whole social structure of Germany, as well as the outlook of the middle class, who would have had to lead such a movement, precluded any possibility of a 'French Revolution' on German soil. Nor, in judging the event, should it be forgotten that no 'French Revolution' has occurred in any great modern state, except in Russia—and there only at the end of a prolonged and disastrous war, and against a system of government even more absolutist in spirit and far less competent in administration than the governments of Germany in 1848.

In face of this situation German liberal-national thinkers for some years lapsed into a sense of helplessness. When their hopes revived they still looked, for the most part, to a liberalized Prussia to carry them into effect and still failed to realize the great strength of the conservative forces, not only in Prussia but in all the German states, opposed to their solution. It was to be Bismarck's triumph to turn their liberal-nationalism into a national-liberalism in which the liberal idea was to be subordinated to the ambitions of conservative Prussia to unite and dominate Germany.

The reaction in Prussia. The remaining years of Frederick William IV's rule are amongst the most depressing in Prussian history. Influenced by a pietistic group of friends the king engaged in a persecution of everything liberal. His Minister of the Interior made ruthless use of government influence against politically objectionable candidates for seats in the Landtag. In alliance with the Junkers the system of local government in the countryside was restored to the situation before 1850, under which the landowners exercised a feudal jurisdiction, whilst prosecutions against intellectuals and politicians were supported by the perjured evidence of police agents. Education from the university to the village school was strictly supervised. If Frederick William had had his way he would have abolished the constitution to which he had sworn observance. Indeed, when he died he left behind him a document in which he adjured his successors, who would not have bound themselves as he had by oath, to abrogate the instrument which he had created.

Nor were Frederick William's achievements in the field of foreign policy during these years any more noteworthy. Indeed, during the Crimean War the king so vacillated that the Czar

Nicholas was constrained to remark that his brother-in-law[1] went to bed 'every night as a Russian' and got up 'every morning as an Englishman'. To some extent this vacillation reflected a cleavage of opinion at the court, where the moderate Conservatives, resentful of the Czar's role in the 'humiliation' of Olmütz, championed the cause of the Western Powers, against the Junkers, who favoured Russia as the possible nucleus of a revived Holy Alliance. On the whole the 'Western' group, who were led by Professor Bethmann Hollweg,[2] and who in *Das Preussische Wochenblatt* traded journalistic blows with the Junker party's *Kreuz-Zeitung*, commanded the greater influence at the Prussian Foreign Ministry.

Yet a third school of thought, represented by Bismarck (then Prussian representative at the Federal Diet), believed that Prussia should woo the Czar, not as the bulwark of reaction, but as a counterweight to Austria. (The latter, ungrateful for the Czar's intervention in Hungary in 1849, tended during the Crimean War to range herself on the side of Great Britain and France, with whom her interests in the Eastern Question coincided.) 'We must look abroad for allies,' Bismarck wrote, 'and among the European Powers Russia is to be had on the cheapest terms; she wishes only to grow in the East, the two others (namely, Austria and France) wish to grow at our expense.' In the cynical school of Federal politics at Frankfurt Bismarck had already learnt that Prussia must sooner or later fight Austria if she desired to unite Germany under her leadership. The policy of friendship with Russia was more than an insurance against the triumph of liberal principles in Prussia. It safeguarded Prussia's eastern frontiers and paid handsome dividends in the struggle with Austria (1866) and France (1870).

[1] Nicholas (as Grand Duke) had married Princess Charlotte Louise, the daughter of Frederick William III of Prussia.
[2] Grandfather of William II's Reich Chancellor.

3. THE VICTORY OF PRUSSIA IN GERMANY, 1858–71

WILLIAM I AND THE CONSTITUTIONAL CONFLICT IN PRUSSIA

In the autumn of 1857 Frederick William IV's mind gave way and in November 1858 his brother William, prince of Prussia, who was already 62 years old, became regent. He was above all things a soldier, a conservative, a Hohenzollern. His attitude to Austria was, at first, hardly less loyal than that of his brother, though it had no romantic trappings. But he was surrounded by liberal influences. His son Frederick, who was married to a daughter of Queen Victoria, wished to see Prussia lead Germany to unity by liberalizing her own institutions and by a policy of moral conquest, and William himself was not wholly averse from this course. His first act as regent was to dismiss Manteuffel, the man of Olmütz, and the rest of his brother's ministers and to appoint a more liberal Cabinet under Prince Charles Anton of Hohenzollern.[1] He also gave instructions that the government influence should no longer be brought to bear at elections. Once again it seemed that a 'New Era' of greater liberalism had set in in Prussia. The success of the Italian struggle for unity against Austria (1859) stimulated liberal-nationalists throughout Germany, and in 1859 the National Association (*National-verein*) was founded by Rudolf von Bennigsen[2] of Hanover and other liberals. As before 1848, and now with even greater strength, the movement for national unity on a liberal basis revived. Propaganda meetings for the national idea and meetings of delegates from different German states to concert plans were held, and expectant liberal eyes were turned towards the new ruler of Prussia.

[1] Father of Prince Charles, later king of Roumania, and of Prince Leopold, the candidate for the Spanish throne in 1870.

[2] Rudolf von Bennigsen (1824–1902), after vainly trying to keep Hanover neutral in the war of 1866, was won over by Bismarck and took his seat as a Prussian in the Diet of the North German Confederation. One of the founders of the National Liberal party, he broke with Bismarck in 1883 over the Chancellor's reactionary policy.

But the regent drew different lessons from the defeat of Austria by France and Sardinia. During the war Prussia mobilized her forces to defend the Federal territory but, even in her hour of need, Austria would not yield the leadership of the German Confederation or of its armed forces into Prussian hands. The result of the Italian war was to reveal Austria's obstinate determination to thwart Prussia in Germany, and also the military weakness of both the German Great Powers. For, if Austria had been beaten by the French and Sardinians, the Prussian mobilization had been slow and inefficient and had strongly reinforced William's conviction that Prussia's greatest need was a drastic reform of her military system.

On 12 January 1860, therefore, in the speech from the Throne to the Prussian Parliament (*Landtag*), army reforms, the work of von Roon,[1] were outlined. Their effect was to increase the field army from 200,000 to 371,000; to lengthen the period of military service from two years to three; to provide for thirty-nine new regiments of infantry and ten of cavalry; and to require an added annual expenditure of $9\frac{1}{2}$ million thalers (about £1,500,000). The reorganization involved, too, a great reduction in the strength and importance of the militia reserve (the *Landwehr*), to which many Prussians were sentimentally attached, and fewer exemptions from the obligation to military service. The Prussian army was also to be equipped with more modern weapons, and the effect of the reorganization, when completed, would be to double the military power of Prussia. William was inflexibly determined that the whole scheme should go through.

The Liberals in the Lower Chamber of the Prussian Landtag at first hoped to secure concessions. They made a provisional grant to cover the cost of the scheme in 1860, but were determined to secure its modification before the next budget. They objected on economic and personal grounds to the lengthened term of service, and on political grounds to the increased power of the crown and the military class which would necessarily

[1] Albrecht Theodor Emil von Roon (1803–79) began his long years of work for the Prussian army after Olmütz, becoming War Minister in 1859 and retiring after the Franco-Prussian War.

44

result from the scheme. But, supported by the Upper House, by his military advisers, and by his own interpretation of his duty, William pressed forward his proposals. On 2 January 1861 he became king on his brother's death. In the same month a new, more democratic, party was founded in Prussia, the Progress (*Fortschritt*) party, and, at the elections at the end of the year, the government was faced with an overwhelming majority against it in the Lower Chamber, to which only twenty-four Conservatives were returned. Early in 1862 this Liberal majority demanded an itemized budget and the reduction of the term of military service to two years. William dissolved the Chambers and used governmental pressure against his opponents at the elections with no success, for only twelve Conservatives were now returned. His more liberal ministers refused to accept his policy and resigned, and William was warned by his son and other advisers not to rule without a budget. There seemed to be only two alternatives—to abandon the scheme of army reform and thus, in effect, to accept the parliamentary system in Prussia, or to abdicate in favour of his son. It was at this critical moment that, following Roon's advice, William decided to send for Bismarck.

Bismarck and his policy. Born in 1815 of an old Pomeranian Junker family, Otto von Bismarck was 47 when he became Minister-President and Minister for Foreign Affairs of Prussia on 22 September 1862. As Prussian representative at Frankfurt he had learnt to know the strength and weakness of Austria and was already convinced that only by defeating Austria in war could Prussia unify Germany. In the years immediately before 1862 he had been Prussian Ambassador at St Petersburg and Paris, and, in both capitals, had strengthened the position of his country and had acquired an intimate knowledge of the foreign policies and probable action of both in a European crisis. In particular he had weighed Napoleon III's character, upon which he passed judgment in the phrase 'People exaggerate his intellect, but underrate his heart'. Bismarck's one consuming passion was the greatness of Prussia, to be achieved by the strength of her army and the subtlety of his diplomacy. When, therefore,

45

his king consulted him, ready to abdicate should Bismarck fail him, Bismarck took office on the understanding that the king would not resign under any circumstances and would give him his full support in the struggle with the Landtag.

That struggle rapidly came to a head. On 30 September, in a speech that was intended to be conciliatory, Bismarck tried to woo the Liberals from their intransigence, but he added, on the national question, that 'Germany did not look to Prussia's liberalism but to her power', and that 'the great question of the time will be decided not by speeches and the resolutions of majorities—that was the mistake of 1848 and 1849—but by blood and iron'. The Prussian Liberals were only the more alienated by this repudiation of their movement for national unity by democratic means, and by the appeal to force. They rejected the budget by a large majority, and were prorogued, whilst Bismarck continued to rule without a budget in defiance of the constitution. When, after a further year's resistance to the government proposals, the Landtag was dissolved in September 1863, Bismarck used every form of government pressure against the Liberal candidates—but in vain. Thus Bismarck's ministry opened as the complete negation of all that German Liberals had hoped for. So far from Prussia seeking to win moral victories by her liberalism, her king and minister had engaged in a bitter struggle with the elected representatives of her people in defiance of public opinion within and without Prussia and at the cost of alienating not only the heir to the Prussian throne, who withdrew for a time from the Crown Council, and the Prussian people, but the minor states and the liberal opinion which was being organized for national unity by the National Association.

Austria's schemes for Federal reform. Bismarck's policy seemed the more foolhardy because Austria was anxious to take advantage both of the revived national movement and of Prussia's difficulties by sponsoring a reform of the Federation. The Emperor Francis Joseph had, indeed, made it clear, when he met William at Teplitz in 1860, that Austria was not prepared to make any concessions in regard to the primacy of the Federation and when, in reply to an impracticable scheme put forward in 1861 by Beust,[1] the Foreign Minister of Saxony, Prussia proposed a narrower union under her own leadership, Austria and some of the lesser states protested (February 1862). The signature by Prussia, in August 1862, of a commercial treaty with France, which greatly diminished Austrian hopes of ultimately entering the Zollverein (see pp. 63–72), rendered Austro-Prussian relations still worse and, in December, Bismarck, during a series of conversations with Karolyi the Austrian Ambassador, bluntly suggested that Austria's proper centre of gravity was Hungary and that she should accept Prussia as her equal in Germany. The serious internal conflict in Prussia, which reached its most acute point in 1863, was, therefore, welcomed in Austria as providing an opportunity of carrying through a reform of the Confederation favourable to Austrian interests. Against the advice of the Austrian Foreign Minister, Rechberg, who was nevertheless weak enough to remain in office, Francis Joseph issued an invitation to the princes of Germany to meet at Frankfurt on 16 August 1863 to discuss a scheme of reform.

The meeting of princes (*Fürstentag*) was duly held under the emperor's personal presidency. But the popular enthusiasm at first shown was damped by the limited nature of the proposals —a chamber of princes under Austrian presidency and a chamber of delegates elected by the parliaments of the several states —and the proposals were accepted only against the votes of a minority of states—Baden, Weimar, Mecklenburg-Schwerin, Oldenburg, and Waldeck. This minority might be unimpressive. But there was not only a minority present, there was a vitally important absentee. Despite an invitation from the whole body of German princes brought to William by the king of Saxony himself, Bismarck would not allow his king to attend. The resolutions of Frankfurt, in Prussia's absence, were, he knew, worth nothing. They only showed, in Friedjung's words, 'how little

---

[1] Friedrich Ferdinand von Beust (1809-86) won the hatred of Bismarck for his opposition to the rise of Prussia. After the war of 1866 Francis Joseph made him Austro-Hungarian Minister of Foreign Affairs. In the war of 1870 he was pro-French, being afterwards, for reasons never divulged, demoted to the Austrian embassy in London.

Austria had to offer'[1] the German nation, and Bismarck countered them brilliantly. Under his direction the Prussian Ministry drew up a set of counter-proposals, by which Prussia was to have an equal place with Austria in the Federal Directory, but in which, too, the chamber of delegates was replaced by a national assembly directly elected on a population basis in every German state. At the height of his conflict with the Prussian Landtag, elected on the Three-Class system, Bismarck appealed to the liberal-national principle of universal suffrage. But, though the proposal was received with scepticism by the Liberals, it was not merely cynical. Given the necessary conservative controls, it represented a genuine intention.

The Schleswig-Holstein Question. Yet the position of Prussia in 1863 seemed hazardous enough in view of her internal dissensions, and she was now to be faced with another critical question, that of Schleswig-Holstein. On 15 November 1863 the death of Frederick VII reopened the whole question of the duchies in an acute form, for the first act of his successor, Christian IX, was to sign a new Danish constitution, by which Schleswig was incorporated in the Danish state, while Holstein, as a constituent state of the German Confederation, remained united only by a personal union with the Danish Crown. The threat of this change in their status had already aroused violent feelings in the duchies, which had always maintained the view that they were entitled to self-government apart from the rest of the Danish kingdom. The position was further complicated by the fact that the new constitution was an undeniable breach of the Protocol of London, signed by Austria and Prussia and the other Powers in 1852 (see p. 39), and still more by the fact that Frederick of Augustenburg, whose father's acceptance of a settlement had been bought in 1852, now claimed the duchies on his own account, on the ground that his father had resigned to him his rights to the succession and that all else in the settlement was personal and could not bind his heirs.

From the outset the main mass of German public opinion,

[1] Cf. Heinrich Friedjung, *The Struggle for Supremacy in Germany, 1859–1866* (trans A. J. P. Taylor and W. L. McElwee, London, 1935), p. 39.

ignoring all legal niceties, passionately supported the claim of Duke Frederick, as he now called himself, and demanded a final settlement of the whole question by the complete separation of the duchies from Denmark and their incorporation as a united state in the German Confederation. This solution, which was backed by the National Association and other bodies, took no account of the recognition accorded to the rights of accession of Christian IX, or of the guarantee of the integrity of the Danish kingdom by the Great Powers under the Protocol of London; and it involved warlike interference by the Federal Diet in the affairs of Schleswig, which had never been part of the Confederation. To be carried out it required the support of either Prussia or Austria since, without this, the forces of the Federal Diet drawn only from the minor states would be insufficient to conduct a war.

On the other hand, Bismarck, from the outset, was clear in his aims. At the first meeting of the Prussian Crown Council after the death of Frederick VII, he reminded William that each of his ancestors had increased Prussian territory and urged him to seize the duchies. The king, Bismarck wrote in his Reminiscences, 'seemed to think that I had spoken under the Bacchic influence of a good lunch and would be glad to have my words consigned to oblivion. But I insisted that they should be placed on record, which was done. While I was speaking the Crown Prince threw up his hands, as though he doubted my soundness of mind; my colleagues sat in dead silence.' Bismarck was, without doubt, fully aware that the king was not ready for any such solution as yet, nor would he himself, at that moment, have pressed for military action. But he intended, if possible, to secure the duchies for Prussia and he sowed the seed of desire in William's mind at the earliest moment. In public, however, whilst refusing the Landtag's request to recognize the Augustenburg claim, since this would close the door to Prussian profit, he pursued the policy of acting with Austria on the basis of the London Protocol of 1852 and of demanding that the Danish king should observe the promises therein made of a special regime for the duchies. Since this involved withdrawing the new Danish Constitution it was very likely that the Danes would provide a *casus belli* by refusing. It was Bismarck's calculation that, if Austria and Prussia then occupied the duchies to vindicate their treaty rights, the other Great Powers could hardly object. At the same time the Federal Diet would be excluded from interference and the Augustenburg claims to the duchies would not have been recognized. The disposal of the duchies would rest in the hands of Austria and Prussia. That this policy ran counter to the declared wishes of the German liberal-nationalists was for Bismarck a positive advantage. He intended to teach them that national aims could best be obtained by the agency of Prussian might.

The Austrian acceptance of this point of view was based on a determination to prevent Prussia extending her sway over the duchies if possible. Joint occupation and ultimate joint disposal of booty appeared the best insurance. And Bismarck's skilful use of the appeal to treaty rights as against radical democratic demands met with a warm response from Francis Joseph, already tired of his Minister Schmerling's[1] constitutional views. Acting together at the Federal Diet, Austria and Prussia were able, in December 1863, to force through by the narrow margin of one vote a motion that a Federal execution should take place in Holstein to oblige the new Danish king to carry out his promises under the London Protocol of 1852.

With the same end in view Bismarck secured a treaty with Austria for joint military action against Denmark if Christian IX refused, as he almost certainly must refuse, the joint Austro-Prussian demand that he should honour the pledges given for the benefit of the duchies in the London Protocol. And in this treaty (16 January 1864) the Austrians also accepted a clause which left the fate of the duchies after the war completely open. Article V provided that: 'In case of hostilities against Denmark

[1] Anton von Schmerling (1805–93) was one of the Austrian representatives at the Frankfurt National Parliament in 1848, becoming an enthusiastic supporter of the *Grossdeutsch* faction. After serving as Minister of Justice under Schwarzenberg (whose reactionary views he found it impossible to tolerate) he took over, in 1860, the Ministry of the Interior, but alienated the Hungarians with his policies of centralization.

and the consequent lapse of the treaties between Denmark and the German Powers, the courts of Austria and Prussia reserve to themselves the establishment of the future condition of the duchies only by mutual agreement.' Under this treaty the claims of Frederick of Augustenburg were ignored, the Federal Diet was excluded from dealing with the disposal of the duchies, and the liberal-national solution of recognizing the Augustenburg claims and admitting the duchies as a united whole to the German Confederation was ruled out in advance unless Austria and Prussia both agreed to accept it. It was in vain that, on 14 January, the Federal Diet rejected by 11 votes to 5 the policy upon which Austria and Prussia under Bismarck's skilful guidance had agreed. On 16 January the two Powers presented an ultimatum to Denmark demanding the withdrawal of the new Danish Constitution and, when this was refused, their troops entered Schleswig.

Bismarck's policy had secured the great advantage to the German Powers of the neutrality of the other Great Powers. By basing their claims strictly on the enforcement of the London Protocol Austria and Prussia had made it almost impossible for Russia and England, who were parties to that instrument, to interfere forcibly on Denmark's side. The Danes, therefore, received no military assistance and, though they fought bravely, the Austro-Prussian forces rapidly overran Schleswig and entered Jutland where, on 18 April, the Danes were defeated. At this point, with the duchies in their hands, Austria and Prussia agreed to a truce and to a Conference of the interested parties in London.

Here Bismarck began by denouncing the London Protocol of 1852 as no longer valid because of the Danish breach of its terms, with the result that the whole future of the duchies was now open for discussion. A series of solutions was examined, but, in the end, as he had hoped, the Conference broke up without reaching agreement and on 25 June the war was resumed. Bismarck had succeeded in his immediate aims. He knew that neither Russia, England nor France was likely to aid Denmark by force of arms. He had torn up the London Protocol of 1852 and, with it, Prussian recognition that the duchies formed part of the Danish monarchy. Now, when the Danes had been finally defeated, the fate of the duchies would depend wholly on an agreement between Prussia and Austria. And, despite negotiations with Frederick of Augustenburg, Prussia was not committed to his claims.

The renewed war went ill for the Danes, and on 20 July 1864 they were compelled to accept an armistice. When the final terms were signed in Vienna, on 27 October, Denmark ceded to Austria and Prussia the duchies of Schleswig, Holstein and Lauenburg—some two-fifths of the area of the Danish monarchy (Map 4). The question of the ultimate disposal of these territories had now to be decided. The condominium of the two German Great Powers was unlikely to prove a satisfactory permanent solution. On his side Bismarck was determined to gain the duchies for Prussia, if possible without war, but if necessary, and if he could carry King William to the point of war, he was prepared to risk the gamble for so rich a prize. But he was in no hurry. Prussia was not, in 1864, ready for hostilities, and the next two years were occupied in a series of negotiations between Austria and Prussia for a solution of the tangled problem.

THE DEFEAT OF AUSTRIA BY PRUSSIA

Bismarck was assisted during these years by the weakness and the vacillation of Austrian policy, but he had powerful forces against him in Prussia itself. The king hated the idea of war with Austria; the Crown Prince and both Prussian and German public opinion at first supported the recognition of Augustenburg's claims; the Prussian Landtag refused obstinately to vote money for the army and would almost certainly not vote war credits. And, though Prussian assistance to Russia in suppressing the Polish insurrection of 1863 as well as the Austrian attitude during the Crimean War (see p. 42) had made Russian intervention against Prussia unlikely, the uneasy ambition and unsatisfied appetite of Napoleon III made a war with Austria a hazardous undertaking. Moreover, the attitude of the other

German states, particularly of Saxony, Bavaria and Hanover, was unlikely to be favourable to a war by Prussia for the annexation of the duchies and for her own aggrandizement at the expense of the national cause. There was every reason for caution.

Map 4. Schleswig-Holstein, 1864. The northern part of Schleswig was ceded to Denmark after a plebescite held in 1920.

During the early months of 1865 war between the two Powers seemed inevitable, for Austria now supported the Augustenburg claim. But in July a change of Ministry took place in Austria and the new government withdrew support from Augustenburg and agreed to the Treaty of Gastein (14 August 1865). By this treaty Prussia acquired the Duchy of Lauenburg for 2½ million thalers, and the joint rule of the Powers in both duchies was superseded by that of Prussia in Schleswig and of Austria in Holstein. Prussia also acquired the harbour of Kiel in Holstein and control of military roads through Holstein into Schleswig. Prussia had the best of the bargain. Yet the treaty made no final arrangement for the duchies—Bismarck described it as 'a papering over the cracks'—though it also had other than material compensations for Prussia. Austria had lost face throughout Europe, as well as in Germany, by abandoning her support of Augustenburg's claims and by yielding much of the Prussian demands.

But if Bismarck was to achieve his final object he yet had to bring William to the point of readiness for war and to ensure Prussia's international position if it came. He began by visiting Napoleon III at Biarritz in October 1865 and left him under the false impression that Prussia might consent to his acquisition of Belgium and possibly even some German territory in the Rhineland in return for French neutrality. Next he signed a commercial treaty with Italy (November 1865), and when the Austrians replied, foolishly enough, by once more allowing the Augustenburg agitation to be conducted in Holstein, Bismarck brought the period of co-operation after Gastein to an end by sending a strong note to the Austrian government denouncing it for allowing a 'seditious agitation' against Prussia to take place in the duchies. This was immediately followed up by negotiations both with France and with Italy, and in March 1866 both Austria and Prussia began a partial mobilization. By 8 April Italy had pledged her support to Prussia for three months, and to this treaty Napoleon III had given the Italians his assent, for he was convinced that Austria and Prussia would exhaust each other and that, probably without war, the threat of French intervention would bring France territorial gains on the Rhine frontier. In this delusion he received every encouragement from Bismarck.

With the signature of the Italian treaty Bismarck's stage was almost set. It remained only to provoke Austria to such a degree that she would provide a *casus belli* and thus persuade King William that she, and not Prussia, was the aggressor. To this end Bismarck now (9 April) made proposals for the unification of Germany under Prussian leadership, with Austria excluded and a national parliament elected on the basis of manhood suffrage. The response of Germany was disappointing and, under pressure from the Crown Prince and from public opinion, William himself began to doubt the wisdom of his minister's policy. Negotiations with Austria continued during May and June and, to prevent Napoleon's immediate intervention in the war, Bismarck at once consented to his proposal for a European Congress, whilst Austria made her acceptance dependent on impossible conditions. At length the Austrian government solved Bismarck's problem for him. Unable to face the cost of prolonged mobilization, the Austrian government suddenly determined to take a strong line in the Schleswig-Holstein question in the hope of securing the support of the smaller German states against Prussia. On 1 June they proposed to the Diet of Frankfurt that the Confederation should decide the fate of the duchies. Bismarck's reply was to say that, Austria having violated the Treaty of Gastein, the earlier system of joint administration was automatically in force, and he marched Prussian troops into Holstein (7 June). The Austrians replied by declaring the entry of Prussian troops into Holstein an act of war and by proposing a Federal mobilization against Prussia. Bavaria, Saxony, Hanover, Württemberg, Baden, the Hesses and Nassau gave qualified support to Austria, and Bismarck therefore declared the Confederation at an end. At last he had his way—and his war. As Cavour had goaded the Austrians into war in 1859, so did Bismarck in 1865–6, and in doing so he had been able to overcome William's last scruples.

The War of 1866 and the peace of Prague. The Six Weeks' War which followed crowned Bismarck's diplomacy and endorsed his political judgment. From the first the Prussian armies were everywhere successful. By the end of June Hanover had been overrun, and on 3 July the main Austrian forces were decisively defeated at Königgratz (Sadowa) in Bohemia. At the cost of under 2000 men killed in this battle, and a little over 7000 wounded, Prussia, if allowed to exploit her victory, had changed the face of Germany and altered the balance of Europe. The danger now was of French or Russian interference. But though Napoleon intervened as mediator, his armies were not ready to act. The speed of the Prussian victory had upset all his calculations and, already weakened by the Mexican expedition, France was in no position to take the swift and decisive action which could alone avail. Napoleon was, therefore, forced to consent to the enlargment of Prussia in north Germany, provided that Austria, apart from Venetia, remained intact. Bismarck has told, in his Reminiscences, of his difficulties in persuading the king and the soldiers to be content with a moderate peace. But, with the Crown Prince's aid, he prevailed, and the final peace was signed at Prague on 23 August and ratified on 30 August. The long struggle between Austria and Prussia for predominance in Germany was over and the 'shame' of Olmütz was most amply revenged.

By the terms of peace Prussia obtained the duchies of Schleswig and Holstein in full sovereignty, with the single reservation that Prussia was to restore to Denmark, after a plebiscite, that part of Schleswig which was Danish speaking. This plebiscite was not held until after Germany's defeat in 1918, and in 1879, when the Austro-German Alliance was formed, Austria renounced the right to demand it. Prussia made no further territorial demands on Austria and received a very moderate indemnity. Bismarck agreed, too, to leave Saxony and the southern states intact. But the treaty, in its second article, recognized Prussia's right to organize north Germany in a new Confederation, from which Austria should be excluded, whilst the south German states were to be free to decide their relation to it. In addition, Prussia annexed outright Hanover, Hesse-Cassel, Nassau and Frankfurt, thus giving her territories unbroken continuity from Königsberg to Cologne. What mattered even more than the gains in territory (1300 sq. miles) and population (3,170,632) was the unchallengeable superiority she now possessed in Germany, and the direct control of the policy and military resources of the other member states of the new North German Confederation (Map 5) provided by the constitution of that body which was passed by the new Reichstag on 16 April 1867.

Bismarck's victory over Austria was also a victory over the forces of liberalism in Prussia, though this was not recognized at

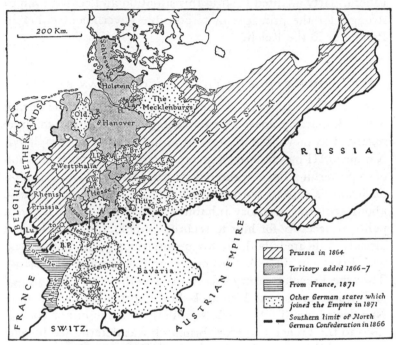

Map 5. The formation of the German Empire, 1864–71

A. = Anhalt; B = Bremen; B.P. = Bavarian Palatinate; Br. = Brunswick; H. = Hamburg; Hesse C. = Hesse-Cassel; Hesse D. = Hesse-Darmstadt; L. = Lübeck; La. = Lauenburg; L.D. = Lippe Detmold; O. = Oldenburg; Thur. S. = Thuringian states; W. = Waldeck.

the time. He sought and obtained from the Prussian Landtag an indemnity for having raised taxes without the Landtag's consent since 1862. But, in asking for the indemnity, he made it clear that neither he nor the king admitted the principle of the responsibility of ministers to the elected house and he asserted the right, and even the duty, of the Crown to act independently if a parliamentary deadlock occurred. After 1866 there was no further progress towards fully responsible parliamentary government in Prussia until the collapse of 1918. It was still more important that the constitutions both of the North German Confederation and of the German Empire followed the Prussian model in practice and that, in course of time, the National Liberal party adapted itself to this situation and ceased even to struggle for the principle of responsible government either in Prussia or in the Reich.

THE COMPLETION OF THE PRUSSO-GERMAN EMPIRE

The three years 1867–70 can only be regarded as a period during which Bismarck prepared for the struggle with France which he regarded as inevitable if German unity were to be completed. Napoleon III had suffered a severe reverse by the mere creation of so powerful a force as the new North German Confederation on France's eastern border. At heart he was not enthusiastic about acquiring territory inhabited by Germans, but it was a political necessity for him to secure compensation, and he had already indicated, both in his negotiations with Austria and with Prussia in 1866, that his eyes were fixed on the Rhineland. That the French treasury was empty and the army ill-equipped and worse organized Bismarck knew, probably better than Napoleon himself. And, whilst willing to make minor concessions to the French emperor, Bismarck was determined to cede no foot of German soil and to be ready for immediate action in case war should become necessary.

During the Austro-Prussian conflict Napoleon, under the influence of his Foreign Minister, Drouyn de l'Huys, had demanded the cession of Mainz, part of the Palatinate, and the Saar territory as compensation for his neutrality. The answer was a blunt refusal, and the further result a series of treaties between Prussia and the southern states providing that the king of Prussia should be commander-in-chief of the German armies in the event of war. Bismarck arranged, too, that Napoleon's demands should 'leak out' in the Paris *Siècle* and, in face of the indignation they caused in Germany, Napoleon drew back, repudiating Drouyn, who resigned from office. But he next sought to negotiate Prussia's consent to his annexation of Belgium and Luxembourg, and at the same time offered Prussia an alliance. Bismarck again allowed him to commit himself— even hinting that Belgium might become 'the rampart of France' and then, at the risk of war, refused to consent. Napoleon, since he dared not fight, fell back on a negotiation with Holland for the purchase by France of the province of Luxembourg, in which, since 1815, the Prussians had maintained a garrison. When Prussia resisted even this compensation, Napoleon III was forced to consent to a conference in London from which he acquired merely the withdrawal of the Prussian garrison from the fortress of Luxembourg and the neutralization of the province itself.

It was Napoleon's last glimmer of success. Between 1867 and 1870 his relations with Italy were worsened by Garibaldi's attempt on Rome, defeated by French troops at Mentana, and his negotiations with the Austrian court were rendered inconclusive by the recent reorganization (1867) of the Austrian Empire on the basis of the 'Dual Monarchy', for the Hungarians were unwilling to fight for a renewal of Austrian predominance in Germany, which had always been associated with German hegemony in the Austrian Empire itself. Thus Napoleon remained isolated in face of the new German Power, for his intrigues to obtain Belgium were not unknown either in Belgium itself or in England, whilst Russia's attention was fixed upon the Balkans and she continued to regard conservative Prussia with benevolence. France, therefore, had every reason for prudence, and Bismarck for confidence, when, in the first days of July 1870, Franco-Prussian relations became acutely strained as a result of information given by the Spanish government to the French ambassador to Spain that Prince Leopold of Hohenzollern-Sigmaringen of the Catholic branch of the Prussian royal family had accepted the proposal that he should be elected king of Spain. To Frenchmen, as the Duc de Gramont (the Minister for Foreign Affairs, 15 May–9 August 1870) declared to the *Corps*

Législatif on 6 July, this was to revive the empire of Charles V and de Gramont's declaration ended with a half-veiled threat of war if Prince Leopold's candidature were not withdrawn.

On 9 July, therefore, Benedetti, the French ambassador, presented the French standpoint courteously but firmly at Ems to King William and received the king's assurance that, as head of the Hohenzollern house, he had already entered into negotiations with Prince Leopold's father and that he would approve the decision if the prince and his father agreed to withdraw the candidature. But, unfortunately for France, de Gramont was now determined to wring from the Prussian king a statement which would show that he had yielded to French pressure and would thus satisfy French public opinion—particularly the Paris press and the right-wing nationalists. Even after it became known in Paris on 13 June that Leopold's father had withdrawn his son's candidature and it seemed that the crisis was over, de Gramont, ignoring the rest of the French Cabinet, instructed Benedetti to seek another interview with King William and to secure his formal assurance that the candidature would not be renewed at any future time.

On 13 July, therefore, Benedetti reluctantly sought to carry out these instructions at a further interview at Ems. But King William refused to give a pledge *à tout jamais* and, although he sent an adjutant to tell Benedetti that he had received confirmation of the withdrawal, he added that he had nothing further to say to the ambassador. These facts were communicated by telegram from Ems to Bismarck in Berlin and, by shortening the message in which they were contained, Bismarck contrived to give his version of the telegram a note of militancy calculated to arouse French resentment still further. He issued his version at once to the press and to all Prussian representatives abroad, with the result that the war party in the French Government easily carried the day and war was declared on Prussia on 19 July 1870.

In later years Bismarck was eager to claim the war of 1870 as his own handiwork.[1] Even though the proximate cause may be

---

[1] Cf. *Bismarck, his Reflections and Reminiscences*, vol. II (trans. A. J. Butler, London, 1898), ch. XXII.

regarded as de Gramont's eagerness to obtain satisfaction for French opinion by inflicting a diplomatic defeat on Prussia, it is now known that Bismarck had been much more active in promoting the Hohenzollern candidature than he cared to admit.[1] In so far as it was the candidature itself which, by threatening France with 'encirclement', was the real cause of the war, his active promotion of it—and his provocative recasting of the Ems telegram at a crucial moment—involve him in a major share of the responsibility for its outbreak, although it seems clear that de Gramont wanted at least to inflict 'on Prussia a humiliation equivalent to a military defeat',[2] and was reckless of the risks involved in his determination to achieve it.

As in 1866, the Prussian army, supported now by Bavaria, Württemberg and Baden, rapidly showed its efficiency and its superiority over the French. Again, in a little over six weeks, the decisive campaign was over. Before the end of August Bazaine, in command of the main French army, was shut up in Metz and, on 2 September, Napoleon and MacMahon were forced to surrender at Sedan, with 80,000 men. Revolution at once broke out in Paris, a republic was declared, and although a government of national defence carried on resistance for some months Jules Favre was compelled to sign an armistice on 29 January 1871. On 26 February Thiers and Jules Favre signed the preliminaries of peace and on 1 March, by a vote of 546 to 107, the French National Assembly accepted them. France yielded Alsace and Lorraine, promised to pay an indemnity of 5000 million francs within four years, and accepted the occupation of certain of her eastern provinces until this indemnity had been paid. The French Second Empire had crashed to the ground. The 'Second Reich' began its history amidst its ruins. For, on 18 January 1871, King William of Prussia, at the request of the ruling princes of all the German states, excluding Austria, was proclaimed German Emperor in the Hall of Mirrors at Versailles. Bismarck had negotiated with the governments of the southern states during the

---

[1] Cf. Eyck, *Bismarck and the German Empire*, pp. 163–8; and G. Bonnin, *Bismarck and the Hohenzollern Candidature for the Spanish Throne* (London, 1957), *passim*.
[2] A. J. P. Taylor, *The Struggle for Mastery in Europe* (Oxford, 1954), p. 205.

autumn and, by making concessions to their particularism, including, in the case of Bavaria, a secretly agreed right to have a representative at peace negotiations and to remain immune from any *Reichsexecution* by the Empire,[1] had secured their adhesion to the new empire (Map 5). The necessary changes were made in the constitution of the North German Confederation and the constitution of the new empire came into force on 1 January 1871.

4. ECONOMIC DEVELOPMENT, 1815-71

ECONOMIC POSITION OF GERMANY IN 1815

At the close of the Napoleonic wars, Germany showed few signs of her future economic greatness. The Germans possessed many qualities necessary for material progress but they were hampered by adverse geographical, economic, political and social factors. Both agriculture and industry suffered from geographical difficulties. Much of the north German plain was infertile. The bogs and heaths west of the Elbe and the swampy valleys east of that river presented special problems to the farmer. Important mineral resources lay on the periphery of the country and could not be exploited until improved transport was available. Germany's chief coastline was on the Baltic, the trade routes of which were of minor importance, and in the days of sailing ships her North Sea ports of Hamburg and Bremen were unable to compete successfully on the Atlantic trade routes with more favourably placed British and Dutch ports.

Further difficulties restricting economic development were presented by poor communications within Germany, by lack of capital for investment in industry, by the survival of medieval social institutions both in the countryside and in the towns, and by the evil effects of political divisions, with their resultant customs barriers. Although Article 19 of the Federal Act of 1815 provided that 'the Confederated States reserve to themselves the

---

[1] These special concessions to Bavaria only came to light in 1918 and 1932 respectively. Cf. Fritz Hartung, *Deutsche Verfassungsgeschichte* (Stuttgart, Koehler Verlag, 1950), pp. 256-7.

right of deliberating... upon the manner of regulating the commerce and navigation from one State to another', the Federal Diet at Frankfurt took no steps to organize German economic life, and the individual states were left to work out their own economic salvation.

PRUSSIAN ECONOMIC POLICY AND THE ZOLLVEREIN

Like the other German states Prussia suffered severe economic depression after 1815. Though she had gained territories, such as the Rhineland and Westphalia, which were to prove of immense economic importance in the future, these were as yet undeveloped, and the great distances between Memel on the east and Trier on the west, combined with poor communications and the lack of territorial continuity between the western and eastern provinces, presented problems of great difficulty. The Prussian state took active steps, by negotiating trade treaties, by building roads and by securing information of technical progress abroad, to overcome them. But the most important step taken was the enactment of Maassen's Tariff Law of 1818.

Under this law many internal dues were abolished and customs duties were now collected at the frontiers, which involved some loss of revenue but facilitated trade between Prussia's two separate groups of provinces. Most raw materials were admitted duty free, whilst manufactured articles paid only 10% import duty *ad valorem* and the products of tropical countries from 20 to 30%. These duties were low enough to make smuggling unprofitable and to avoid offending powerful neighbours. Goods which crossed Prussian territory (without being consumed) paid 1s. 6d. a cwt., a tax on international commerce which was a useful source of revenue as well as a weapon which could be used against small German neighbours.

The Tariff Law brought no immediate relief to Prussia's agriculture or industry, but ultimately it facilitated economic expansion. Shortly afterwards various small enclaves were absorbed into the Prussian customs system. They accepted the Prussian tariff (administered by Prussian officials) and received a share of

the joint revenue calculated upon the ratio between their population and that of Prussia's eastern provinces.

Customs unions (Map 6). The existence of many independent
tariff units was so inconvenient that several states undertook
negotiations in the 1820's for the formation of customs unions.

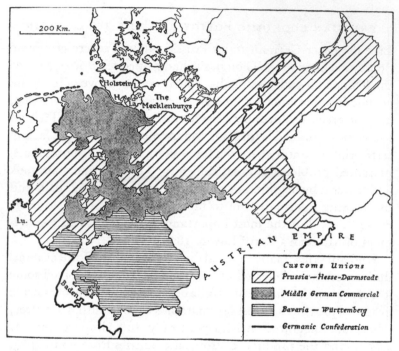

Map 6. The three customs unions of 1828

H. = Hamburg; L. = Lübeck; La. = Lauenburg; L.D. = Lippe Detmold;
Lu. = Luxembourg; W. = Waldeck.

Three were formed in 1828. The first—between Bavaria and
Württemberg—fell short of the great South German Union
originally planned. The second was between Prussia and Hesse-
Darmstadt, and was on the same lines as the arrangements made
to include enclaves in the Prussian customs system, except that
Hesse-Darmstadt retained her own customs officials. The third
was the Middle German Commercial Union which included
Hanover, Brunswick, Saxony and several small states in central

Germany. It had no common tariff and its object was to prevent Prussia from controlling the main roads from the North Sea ports to the markets of Frankfurt-am-Main and Leipzig. But Prussia defeated the union's plans. She facilitated commerce between north and south Germany by herself constructing roads through

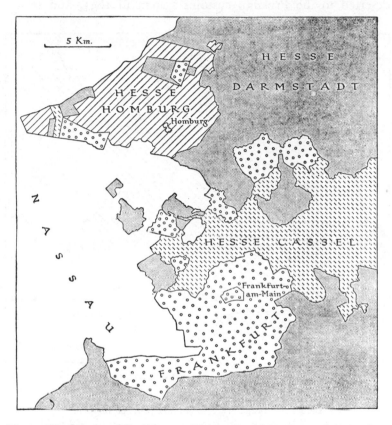

Map 7   The free city of Frankfurt-am-Main and neighbouring territory in 1833. The map well illustrates the territorial confusion in Germany at this time.

the principalities of Meiningen and Gotha from Prussia to Bavaria, Württemberg, and Frankfurt-am-Main, and by taking the lead in negotiations with the Dutch for reducing the tolls levied on shipping on the Rhine. This was the work of Motz, who was Prussian Finance Minister between 1825 and 1830. The extreme confusion in tariff boundaries involved in the territorial divisions of the German states is illustrated by the case of Frankfurt (Map 7).

Prussia and the foundation of the Zollverein. The Middle German Commercial Union collapsed under these blows. Hesse-Cassel deserted to the Prussian customs system in 1831, and so an

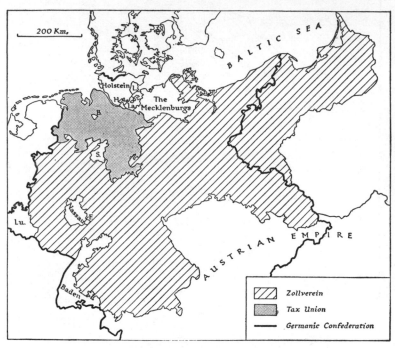

Map 8. The Zollverein and the Tax Union, 1834

B. = Bremen; H. = Hamburg; F. = Frankfurt-am-Main; L. = Lübeck;
La. = Lauenburg; S. = Schaumburg principalities, etc.

economic link was forged between Prussia's eastern and western provinces. Saxony and the Thuringian states followed suit. Meanwhile Prussia and the southern states were drawing closer together. In 1834 Bavaria and Württemberg formed a customs union with Prussia and the two Hesses. This union—the Zollverein—had an area of 162,870 sq. miles and a population of nearly 23½ millions (Map 8). Within eight years it had been joined by Baden, Nassau, Frankfurt-am-Main and Luxembourg. But Hanover, Brunswick and Oldenburg, the rump of the defunct Middle Union, remained aloof and formed the Tax Union, whilst other states which retained their economic independence were the three Hanse towns (Hamburg, Bremen and Lübeck), the two Mecklenburgs, Schleswig and Lauenburg. Between 1837 and 1844 the Brunswick lands joined the Zollverein (Map 9).

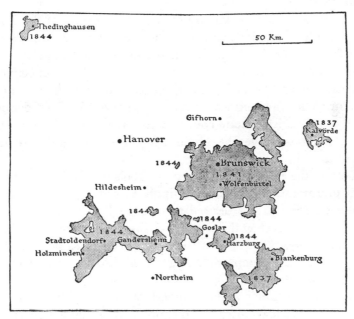

Map 9. The adhesion of Brunswick to the Zollverein, 1837–44.
The dates indicate when various Brunswick lands
entered the Zollverein.

The establishment of the Zollverein was not the direct result of the growth of German national consciousness. Many states entered the Prussian customs system only because they could in no other way alleviate their financial and economic embarrassments. They jealously guarded their sovereign rights and prevented Prussia from gaining any substantial political advantages from her position as the leading state in the Zollverein. Only slowly did the beneficial effects of the Zollverein on industry and trade become apparent, but the financial advantages derived from membership of the Zollverein were more immediately obvious. With the exception of Saxony and Frankfurt-am-Main nearly all members of the Zollverein normally drew more revenue from the customs union (calculated on a population basis) than they collected in duties. This, more perhaps than any other factor, prevented recalcitrant members from breaking away from it.

There were two weaknesses in the organization of the Zollverein. First, unanimity and not a majority decision was necessary for a proposal to be passed by the Zollverein Congress. This *liberum veto* was a weapon which small states could use effectively against Prussia. Secondly, the original Zollverein treaties only ran for eight years and were subject to renewal for fixed periods so that a dissatisfied state could try to remedy its grievances by threatening to leave the union when the Zollverein treaties expired.

Both in the early 1850's and early 1860's the Zollverein came near to dissolution. The assaults upon it were inspired by mixed motives. Some states desired to weaken Prussia by wrecking the Zollverein even at the cost of reviving tariff barriers throughout Germany. Others wanted the Zollverein to be absorbed into a greater union including all Germany and Austria, just as they desired a *Grossdeutsch* solution of the problem of political unity. The popular demand for the complete economic unification of the country found expression during deliberations of the Frankfurt National Assembly in 1848–9, and the draft constitution of March 1849 provided that the Reich 'shall be united for purposes of commerce and tariffs and shall be surrounded by a customs frontier. All internal dues shall be abolished'. But 'the Federal authority may exclude certain places and districts from the customs union'. The attempt to establish a unified Germany failed and the constitution of 1849 remained a dead letter.

AUSTRIA AND THE ZOLLVEREIN

After 1850 Austrian statesmen were anxious to wrest from Prussia the economic as well as the political leadership of Germany, and the attempt was made by Bruck, who had helped to found the Austrian Lloyd shipping company, and was one of the ablest leaders in the growing Austrian world of business. He became Austrian Minister of Commerce in November 1848 and prepared to abolish the Austro-Hungarian customs frontier and to reform the prohibitive Hapsburg tariff as necessary preliminaries to the establishment of a customs union with Germany. He planned the economic unification of the Hapsburg Empire, the Zollverein, the Tax Union and those German states which still retained their economic independence. In the Hapsburg Empire Bruck's scheme was supported by the Magyar landowners (who welcomed the prospect of wider markets for their agricultural products) and by those manufacturers who did not fear German competition. But it was opposed by industrialists in Lower Austria and Bohemia. In Germany Bruck's scheme was sympathetically received by protectionists and was opposed by free traders. The southern states would have accepted the plan only if they got as much revenue from it as they received from the Zollverein. Prussia was implacably hostile for, if Bruck's scheme had succeeded, Prussia would have fallen under Austrian control in economic policy. In Delbrück, a brilliant young official in the Prussian Ministry of Commerce, Bruck met his match.

Delbrück strengthened Prussia's position by securing the adhesion to the Zollverein of Hanover and her associates. Hanover was given 75% more of the Zollverein revenue than she would have secured on the basis of population. But Prussia made the financial sacrifice to gain a useful free-trade ally in the struggle with protectionist Austria and to complete the economic links between her eastern and western provinces. If the southern states deserted her, Prussia was at least assured of the economic control of Germany north of the Main. The southern and central states, however, eventually renewed the Zollverein treaties and no Austro-German customs union was founded. All that Austria secured in the Austro-German commercial treaty of February 1853 was that negotiations for such a union should begin in 1860, and that new tariff concessions made by one of the contracting parties to a third state were to be automatically enjoyed by the other contracting party.

Prussia had kept Austria out of the Zollverein and had absorbed the tax union. While in the political field Austria had recovered her ascendancy in Germany at Olmütz (see pp. 37–8), in the economic sphere she failed to shake Prussia's supremacy. Further commercial negotiations in the late 1850's between Prussia and Austria resulted only in the formation of a German monetary union which sought to fix the relationship between the country's three main currencies.

In 1862 Prussia endeavoured to make an Austro-German customs union impossible by signing a commercial treaty with France which was to come into force three years later. Provision was made for changes in the Zollverein tariff, many import duties being reduced. In return France agreed that normally her imports from the Zollverein should pay duty at the reduced rates recently conceded to Britain and Belgium. While Saxony welcomed the proposed changes in the Zollverein tariff, Bavaria, Württemberg and Hanover at first refused to agree to them and, in July 1862, Austria revived Bruck's proposal for an Austro-German customs union with a protectionist tariff. She desired far higher import duties than those proposed by the Franco-Prussian commercial treaty. Prussia rejected this proposal since it involved the loss of her supremacy in the Zollverein and the sacrifice of the French commercial treaty.

On the Prussian side the negotiations were skilfully conducted. Bismarck, who became Minister President in 1862, appreciated the political necessity of keeping Austria out of the Zollverein, and the southern states were brought to heel by giving them the choice of accepting the French treaty or of leaving the Zollverein, with the result that the Zollverein was renewed by all its former members in October 1864.

Austria and Prussia came to terms in April 1865. The preamble of the treaty referred to a future 'general German customs union' but no one seriously imagined that this could now be achieved. The preferential duties of the treaty of 1853 were replaced by a most-favoured-nation clause, and Austria, even before her military defeat by Prussia, surrendered the dominating position

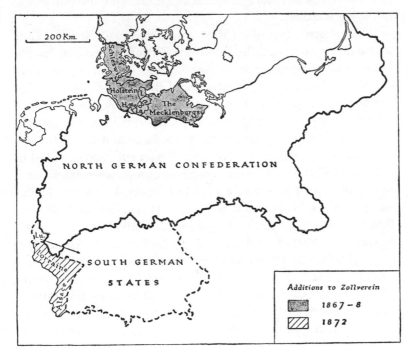

Map 10. The new Zollverein, 1867

A. = Altona; B. = Bremen; L. = Lübeck; La. = Lauenburg; Lu. = Luxembourg.

The constitution of the North German Confederation provided for a customs union, except that Hamburg, Bremen, and the Prussian city of Altona, though within the confederation, were outside the customs union; they paid a special contribution to the exchequer of the North German Confederation in lieu of customs duties. The South German states and Luxembourg (not members of the North German Confederation) joined the new Zollverein by various treaties.

in German economic affairs that Bruck had sought to win for her.

The defeat of Austria and her allies in the Six Weeks' War followed in 1866, and Prussia's political and economic supremacy in Germany was now unquestioned. The Zollverein treaties had automatically ended when hostilities began, and legally the customs union was dissolved, though actually it remained in being. Customs duties continued to be collected, and the proceeds were sent to Berlin and were shared between members of the Zollverein as before, a remarkable example of 'business as usual' in wartime.

The Zollverein after 1866 (Map 10). The North German Confederation under the domination of Prussia, swollen by the annexation of Hanover and other German territories, was also a customs union, though Hamburg and Bremen, whilst becoming members of the Confederation, retained economic independence. The states south of the Main, though politically independent of the Confederation, joined with it to form a new Zollverein. The old General Congress (with its *liberum veto*) was replaced by a Federal Customs Council where decisions were taken on a majority vote. Moreover, a popularly elected Customs Parliament was established and held its first meeting in 1868—the first meeting of popularly elected representatives from the whole of Germany excluding Austria since the Frankfurt Assembly of 1848. But it was the scene of serious disputes on political and economic matters between the northern and southern states, which showed that differences still existed between the states on either side of the Main. The gulf was only bridged by the Franco-Prussian War and the creation of the German Empire in 1871.

DEVELOPMENT OF COMMUNICATIONS AND SHIPPING

The development of the Zollverein had an important influence on the genesis of the German industrial revolution. Equally important was the improvement of communications. In the early nineteenth century the poor transport facilities—particularly east of the Elbe—hampered economic progress. The first German metalled road had been made in Bavaria in 1753. Prussia began to improve her main roads forty years later. Napoleon constructed military roads in western Germany—such as the one from Metz to Mainz and Bremen. In the 1820's Prussia embarked on a road-building programme to foster industry and trade and to defeat the plans of the Middle German commercial union. Over 2800 miles of new main roads were built between 1817 and 1828. By 1845 an English traveller was referring to roads in the Rhineland as 'luxurious'. But the great age of Prussian road-building was from 1845 to 1870, when the total length of the Prussian main roads rose from 8000 miles in 1837 to 18,000 miles in 1862. Whereas Britain and France had completed their networks of main roads before the coming of railways, in Germany the development of roads and railways went hand in hand.

Since many roads were so poor in the early nineteenth century the rivers—particularly the Rhine and the Elbe—were a useful means of transport. But the main rivers crossed the frontiers of various German and foreign states and transit duties hampered the expansion of their traffic. Agreements made between 1821 and 1831 regulated dues on the Rhine, Elbe and Weser, but it was not until the 1860's that these vexatious impositions were either greatly reduced or abolished on the principal rivers. A steamship made the journey from Rotterdam to Cologne in 1816. Fourteen years later a dozen steamships plied on the Rhine. Steamship traffic also appeared on the Danube. The first river steamers carried passengers, but subsequently the transport of goods, such as coal from the Ruhr, became more important. In 1841 a company provided a service of tugs to draw barges on the Rhine. In addition to the improved facilities for river traffic some canals were also constructed, the most ambitious being that joining the Rhine, Main and Danube, which took nine years to build (1836–45) and cost £1,500,000.

The development of railways. It was the railways, however, that really made possible Germany's modern industrial development. They 'first shook the nation out of its economic stagnation, completing what the Zollverein had surely begun. So vigorously did they influence all habits of life that by the 1840's Germany had already assumed a completely different aspect' (Treitschke). The first German railways were short suburban lines—Nuremberg-Fürth, Berlin-Potsdam and Brunswick-Wolfenbüttel—but in 1839 Dresden, the capital of Saxony, was joined by rail to Leipzig, the chief commercial city of the kingdom, 70 miles away, and at the end of 1846 over 2000 miles of railways were open. By the 1860's the trunk lines were complete. Three railway systems linked west and east Germany—one across the north German plain (Aachen-Berlin-Königsberg), one through central Germany (Essen-Dresden-Beuthen), and a third in the south (Mannheim-Munich-Vienna). Three systems linked north and south Germany, one in the east (Stettin-Berlin-Prague), one in central Germany (Hamburg-Cassel-Munich) and one in the Rhine valley (Amsterdam-Cologne-Basle). Railway building fostered the heavy industries, for rails and sleepers had to be constructed, engines and carriages had to be built, and coal had to be provided —though here, as elsewhere, keen foreign competition had to be met. When the railways were completed there were new opportunities for the development of Germany's economic resources— particularly in frontier regions such as Silesia. The railways helped to bring closer together Germans living in different states, and weakened the particularism which was so characteristic of Germany's political and social life in the nineteenth century. 'The German Empire', declared Wilhelm Raabe, 'was founded with the construction of the first railway system between Nuremberg and Fürth.'

The growth of shipping. While the railways promoted internal trade, the mercantile marine fostered overseas commerce. Recovery from the paralysis produced by Napoleon's continental system was slow, and for some time Germany's sea-borne trade was largely in British and Dutch hands. The petty rivalries of the German coastal states, the stringent navigation laws and differential harbour dues of her rivals hampered the development of German shipping. In the 1830's and 1840's Prussia's shipping expanded with the revival of the Baltic corn trade. More important was the rise of the shipping of Hamburg and Bremen in the Atlantic trades, and between twenty and thirty German vessels were bringing sugar and coffee from Brazil in the early 1830's. At this time Bremen was Germany's leading port. Under Burgomaster Smidt's able leadership Bremen constructed the outport of Bremerhaven in 1827 and became the principal port from which emigrants left for the new world; in 1852 nearly 60,000 of them passed through the harbour.

While Bremen was primarily a shipping centre, Hamburg was mainly a commercial centre. It has been said that in the first half of the century the Hamburgers were merely 'the commission agents of England', and certainly her trade and shipping at that time were dominated by British interests. Her prosperity was temporarily checked by the fire of 1842, but the founding of the Hamburg-America Company (1847) and the North German Lloyd (1857) marked the beginning of a new era of prosperity for the Hanse towns. By the 1850's Hamburg firms—particularly those of Wm. O'Swald and Carl Woermann—were active in West and East Africa, and a commercial agreement was made with the sultan of Zanzibar. The Hamburg house of Godeffroy was gaining control of the Samoan copra trade in the late 1850's. These were only modest beginnings, and as late as 1870 the German mercantile marine was still smaller than that of France and her steam tonnage was quite insignificant in comparison with that of Britain.

Mercantile tonnage of Germany, Britain, U.S.A. and France

		1870	
	1850	Total tonnage	Steam tonnage
Germany	139,000*	982,000	82,000
France	688,000	1,072,000	154,000
Britain	3,565,000	5,691,000	1,113,000
U.S.A.	1,586,000†	1,517,000	193,000

* Hamburg and Bremen only.   † Foreign trade only.

Source: Sir J. H. Clapham, *Economic Development of France and Germany* (Cambridge, 1928), pp. 112, 356.

GROWTH OF CAPITAL AND MACHINE INDUSTRY

Another factor influencing the genesis of the Industrial Revolution was the provision of capital. In the early years of the nineteenth century Germany was a poor country compared with Britain and France. Capital for industrial enterprise was

75

provided by the states (e.g. various royal mines in Silesia and the royal foundry in Berlin) and by individuals and families (e.g. manufacturing establishments set up by Krupp at Essen, Borsig at Berlin and Harkort at Witten). Then came sleeping partnerships—particularly in the mining industries—and joint-stock companies. Except in the Hanse towns (which had adopted the French commercial code) joint-stock companies in Germany each required at first a special state charter. But a railway company law was passed in Prussia in 1838 and a general law for joint-stock companies in 1843. In the 1850's financial institutions were established on the lines of the French *Crédit foncier* (which made advances on the security of land) and of the *Crédit mobilier* (which promoted joint-stock enterprises). The Austrian Credit Institute and the Darmstadt Bank were organizations of this kind. In Prussia banks of a rather different type were established (e.g. the *Diskontogesellschaft, Berliner Handelsgesellschaft* and *Schlesischer Bankverein*). The share capital of banks founded in Germany in 1853–7 amounted to £30,000,000. By 1860 there were in Germany some 320 recently founded companies (joint-stock and sleeping partnerships) with an estimated capital of £120,000,000. It was at this time, too, that Frankfurt became an international centre for the exchange of state bonds.

Foreign capital, too, played its part in the rise of Germany's industries. In the middle of the nineteenth century British, French, and Belgian companies were established in western Germany. At least nineteen English mining companies were founded along the Rhine in the 1850's. The 'Hibernia' and 'Shamrock' mines flourished under the management of an able Irishman (W. T. Mulvany). For a generation Prussia had tried to learn from those of her neighbours with industries more advanced than her own. Beuth, an official who has been described as the 'schoolmaster of Prussian industry', encouraged the formation of the Association for the Promotion of Industrial Knowledge (*Verein zur Beförderung des Gewerbefleisses*, 1821), and established technical schools in Berlin and the provinces. He picked the brains of English manufacturers in every way possible, and he was not too scrupulous in his methods.

The rise of heavy industry. The exploitation of Germany's coal and lignite resources and the development of her iron, steel and allied industries laid the foundations of her industrial expansion. 'The German Empire was built more truly on coal and iron than on blood and iron' (Keynes). The Ruhr, Saar and Aachen coalfields were worked effectively on a small scale in the late 1830's. In 1846 Prussia produced only 3,200,000 tons a year—much less than either France or Belgium—but as the German network of railways was completed, so the production of coal increased. Lignite, too, was successfully exploited. In the 1860's Germany had drawn ahead of her continental rivals as a coal producer, but was still far behind Britain.

Output of coal (metric tons)

	Britain	Germany and Luxembourg		France	Belgium
		Coal	Lignite		
1860	81,300,000	12,300,000	4,400,000	8,300,000	9,600,000
1871	118,000,000	29,400,000	8,500,000	13,300,000	13,700,000

Source: Sir J. H. Clapham, *Economic Development of France and Germany* (Cambridge, 1928), pp. 280–1.

The German coal industry was capturing the home markets— the Rhine valley, where Belgian and even English coal were competitors, and south Germany, where wood had been used as fuel. Only in the coastal towns did English coals hold their own.

In the early nineteenth century the craftsmen engaged in the old-established metal industries still possessed a considerable degree of traditional skill, but when the gild system was abolished the efficiency of the workers declined. The ironworks of Silesia and the Siegerland, the steelworks of Solingen and the silver mines of the Harz were small concerns run on the handicraft system, but by the 1840's a few large-scale iron, steel, engineering and machine-making establishments had already been set up. A new era in these industries was heralded by the development of railways and by the increased use of coke instead of charcoal for smelting. The railways themselves needed iron and steel goods. They helped to bring iron and coke together and linked the metal industries with new markets.

It was, however, only after 1860 that these industries expanded rapidly as modern large-scale enterprises. Whereas in 1850 Germany produced only 529,000 tons of pig-iron as compared with France's 898,000 tons, by 1875 Germany produced 2,000,000 tons and France only 1,448,000 tons. The growth of the manufacture of machines paved the way for the modernization of other industries such as textiles.

The textile industries. In the textile industries progress was uneven. The manufacture of linen, hemp and wool, which involved the use of home-produced raw materials, long remained in the hands of peasant craftsmen who worked at home. In the woollen industry the professional urban handicraft weaver was becoming more important than the part-time peasant weaver. On the other hand, the manufacture of cotton and silk, where the raw materials were imported, was necessarily conducted on a larger scale. The organization of the distribution of the raw materials to spinners, weavers, and dyers could be done only by clothiers who were the middlemen (*Verleger*) possessed of some capital. Factories were still small and primitive. In the 1840's only two of the ten cotton mills in the Krefeld district were worked by steam, six of the others by hand and two by horsepower. It was not until after 1845 that power-driven mills were gradually introduced into the linen and woollen industries, and spinning by hand survived the founding of the Empire. Between 1850 and 1870 important changes in woollen manufacture were introduced and, as modern technical knowledge was applied on a large scale in the later 1860's, the home production of wool failed to keep pace with the demand for raw material. The cotton industry also developed rapidly after 1840. At that time only 15,000–16,000 tons of raw cotton were imported annually, but twenty years later (1861) the amount had risen to 67,000 tons. There were over 300 cotton-spinning factories running two and a quarter million spindles and employing 34,663 persons: there were also over 150,000 hand-loom weavers. The depression caused by the shortage of cotton, when the southern ports of the United States were blockaded during the American Civil War, had important results upon the development of the industry.

Spinners had to adapt more of their machinery to Indian cotton. In Saxony large factories with modern machinery replaced small concerns. The introduction of power for spinning and weaving was encouraged by the drifting of hand-loom weavers to other industries and by the temporary cheapness of English textile machinery. An official Prussian report stated that the cotton famine had 'considerably furthered technical improvements, particularly in spinning'. By the early 1870's the industry was using 116,000 tons of cotton a year—rather more than one-sixth of the consumption of the British industry.

The chemical and electrical industries. The development in the 1850's and 1860's of two other groups of manufactures—the chemical and electrical industries—was of special significance for the future. Scientific research in the first half of the century provided the knowledge indispensable to the growth of these industries. Germany was richly endowed with the raw materials of the chemical industry. The Stassfurt deposits of potash salts for example were rapidly developed after 1861, and the output of crude salts rose from 2000 tons in that year to 375,000 tons ten years later. In the electrical industry the period of preliminary research fell in the 1860's, when Werner von Siemens invented the dynamo, and that of the growth of manufacture in subsequent decades.

Agriculture. The period under review also saw substantial progress in agriculture. Between 1840 and 1870 the open-field system under communal management (with its three-course rotation of rye, barley, fallow) gave way to enclosed fields under individual management. The improvement of agriculture owed much to the work of Albrecht Thaer and Justus von Liebig. Thaer stressed the importance of such reforms as enclosures, deep ploughing, improved crop rotation and better implements. Liebig was the father of modern agricultural chemistry. He showed how chemical manures could improve soils and increase the yield of crops. This new scientific knowledge was spread through the experimental stations of university agricultural departments, agricultural schools and special 'winter schools' where short courses were held at a time of year convenient to young farmers. The success of these efforts to educate the German farmer is illustrated by the development of the sugar-beet industry, which makes unusual demands upon the skill and knowledge of the cultivator. In the late 1860's two and a half million tons of beet were handled and 211,000 tons of raw sugar were produced every year.

SOCIAL EFFECTS OF INDUSTRIAL DEVELOPMENT

Growth of population. These changes in industry and agriculture were influenced by, and in turn themselves influenced, the growth and movement of Germany's population. At the beginning of the nineteenth century Germany had a population of less than 25 millions. By the middle of the century it had risen to 35 millions, and when the empire was founded it was 40 millions.

Growth of Germany's population, 1815–70

	Germany	Prussia	Saxony	Bavaria	Württemberg
1815	24,833,000[1]	10,319,993	—	3,707,966[2]	1,410,327
1825	28,113,000	—	—	—	—
1835	30,802,000	13,692,889[3]	1,595,668[3]	4,251,118[3]	1,627,122[3]
1845	34,290,000	—	—	—	—
1855	36,138,000	17,202,637	2,039,176	4,547,239	1,669,720
1865	39,548,000	19,254,649[4]	2,337,192[4]	4,807,192[4]	1,747,187[3]
1875	42,518,000	—	—	—	—

[1] 1816.　　[2] 1818.　　[3] 1834.　　[4] 1864.

Sources: P. Benaerts, *Les Origines de la Grande Industrie Allemande* (Paris, 1933), p. 136; G. Stolper, *German Economy 1870–1940* (London, 1940), p. 38.

This increase was due mainly to the high birth-rate and not to any decline in the death-rate. An analysis of the composition of age groups shows that Germany was a country of young people. In 1868, 45% of Prussia's population was under 20 years of age. The growing population provided the manpower necessary for the expanding industries and increased the size of the home market for manufactured goods. On the whole, urbanization proceeded at a leisurely pace. In Prussia the urban population only increased from 26·5 % of the total population to 32·5 % between 1816 and 1870. In the 1860's, however, the modern population map of Germany was clearly emerging. There were three chief concentrations of population, the Rhineland, Saxony and Upper Silesia, though the state capitals and old medieval cities were still much larger than the new industrial centres.

Growth of certain German towns, 1800–80

	1800	1850	1880
Munich	30,000	110,000	230,000
Cologne	50,000	97,000	145,000
Essen	4,000	9,000	57,000
Chemnitz	14,000	32,000	95,000
Düsseldorf	10,000	27,000	95,000

Source: W. G. East, *An Historical Geography of Europe* (London, 1935), p. 415.

Social problems. In the growing towns were to be found the social problems which generally accompanied the industrial revolution. In the 1840's 'complaints were already rife concerning starvation wages, child labour, the maltreatment and exploitation of workpeople' (Treitschke). Wages declined in the early 1850's but subsequently rose steadily. There was, however, much distress among the worse paid men and those who clung to dying trades. The 1860's saw the founding of Lassalle's General German Labour Union (which disappeared shortly afterwards) and of the Social Democratic Party (1869) which was to play a significant part in the politics of the country.

Neither industry nor agriculture expanded rapidly enough to enable the whole of the increased population to maintain its existing standard of living. There was considerable emigration from Germany in the middle years of the nineteenth century, particularly between 1847 and 1854. In 1847 alone some 90,000 persons left the country. This migration has sometimes been ascribed to political causes but, in fact, these causes were of only subsidiary significance. The main cause was the unsatisfactory conditions in certain agricultural districts. Political revolution and reaction occurred all over Germany in 1848–54, but emigration was mainly from the rural districts in the south-west of the country. Between 1830 and 1860 over a million Germans went to the United States—most of them settling in the old North-West (north of the Ohio and east of the Mississippi) and in Texas. Others went to the provinces of Rio Grande do Sul (Brazil) and Valdivia (Chile). Several societies were founded to exercise some control over German emigration.

Overseas emigration from Germany, 1821-70

1821–30	8,500	1851–60	1,075,000
1830–40	167,000	1861–70	832,700
1841–50	469,300		

Source: G. Stolper, *German Economy 1870–1940* (London, 1940), p. 39.

'Booms' and 'slumps'. As Germany became more industrialized she began to experience that more or less regular recurrence of ebb and flow in trade and of periodic commercial panics which constitute the 'trade cycle'. This puzzling and disquietening phenomenon had been observed and discussed by economists and statesmen in England since the end of the eighteenth century. When Germany began to take her place among the manufacturing states of the continent it became evident that similar forces were at work. There was distress in 1817, 1847, 1857 and 1866. The distress in 1817 marked the beginning of a depression in farming which lasted throughout the 1820's. The depression of the late 1840's was also mainly agrarian in origin—the potato harvest of 1845 had been a failure—but the collapse of firms in Hamburg, Bremen, Frankfurt-am-Main, Karlsruhe and Mannheim was connected with the English financial crisis of 1847. The depression of 1857 showed how closely the fortunes of German commerce were being linked with world trade. It was a financial crisis and it hit Hamburg with special force. A hundred and fifty firms collapsed with total liabilities of £15,000,000. The important firms of Palmié Brothers (Berlin) and Boskowitz (Vienna and Budapest) went bankrupt. The depression of the early 1860's was largely confined to the cotton industry and was due mainly to the sudden shortage of the raw material during the American Civil War. The crises between 1847 and 1866 caused much distress, but they led to the disappearance of small firms working with out-of-date machinery and so ultimately promoted industrial efficiency.

82

GERMAN SOCIETY IN 1871

At the foundation of the empire, Germany, excluding the Austrian empire, had already laid the foundation of the industries which, during the next fifty years, were to make her the greatest industrial nation in Europe. By the creation of the Zollverein and because the new industries, particularly the heavy and chemical industries, drew their raw materials from her soil and the technique of their manufacture from the brains and vigour of her scientists and entrepreneurs, Prussia increased the predominance which her size and population gave her in any case in the empire which, under Bismarck's direction, she had created. The annexation of Alsace-Lorraine in 1871 brought with it new forces of industrial power, in the shape of the iron ore of Lorraine and the textile industry of Alsace. These in turn hastened the rapid industrial development already in progress and enabled Germany to outstrip France and to rival both England and the United States as a manufacturing country before the war of 1914–18 (see pp. 103–117).

Yet the late impact of the Industrial Revolution upon Germany could not change the authoritarian-feudal outlook of her governing classes. In the Prussian eastern provinces the large landowners, from whom the officers of the Prussian army and the administrators of the Prussian state were largely drawn, continued to exercise an authority over their labourers far more stringent than that of any French or English landowner. The 'Gutsherr' (lord of a manor) in East and West Prussia was not only 'the master' in an economic sense, but he represented also the public authority through his rights of jurisdiction, and was, in many cases, judge in his own cause. Moreover, the Servants' Ordinance (*Gesindeordnung*), promulgated at the time when the edict of emancipation from feudal services was to become operative (1810) and reinforced by a law of 1854, placed the landless labourers so much at the mercy of their lords that Dawson could say in 1908 'though the name of serfage is no longer used, this condition exists in spirit and to some extent in fact'. Nor was this state of affairs confined to Prussia, for 'most of the German states

83

have their Servants' Ordinances'[1] and the legal process of emancipation from feudal dues was actually later in Bavaria than in
Prussia itself.

In addition to the labourer's disabilities in face of the rural
lord it must also be remembered that the right of free migration
to the towns and to industrial employment was not granted until
after the establishment of the North German Confederation, and
that, in the towns themselves, the gild system, including compulsory apprenticeship, outlived the revolutions of 1848 and in
Prussia was given new life by a law passed in 1849.

Both in town and country, therefore, despite the relatively
freer society of the Rhineland, on which the influence of French
occupation and of the Napoleonic code had left its mark, the
Germany which was united in 1871 was still in certain respects
a profoundly conservative society from the economic as well as
from the political point of view. The enterprising capitalists, who
organized the new machine industry, were, indeed, far from
conservative in their adoption of the most advanced industrial
techniques. But in their relations to the 'hands', who flowed into
industry from the countryside to 'better themselves', the entrepreneurs were ready to adopt the authoritarian principles of the
landowners towards their labourers, whilst the 'hands' themselves, many of them only a generation removed from serfdom
and none of them accustomed to a free society, were ill qualified
to struggle either for social or political rights. The fact that the
industrial revolution, with the organization of large units which
it involves, came to the German people whilst they were still so
largely influenced by feudal institutions and ideas and before
they had ever tasted civil, still less political liberty, is of great
importance in their later development.

[1] Cf. W. H. Dawson, *The Evolution of Modern Germany* (Fisher Unwin, London,
1908), pp. 275–6.

CHAPTER II

THE GERMAN EMPIRE IN PROSPERITY AND DEFEAT, 1871–1918

1. THE AGE OF BISMARCK

THE BISMARCK SYSTEM

'THE domestic and foreign policy of a state cannot be distinguished from one another since both alike are the expression of the social forces in power in the state.' These words of an acute German historian apply with particular force to the German Empire as Bismarck constructed it, and the history of Germany since 1871 is unintelligible without some understanding of the disposition of political forces not only as provided for in the Imperial constitution but as they operated in practice. The essential feature of Bismarck's work was that Prussia dominated the new Empire, and that Prussia remained unchanged, ruled itself by the king, so far as he had enough strength of character to enforce his will, and by the largely noble military-bureaucratic caste. The Three-Class system of voting (see p. 32 n. 2) maintained the ascendancy of the Prussian Conservatives in the elected house of the Prussian Landtag, whilst the Upper House was their preserve. Prussia had an absolute veto in the new Federal Council (*Bundesrat*) upon any constitutional change, and by her influence over the smaller states could be practically certain that no measure to which the Prussian government objected would ever become law. Further, whilst Prussia had nothing to fear from the opposition of the smaller states, their preservation in a monarchical-conservative form served to buttress the power of the Prussian king himself within the boundaries of his own state. The preamble to the constitution of 1871 makes clear the conservative nature of the new Prusso-German Empire. It does not emanate from the German people. It is a grant from the rulers of the several states. Bismarck had arranged that Prussia should not 'merge' into Germany, particularly into a democratic Germany. The preservation of the lesser dynasties was, in itself, an insurance for the Hohenzollern kingship of Prussia.

In the new Prusso-German Empire, then, the king of Prussia remained the Commander-in-Chief of the Prussian army, and personally controlled the appointment of its general staff and superior officers. He became also in 1871, with some limitations on his control in Bavaria and the southern states, the War Lord of united Germany. The methods and discipline of the Prussian army were extended to the contingents of the other states, and the influence of the social outlook of the ruling classes in Prussia was spread over the Empire. The power to declare war and to make peace were in the Kaiser's hands and, since Prussia formed three-fifths of the Reich, none of the lesser states was likely to oppose his will. The popularly elected Reichstag had formally wide powers of legislation and budget control. But the active head of the government, the Imperial Chancellor, was not responsible to it, but to the Kaiser, and, as Minister-President of Prussia and President of the Federal Council, spoke to it with a voice of impressive authority. Divided from the first into many parties, with no clear and united majority ever likely to emerge in time of peace, the Reichstag was powerless to control policy, although it could to some degree influence it, and has been justly described as no more than 'a democratic plaster' applied to the iron structure of Prusso-Imperial government. Bismarck, in framing the Imperial constitution, had institutionalized himself. He was, under William I, subject to fewer restraints than either an American President or an English Prime Minister. By his services and his personal force he had made himself indispensable to William I, whom he could always bring to heel by threats of resignation. In effect, therefore, he wielded himself the great political powers of the sovereign as well as those attached to his own office. He towered over his colleagues in the Prussian Ministry, whilst the Imperial Vice-Chancellor and Under-Secretaries were definitely his subordinates. All policy, domestic and foreign, was in his hands, and, apart from the wishes of the Kaiser, the sole limitation on his power was the need to maintain working majorities in the Lower House of the Landtag and in the Reichstag.

There were two deep flaws in Bismarck's system. The enormous powers which he, quite literally, enjoyed as well as exercised, depended on the Kaiser's will, and either he, or a future Chancellor, might find a new Kaiser less easily controllable than William I. In that event Germany, and Europe, might be endangered if the new Kaiser's character or ability was unequal to his task. In the second place, the dominance of the Prussian army and Junker class was bound to cause a political cleavage in the Reich itself. The development of democratic ideas in the Reich and in Prussia could not fail to create a demand that the very basis of Conservative power—the Three-Class suffrage in Prussia—with its gross inequalities should be assimilated to the system of manhood suffrage granted by Bismarck himself for elections to the Reichstag. No logical justification could be found for a system in which a Prussian citizen was, in Prussia, unable to secure fair representation for his views, whilst in the Reich he could do so.

BISMARCK'S POLITICAL ALLIES AND OPPONENTS

In fact, immediately the new Empire began to function, the grant of manhood suffrage and of the secret ballot gave rise to a misunderstanding and an inner conflict. His old Conservative friends in Prussia feared that Bismarck had decided to move towards Parliamentary government; his new National-Liberal allies hoped through their powerful representation in the elected house to extend the slender powers granted to the Reichstag in the constitution. Both were deceiving themselves. Bismarck was as determined as any other Prussian Junker to maintain the power of the monarchy and the ruling class, but he had seen in 1866 the need to enlist the support of the wider movement for national unity represented by the National-Liberals in his task of unifying Germany, and, especially from 1866 to 1870, he was anxious to secure the support of the Liberals in the southern states. He was determined, however, to make no further concessions to liberalism. He intended to stand himself, and to keep the monarchy, above all parties, including even the Conservative parties, and to use them all, except those which he regarded as fundamentally hostile to the state, for the state's purposes. The years 1870–8, which have been regarded as Bismarck's 'liberal' period, do not, in fact, deserve the title. It is true that he relied largely on National-Liberal votes, both in the Prussian Landtag and in the Reichstag, for carrying through his domestic policy. But it was what he regarded as the factious opposition of his old Prussian supporters, their failure to understand the absolute necessity of a minimum of concession to liberalism, in order to secure the unity of Germany without sacrificing the basic conservative-monarchical institutions of Prussia, which forced him to rely more than he desired upon National-Liberal support.

Anti-liberal aspects of Bismarck's policy. Not that his policy was more than superficially liberal. His attack on the Catholic Church, in the *Kulturkampf*, was directed against what he regarded as a political monstrosity—a political party on a religious basis. Moreover, this Catholic party, the Centre (*Zentrum*), represented every anti-Prussian force, both in external and internal affairs. As Catholic it might ally itself with the *Grossdeutsch* forces in recently defeated Austria, or with the Catholic monarchists in France. It was openly in alliance—and the alliance was personified by Ludwig Windthorst, the former Hanoverian Minister of Justice and now the virtual leader of the Centre party—with the Poles of Prussia's eastern provinces, with the irreconcilable representatives of the newly annexed Alsace-Lorraine and with the Hanoverian legitimists who protested against Prussian annexation of their state. The attack upon Catholicism was, indeed, supported enthusiastically by the National-Liberals, with whom Falk,[1] the Prussian Minister of Public Worship and author of the 'May Laws' (1873), was in close touch. The National-Liberals, like Bismarck himself, were more concerned for the defence of the national state against the threat from a foreign Power contained, in their eyes, in the

---

[1] Adalbert Falk (1827–1900) entered the Prussian state service in 1847, becoming public prosecutor at Lyck. He was Prussian Minister of Public Worship from 1872–79. Retiring from politics in 1882, he became President of the Supreme Court at Hamm.

doctrine of Papal Infallibility, declared as an article of faith by the Vatican Council on 19 July 1870, the day France declared war on Prussia, than for truly liberal principles. A liberal party which supports exceptional measures directed against the convictions of a religious community is likely to find itself in grave difficulties when similar measures are proposed against a political party.

The Kulturkampf. The *Kulturkampf*, or cultural struggle,[1] originated, in part at least, in the determination of the Prussian government to protect in their spiritual offices those Catholics— the so-called 'Old Catholics' (*Altkatholiken*)—who rejected the new dogma of Papal Infallibility. The first blow was struck in July 1871, when Bismarck suppressed the Catholic Section in the Prussian *Kultusministerium*. Four months later the Reichstag adopted, for the Empire as a whole, a new clause in the criminal code (the so-called *Kanzelparagraph*) imposing penalties for clergy who misused their pulpits for political ends. But it was in Prussia —which had the strongest tradition of religious tolerance of all the German states—that anti-clerical legislation was fully developed. In March 1872 the Prussian Landtag passed a law placing the supervision of all schools in the hands of the state, and in June, by an administrative decree of doubtful legality, the new and vigorously anti-Catholic Prussian Minister of Public Instruction, Falk, forbade all members of religious orders to teach in schools. In the following year the struggle reached its climax when, by securing the adoption of the notorious 'May Laws', Falk succeeded in subordinating all Church life to state regulation. Meanwhile, on 4 July 1872, in response to a popular petition, the Reichstag had passed a *Jesuitengesetz*, banning the Jesuits from Reich territory.

So severe were these measures that even the Evangelical Supreme Council, as well as the Catholic episcopate, was constrained to protest. As for the Roman Catholics, they continued to act as though the May Laws had not been passed, and the

---

[1] The term *Kulturkampf* originated in an election appeal of Rudolf Virchow of March 1873, referring to the struggle against the Catholic Church as a 'struggle for culture' (*Kampf für die Kultur*).

Prussian state was forced both to imprison them and to pass further laws to deal with the administration of dioceses and livings whose bishops and priests had been arrested. More state pressure was applied by a Prussian Landtag law of 9 March 1874 (supplemented by a Reichstag law of 6 February 1875) introducing compulsory civil marriage, and by the Prussian *Klostergesetz* of May 1875, providing for the dissolution within six months of all monastic orders inside Prussia.

Yet, despite these measures, which a Papal encyclical of 5 February 1875 declared invalid, Catholic resistance continued. By 1876 nine Prussian sees were vacant, and over 1400 parishes were without lawfully appointed priests. Feeling was running high enough among the Catholic population to provoke the Catholic apprentice, Kullmann, to try to assassinate Bismarck in July 1874. By now the Chancellor himself had begun to realize that the whole policy was misconceived. After the death of Piux IX in February 1878, he opened negotiations with his more conciliatory successor, Leo XIII. In 1880, 1882 and 1883 laws substantially modifying the 'May Laws' were passed, and in 1886–7 further legislation restored many of the rights previously enjoyed by German Catholics. Some losses which the Catholic Church in Prussia had suffered were not made good, the anti-Jesuit law, for instance, not being fully repealed until 1917. The state, too, retained the right to object to all ecclesiastical appointments. But, in the main, the end of the *Kulturkampf* came as a defeat for Bismarck and for the nationalist Protestants who had supported it. Bismarck's slow and cautious retreat from the uncompromising position taken up against the Catholics in 1871 could not conceal the fact that his promise to the Reichstag early in the conflict—'We shall not go to Canossa'—had not been satisfactorily observed.

The breach with the National-Liberals. Apart from his need to end the *Kulturkampf*, Bismarck also wished to free himself from any dependence on the National-Liberals whose leader, Bennigsen, when invited to join the Prussian government in 1877, sought to bring in with himself several other prominent National-Liberals. These negotiations, carried on by Bismarck without consulting the Kaiser, earned him a sharp reprimand, but they also revealed the National-Liberals' hopes of a further approach to parliamentary government. When, therefore, a Reichstag majority in favour of protective tariffs emerged during the winter of 1877–8, consisting of Conservatives, Centre and some National-Liberals,[1] Bismarck saw the means of reconciling himself with his old friends and of dividing the National-Liberals on the tariff issue. At the same time, two attempts on the Kaiser's life in the spring and summer of 1878 gave him a further rallying cry for the Conservative forces. By pinning the responsibility for the attacks on the Social-Democratic party and demanding an anti-Socialist law for their suppression, he could still further bind the Conservatives to him and still more effectively split the Liberal forces. At the same time the Centre, essentially conservative in its leaders—Catholic prelates, nobles and industrialists—could be gradually brought into the circle of government supporters.

The attack on the Socialists. In addition to these reasons of political expediency the international character of the new Social Democratic party was as repugnant to Bismarck as were its political and economic doctrines which struck at the very foundations of the existing state. With the example of the excesses of the Paris Commune vividly in his mind he had ceased to have any sympathy or tolerance for a movement with which, when presented to him by Ferdinand Lassalle in a more nationalist form, and one which seemed to offer a common front against the hated Progressive party, he had flirted in the 1860's. In 1878, therefore, after a national election in which the Conservative parties gained heavily, a stringent anti-Socialist law was passed, and renewed at intervals until 1890, which sought to repress every public activity of the Social-Democratic party and of the trade unions allied with it. An attack on the rapidly increasing urban proletariat was substituted for the attack on the Catholic minority. In 1879 a law for protective tariffs was passed, at the expense of this same section, but to the advantage of the Junkers

---

[1] The Prussian agrarians had found themselves threatened by American, Canadian and Russian competition, and in 1875 the German manufacturers, after the temporary boom resulting from the French indemnity, had formed the Central Union of German Industrialists and had begun to agitate for tariffs.

4-2

and peasant proprietors, who now began their alliance with the new industrial magnates, particularly in the heavy industries, which has had such sinister consequences for Germany and the world. One mitigation, indeed, Bismarck offered to the working classes, a system of social insurance against sickness, accident and old age, initiated by a special message from the Kaiser in 1881, and carried out in laws passed in 1883, 1884 and 1889. But, so far as their purpose was to wean the working class from Social-Democracy they failed, and the view expressed by Liebknecht that they merely represented 'the night-watchman state, the beadle state, which stands as a prison guard over the subject people' was widely shared.

The Conservative system established. By 1881, then, the essential features of German government at home had been worked out in practice and, thereafter, continued unchanged, except for a brief interval under Caprivi, until 1918. Bismarck had renewed his alliance with the Prussian Conservatives, had widened the alliance by including the right-wing National-Liberals, and, in a less cordial relationship, the Centre. He had preserved his independence of all these allies, had broken the National-Liberals and induced his supporters amongst them tacitly to abandon their remaining shred of liberalism, the demand for responsible parliamentary government. Through the controlled press and at elections the whole influence of government was thrown against the parties of the Left, whilst the Socialists had to face the provisions of the anti-Socialist law. The bureaucracy and the police, armed with powers far wider than in this country, were a further force of government repression, whilst the educational system, from the university downwards, was carefully supervised and its teachers controlled. Behind all was the alliance of the agrarians and industrialists, who supplied the members of the officers' corps, the higher bureaucracy and the directors of industry. To the interests of all these alike responsible parliamentary government spelt danger unless they could, as in England, organize a great national party, which, by a system of compromise and concession, should create a unity transcending class differences. But the Prussian Junker retained his feudal outlook and had no gifts of compromise or sympathy, and the new lords of industry, bred in the same system of ideas, extended the master-subject relationship from the farm to the factory. Commanding the Prussian Landtag they clung to an anti-parliamentary system, since they feared their own countrymen of the working class, increasingly attached to the Marxian doctrines of Social-Democracy, as well as the national minorities —Poles, Danes and Alsace-Lorrainers—of east, north and west. They found bargaining with an irresponsible Chancellor safer and more profitable for their interests than an attempt to build a majority of their countrymen into active support of the state.

THE NATIONAL MINORITIES

The Poles. The tension inherent in this situation inside Germany was increased by Bismarck's policy towards the national minorities within the Empire—the Poles on the east, the inhabitants of Alsace Lorraine on the west. The abandonment of the attack on the Catholic Church involved no relaxation of Bismarck's policy of repression towards Polish political aspirations, and in 1886 he adopted the idea of 'internal colonization' of the Polish provinces by a process of land purchase by the Prussian state, for which 100 million Reichsmarks were allotted, and of the settlement of Germans on the lands purchased from Polish ownership. The results were disappointing, for the German settlers were not of the highest quality and some married Polish wives and their children became Polonized. But, in addition, the Poles were stirred to greater activity in self-defence and began to organize co-operative societies and to develop a greater consciousness of their separate nationality.

Alsace-Lorraine. In Alsace-Lorraine Bismarck's policy was equally unsuccessful. The annexed provinces were given a special constitutional status as a 'Reichsland' directly under the authority of the Kaiser, represented by his Viceroy (*Statthalter*) at Strasbourg. But the hard terms offered to those who opted for French citizenship, the restrictions imposed on the use of the French language in the schools and in official intercourse, and the stringent control of the schools themselves, to which only German teachers were now appointed, were not calculated to win over the affections of the population to their new rulers. The attachment of the provinces to France continued to be strong and when, in 1874, they were allowed representation in the Reichstag they sent a *bloc* of fifteen deputies who had to be added to the other irreconcilable groups, the Poles and Social-Democrats, to whom the German Empire in its existing form was, for national or social reasons, unacceptable.

The Danes of Schleswig. Bismarck's treatment of the Danes of Schleswig was no more tactful. The plebiscite provided for in the Treaty of Prague, by which the Danes of North Schleswig were to be given an opportunity of deciding their own fate, was not held, and release from the obligation to hold it was one of Bismarck's conditions in the alliance made with Austria in 1879 (see p. 97). The Danish 'optants', who had the right to choose Danish citizenship, were forced to do military service in the Prussian army or to leave the country, and the Danish language was steadily displaced by German in the schools. Though the Danes of Schleswig presented no military danger to the Empire, his treatment of them remained a moral stigma on Bismarck's policy. Wherever, on its frontiers, the German Empire included non-Germans there were harshness and repression on the one side, discontent and hostility on the other.

EFFECTS OF BISMARCK'S SYSTEM ON THE PARTIES

The results of Bismarck's determined opposition to any extension of parliamentary government in the new Empire, or in Prussia, were serious. The parties, deprived of any responsibility for the policy of the state or of any opportunity of learning by experience the art of government, increasingly became mere interest groups, whose main function was to exert pressure on the Chancellor on behalf of the sections of opinion which they represented. The Conservatives, and to a lesser extent the Free Conservatives, represented agrarian interests; the National-Liberals, 'big business'; the Left Liberals, the professions and those in commerce who were in favour of free trade; the Centre, the defence of Catholicism; the Social-Democrats, the interests of the working class. As a result the parties considered every question rather from the angle of tactical advantages for themselves than from that of the national welfare as a whole.

Moreover, the divorce of the parties from the practical work of government helped to strengthen the grip of the central Party Committees, consisting of the established leaders, over their followers since new talent for the task of administration was not required. The unreality of party strife under Bismarck's system compared with that of a country like our own in which the fate of the government is at stake, encouraged the German tendency to regard each political party as an expression of a *Weltanschauung* (philosophy of life), and to insist on its separateness from all other parties.

Even Bismarck found his system difficult to work. After 1879 he was able to rely on the steady support of the Conservatives and National-Liberals, but the Centre, still smarting from the *Kulturkampf*, was never a reliable ally, and the Left Liberals still hoped that the Crown Prince Frederick would admit the principle of parliamentary government when he succeeded to the throne. But, by appeals to patriotism, as after the attempts on the Kaiser's life (1878) or over the danger of a French attack (1887), Bismarck was able to maintain a majority for his measures. And, at the worst, he was prepared to consider more drastic steps towards reaction such as he recommended to the young Kaiser in the early months of 1890 (see p. 102).

BISMARCK'S CONSERVATIVE FOREIGN POLICY

Basic ideas. Whilst Bismarck was moulding the internal forces of the new Empire into the conservative pattern just described, he was also engaged in the task of guiding the Empire in its external relations. Here, too, he started from an essentially conservative outlook in two senses. Not only was he anxious to secure the support of the Russian and Austrian Empires, both representing the autocratic principle, but, having accomplished German unity, he regarded the German Empire as a 'satiated state' which must refrain from adventures and devote its energies to the task of conserving the territories and the position it had won.

Above everything, therefore, Bismarck aimed at preventing any coalition of states which might threaten his creation. To this end he set out to isolate France, where dreams of revenge for 1870 were bound to arise, and to draw both Russia and Austria into the German orbit. Since, at first, he steadily refused to consider a policy of colonial expansion, it was possible to remain on good terms with England and to divert France from the idea of recovering the lost provinces by encouraging her colonial aspirations in Indo-China and Africa.

These basic ideas of foreign policy were not consistently followed out by Bismarck himself, for the logic of events was too strong for him. The idea of a conservative Three Emperors' League (*Dreikaiserbund*) was given some substance, but no documentary form, by conversations in 1872 in Berlin between the three rulers and their Foreign Ministers, and later on, in 1881, it took written form in a treaty between the three empires, by which Russia's special interest in Bulgaria was recognized and Austria's in Bosnia-Herzegovina. The treaty also provided for the benevolent neutrality of the other partners if one of the three was attacked by a fourth Power.

French revival after 1871. But, before the agreement of 1881, two events had shown the difficulty of isolating France effectually, and of persuading Russia and Austria to work together. The rapid recovery of France after 1871, the payment of the indemnity (1873) and the consequent withdrawal of the German troops of occupation, were followed by provocative articles in the French press which led both Moltke and Bismarck to think of a preventive war. But, when a kite was flown in the Berlin *Post* in April 1875 by an article headed, 'Is war in sight?', both Queen Victoria and the Czar intervened personally with Emperor William, and, the war scare having died down, the Russian Foreign Minister, Gortchakoff, issued a despatch to all the Russian legations in Europe saying, 'Maintenant la paix est assurée', implying both that Bismarck had desired war and that he had been prevented by Russian intervention from carrying out his designs. The incident showed clearly that France's isolation was only relative, and that Russian policy was set against further Prusso-German aggrandisement.

Germany and Russia. Further, Bismarck's attempt to act 'the honest broker' at the Congress of Berlin (1878) brought upon him and upon Germany the resentment of the Czar and of wide circles in Russia, to whom it seemed that his influence was exerted almost wholly on the Austrian side. The painful necessity to give up, under pressure from England and Austria and with little or no help from Bismarck, some of the gains won from Turkey by the Treaty of San Stefano (1878) was regarded by Russia as a poor return for her benevolent neutrality towards Prussia in 1866 and 1870–1. So strongly did the Czar express himself that, in 1879, Bismarck opened negotiations for a defensive alliance with Austria and, by threats of resignation, forced William I to accept this alliance in October 1879. The existence of the treaty became known in Russia before the end of the year, and the old relationship of confidence between Russia and Germany was never fully re-established. The *Dreikaiserbund* of 1881 represented a *détente* between the three empires, but, though renewed in 1884, it failed to prevent an acute crisis in 1885–6, when the Serbs, then under Austrian protection, attacked Russia's Bulgarian protégés, and was not renewed again in 1887. The rivalry between Russia and Austria in the Balkans was too acute for Bismarck's idea of the alliance of the three conservative Powers to retain much vitality, for movements of nationalist sentiment —Pan-Slavism *v.* Pan-Germanism—were beginning to appear. He was, indeed, able to 'keep the wire open' to St Petersburg by his so-called 'Reinsurance Treaty' of 1887. But that treaty was extremely difficult to reconcile with Germany's obligations to Austria and was kept strictly secret, whilst its limited effectiveness was shown, before Bismarck's fall, by the first steps, in the form of loans and sale of rifles, to a rapprochement between Russia and France. Despite all his skill Bismarck's nightmare of a coalition hostile to Germany was beginning to acquire form and substance.

97

Formation of the Triple Alliance. As against the increasing difficulty of keeping both Russia and Austria in alliance with Germany, Bismarck could set the widening of the Austro-German Alliance into the Triple Alliance by the inclusion of Italy (1882), and also the Austro-Roumanian Treaty of 1883, to which Germany acceded in the same year. But both treaties tended to drive Russia and France still more into each other's arms, and the value of Italy's signature depended largely on the maintenance of good relations with England, for it was qualified by a Mediterranean agreement (1887) between Italy, Austria and Great Britain, and by the firm determination of every Italian Foreign Minister before Mussolini to risk no action which might entail a conflict with British naval power.

THE BEGINNINGS OF EXPANSIONISM

Bismarck and the Colonial Question. If Bismarck's union of conservative Powers and his attempt to isolate France proved difficult to accomplish, he himself began to abandon his basic principle that the German Empire was a 'satiated' Power during the 1880's, and entered into the competition for colonial expansion in Africa and the Pacific which made more difficult his own, and his successors', task of preventing combinations hostile to Germany. As late as 1880 Prince Hohenlohe, then Statthalter of Alsace-Lorraine, after a conversation with Bismarck, wrote: 'Now, as before, he will not hear of colonies. He says we have not an adequate fleet to protect them....He also spoke of my report on the French designs on Morocco, and declared that we could only be pleased if France took possession of the country.'[1] In accordance with this policy Bismarck encouraged the French declaration of a protectorate over Tunis (May 1881), which had the further advantage from his point of view of embroiling France with Italy, and was equally benevolent towards the British intervention in Egypt (1882) which ultimately led to the establishment of British control. But there were forces developing in

[1] Fürst Chlodwig zum Hohenlohe-Schillingsfürst, *Denkwürdigkeiten* (Deutsche Verlags-Anstalt, Stuttgart & Leipzig, 1907), vol. II, p. 291.

Germany, such as those which founded the German Colonial
League in 1882, which led Bismarck to change his views radically
in the next few years. The rapid process of the partitioning of
Africa and the claims of German explorers, missionaries, and
merchant-traders for government backing raised the question

Map 11. German colonies in Africa, 1914

B. = Basutoland (British Protectorate); F.P. = Fernando Po (Sp.); K. = Kabinda
(Port.); P. = Pemba (Brit.); R.M. = Rio Muni (Sp.); S.T. = São Thomé (Port.);
Sw. = Swaziland (British Protectorate); W.B. = Walfish Bay (Brit.); Z. = Zanzibar
(Brit.).
Note the change in the boundary of the Cameroons in 1911.

whether Germany ought not to claim her share of the spoils. At
the same time German overseas emigration, which had been
very small in the 1870's, was increasing rapidly until, in one
year, 220,000 Germans passed under foreign jurisdiction. In
response to these facts Bismarck changed his attitude. In 1882
he gave a pledge to Lüderitz, a Bremen merchant imperialist, of

99

government support in what was to become German South-West Africa, and, as a result, Lüderitz and his colleagues acquired, by treaties with the native chiefs, rights over most of the coast between Portuguese West Africa and Cape Colony during the next two years.

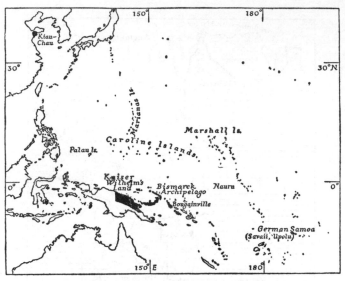

Map 12. German colonies in the Pacific, 1914

Only German colonies are named.

The German Colonial Empire (Maps 11, 12). Between 1884 and 1890, when Bismarck fell, the bulk of the German colonial empire had been acquired. German South-West Africa, Togoland and the Cameroons were all annexed in 1884, and the Marshall, Brown and some of the Solomon Islands in 1885. In 1884 also, acting in agreement with France, a conference was held in Berlin which placed the whole of the Congo basin in the hands of the African International Association, created by King Leopold of Belgium, as the Congo Free State, and thwarted British ambitions for control of the mouth of the Congo. Again, in 1885, an agreement with England recognized German sovereignty over a large part of New Guinea (Kaiser Wilhelm's Land) and over the Bismarck Archipelago in the Pacific. Finally, the conversations which led to the agreement with regard to German East Africa (Tanganyika), concluded by Caprivi in July 1890, had been begun before Bismarck's fall.

This rapid expansion overseas had not been accomplished without a severe strain on Anglo-German relations. British governments resented, somewhat unreasonably, the appearance of a new rival; the Australians felt bitterly the absorption by Germany of the islands off their coasts. The new policy was a flat contradiction of Bismarck's earlier principles. It marked the vigorous beginning of a new German expansionist movement. But, in one fundamental respect, Bismarck set bounds to German ambitions. He took no steps to construct a fleet capable of being a challenge to British naval supremacy, and there can be no doubt, from many of his utterances, that he would have refused to engage in war on a colonial question. The difficulties of Germany's European position were too constantly in his mind. Nor should it be forgotten that it was Bismarck who said: 'The most important political fact in the modern world is that the British and Americans speak the same language.' It is possible that the bitter experience of two great wars may at length convince Bismarck's successors of the truth of his remark.

BISMARCK'S FALL

The accession of William II. The death of the aged Emperor William I in 1888, and of his son and successor Frederick III in the same year, brought to the throne Frederick's son, William II, then 29 years old. Vain, romantic, versatile, self-willed, rash in utterance, alternating between excessive self-confidence and nervous depression, William II had qualities strongly reminiscent of his great-uncle Frederick William IV, and his character exercised a powerful influence on events. For he loved the *métier du roi*, and, without the capacity for unremitting toil and close attention to affairs which had made Frederick II 'the Great', he was determined to enforce his will and to see that his Chancellor obeyed it. Bismarck, now over 70, accustomed to regard himself as indispensable and to be the controller and initiator of policy, was unlikely to fit easily into the new situation.

William II's breach with Bismarck. After a brief 'honeymoon', during which the new Kaiser paid a round of visits, difficulties began to emerge during the winter of 1889–90. There were those in the Kaiser's entourage who whispered that the real issue was whether the Bismarck dynasty or the Hohenzollern was to rule Germany. And, at bottom, the issue was that of the final control of policy. The immediate cause of the breach was that the Kaiser wished to pursue a policy of social reform and conciliation, whilst Bismarck urged upon him a policy of conservative resistance and, if necessary, an open breach with the constitution of 1871, a concerted declaration by the rulers of the German states abolishing universal suffrage, and the promulgation of a new constitution with a great reduction in the rights of the Reichstag. It is difficult to decide how seriously Bismarck meant his proposals to be taken, but their effect was to reveal sharply the underlying issue. Was the Kaiser or the Chancellor to control policy? When William, to assert his authority, demanded the abrogation of a Prussian Cabinet Order of 1852, which gave the Prussian Minister-President the right to be present at any audience between the king and another minister, the naked issue appeared. In face of Bismarck's resistance the Kaiser demanded his resignation and, on 18 March 1890, the great Chancellor resigned. The critical moment in the history of the Prusso-German Empire had arrived, and the famous *Punch* cartoon 'Dropping the Pilot' indicated its nature.

Bismarck's legacy. So long as Bismarck was Chancellor the Prusso-German Empire had had unity of direction, for he had dominated the Kaiser, the soldiers, the Prussian Ministers and bureaucrats, the rulers of the lesser states and the Reichstag alike. Now control was to pass into the young Kaiser's inexperienced hands, and the new ruler's instability of mind and temperament made it probable that he would neither show Bismarck's wisdom nor be able to provide the coherence in policy and control of affairs which the great Chancellor's personality had enforced.

Moreover, the legacy Bismarck left was a difficult one. At home and abroad he had acted on the principle 'divide and rule'. But, abroad, the outline of a coalition against Germany was beginning to take shape, and he had by his colonial policy whetted German desires for expansion. And at home, though the internal divisions of party, nationality, creed, class, and local loyalties remained unhealed, a great industrial development was in progress which gave new force and urgency to the desire for expansion but also sharpened the social antagonisms within the state. Before the reign of William II is reviewed it is necessary to consider the background of economic expansion which profoundly affected Germany's policy in the years before 1914.

2. GERMANY'S ECONOMIC DEVELOPMENT, 1871–1914

THE NEW EMPIRE

Between 1871 and 1914 the development of industrial capitalism in Germany, the beginnings of which have already been described (see pp. 75–80), proceeded with such rapidity that she caught up and, in certain spheres, passed countries like Great Britain, where the industrial revolution had begun earlier. A very rapid growth in population assisted this development by providing the necessary 'hands' for industry. Whereas in 1871 Germany's population was 41 millions, it had by 1915 increased to nearly 68 millions, whilst that of France, which, then including Alsace-Lorraine, had been larger than that of Germany before 1870, had only reached 40 millions on the eve of the war of 1914–18. This rapidly expanding population, of whom, in 1915, one-third were under fifteen, produced in Germany a sense of the need for an equally rapid and continuous expansion in new markets to meet the increasing production of German industry.

The establishment of the German Empire, in 1871, contributed to this rapid expansion. For the annexation of Alsace-Lorraine provided large new iron-ore deposits, which could be worked in conjunction with the existing heavy industry of the

Ruhr and Saar basin and with a flourishing cotton industry, whilst in the 1890's the valuable potash deposits of Alsace were discovered and began to be developed.

The political unity achieved in 1871 also produced effects which encouraged economic expansion. The unified customs administration, post office and consular service all contributed to stimulate economic activity. The chaotic systems of currency and of weights and measures were swept away; the *Thaler* and *Gulden* gave place to the *Mark*, and the metric system of weights and measures was adopted. Although the system of taxation under the Federal government left direct taxes to the individual states, and special privileges to some of them, the Imperial control of tariff policy was a most important factor in German trade expansion, and, before 1914, the Imperial government had acquired, to meet its increasing needs for the armament programme, a share in the estate taxes and, in 1913, a special 'defence contribution' from the whole country.

The late date at which the great development of German industry took place enabled her manufacturers to profit by the experience, and mistakes, of their rivals in other countries. Veblen has pointed out that Germany was 'not committed to antiquated sites and routes for its industrial plant', and that 'having no obsolescent equipment and no out-of-date trade connections', her directors of industry 'were also free to take over the processes of the new industry at their best and highest efficiency, rather than content themselves with compromises between the best equipment known and what used to be the best a few years or a few decades ago'.

The immediate results of the victory over France in 1871 were not wholly favourable. Germany obtained an indemnity of £200,000,000 after the war, and, as she contemplated the adoption of the gold standard for her currency, she added to her reserves that part of the indemnity which was paid in gold. But the receipt of the indemnity accentuated a tendency to speculate which was to be expected in a people enthusiastic over their victories and newly-won unity. There was an unhealthy boom in 1873-4, particularly in railway construction and the heavy industries. When the crash came, 160 out of 857 recently founded companies failed, and agriculture and industry both remained depressed throughout the 1870's. Then, assisted to some extent by the higher tariff of 1879, German industries revived so that within a quarter of a century Germany had become the leading manufacturing state on the continent and competed successfully with Britain in various overseas markets.

THE HEAVY INDUSTRIES (COAL, IRON AND STEEL)

Coal production. The exploitation of Germany's coal resources was one of the foundations of the country's industrial strength. In 1871 production was less than 38 million tons of coal and lignite as against Britain's 118 million tons of coal. But in 1913 Germany produced 279 million tons of coal while Britain produced 292 million tons. The production came mainly from four coalfields: the Ruhr, the Saar, Lorraine and Upper Silesia. The Ruhr was the most important, its production rising from rather less than half of the total German production in 1860 to more than 60% in the present century. It supplied coal and coke to the iron and steel industries of Westphalia, the Rhineland, Lorraine, Belgium, Luxembourg and northern France. The coal handled at the river ports of Duisburg and Ruhrort increased from 1,640,000 tons in 1870 to 18,262,000 in 1913.

Coal mining in Germany and Britain, 1871–1913

| | Germany | | Great Britain |
	Output of coal and lignite (tons)	Number of miners	output of coal (tons)
1871	37,900,000	125,000	118,000,000
1880	59,100,000	179,000	149,000,000
1890	89,100,000	262,000	184,000,000
1900	149,800,000	414,000	228,800,000
1910	192,300,000	621,000	268,700,000
1913	279,000,000	689,000	292,000,000

Sources: Columns 1 and 3—Sir J. H. Clapham, *The Economic Development of France and Germany* (Cambridge, 1928), p. 281. Column 2—M. Baumont, *La Grosse Industrie allemande et le Charbon* (Paris, 1928), p. 528.

Since the great expansion of the German coal industry occurred so late in comparison with that of Britain, large units of production were established using up-to-date methods. As early as 1895 the average coal-mining concern employed no fewer than 500 men. In the early years of the present century Germany exported coal to France, Belgium, Holland and Switzerland, though she still imported it from Britain and Austria.

Coal production of the four main German coalfields in 1910–1913 (metric tons)

	Ruhr	Upper Silesia	Saar*	Alsace-Lorraine
1910	89,315,000	34,461,000	10,823,000	2,686,000
1911	93,800,000	36,623,000	11,459,000	3,033,000
1912	103,093,000	41,543,000	11,663,000	3,539,000
1913	114,487,000	43,801,000	12,223,000	3,796,000

* That part of the Saar in Prussia.

Source: M. Baumont, *La Grosse Industrie allemande et le Charbon* (Paris, 1928), p. 36.

The Ruhr—iron and steel. The Ruhr was the chief centre not only of Germany's coal mining but also of her iron and steel industries. By 1900 half of her pig iron was produced in this area, 30% in Lorraine and Luxembourg and 15% in Silesia and the Saar. But the allied trades—the manufacture of tools, machines, engines and so forth—were more dispersed. The annexation of Lorraine gave Germany great deposits of *minette* iron ores, the extent of which was not at first fully known. The boom in the iron trades in the early 1870's was followed by a collapse, and by 1876 nearly half of Germany's 435 blast furnaces were idle. But revival came with the introduction of the Thomas Gilchrist process for making steel from phosphoric ores, which were plentiful in Lorraine and Luxembourg, and the 1880's saw a vast increase in Germany's iron and steel production. Between 1880 and 1890 her pig-iron and steel production increased from 2,729,000 to 4,658,500 tons, and her steel output rose from 1,548,000 to 3,164,000 tons. The German ironmasters and metal manufacturers learned much from their British rivals. They paid careful attention to the problem of the location of their plants, and they appreciated the importance of concentration in their industry. Collieries, furnaces and engineering works began to come under united control in the 1890's, and great iron and steel works were established by the combination of small firms. By 1910 Germany had outdistanced Britain and her continental rivals with an output of 14,794,000 tons of pig iron and 13,149,000 tons of steel, and, despite the ore of Lorraine, did not produce all the iron ore that her industries needed: nearly 10 million tons were imported, of which one-third came from Sweden. The establishment of great shipbuilding industries at Hamburg, Bremen and Stettin was but one aspect of the remarkable progress of the iron and steel industries of which the manufacture of armaments of all kinds was another not less important. In addition, a great variety of iron and steel goods were exported from Germany, their value in 1913 being over £100,000,000.

Output of German pig iron and steel, 1880–1938 (metric tons)

	Pig iron	Steel	
1880	2,729,000	1,548,000	
1890	4,658,500	3,164,000	Including
1900	8,521,000	7,372,000	Luxembourg
1910	14,794,000	13,149,000	
1929	13,190,000	15,990,000	
1933	5,180,000	7,440,000	Frontiers of 1919
1938	18,497,000	23,219,000	

Sources: Sir J. H. Clapham, *The Economic Development of France and Germany* (Cambridge, 1928), p. 285; H. Levy, *Industrial Germany* (Cambridge, 1935), p. 46; *League of Nations Statistical Yearbook*, 1938–9 (Geneva, 1939), pp. 146–7.
N.B. 1880–1910 figures include Luxembourg (in German customs union); 1929–33 figures include territory of 1919 (excluding Saar); 1938 figures are for Greater Germany (including Saar and Austria, but not Sudetenland).

CHEMICAL AND ELECTRICAL INDUSTRIES

Two new groups of manufactures had an important place in Germany's economic structure—the chemical and electrical industries. As early as 1840 Dr John Bowring, in a report on the Zollverein, had observed that in Germany 'chemical knowledge in its various branches is further advanced than with us'. In the 1860's the crude potassium salts of Stassfurt-Leopoldshall (south of Magdeburg) began to be systematically exploited. The basic (heavy) chemical industry produced chemicals in bulk partly for manufacturing purposes, including munitions, and partly for agriculture (artificial manures). Intensive scientific research—particularly into the utilization of coal by-products—paved the way for the development of the fine (light) chemical industry of which the two main branches were the preparation of dyes and pharmaceutical products. The products of the German dye industry achieved world-wide fame, and the value of the exports was nearly £10,000,000 in 1913. The manufactures of the pharmaceutical industry also had a high reputation. The chemical industries employed some 150,000 workpeople in 1903. The great chemical concerns co-operated even in the early stages of the industry. Two important 'communities of interest' were formed in 1904 and united in 1916, and subsequently the *I.G. Farben* (*Interessengemeinschaft Farbenindustrie Aktiengesellschaft*) cartel was established which dominated the whole industry.

The German electrical industry sprang up in the 1880's and 1890's. German experiments and inventions—particularly those of Werner von Siemens—helped to lay the foundations of the industry, but it was the practical application of electrical inventions in America that inspired German manufacturers to exploit the new form of light and energy. As in the chemical industries the establishment of large concerns was, almost from the first, a feature of the electrical industry. This was accentuated by the necessity for reviving the industry after the depression of 1900–2. On the eve of the war of 1914–18 two concerns—founded by Werner von Siemens and Emil Rathenau—were in a dominant position. They were Siemens and Halske (Berlin-Nuremberg) and the *A.E.G.* (*Allgemeine Elektrizitäts Gesellschaft*) which had developed from the German Edison Company. The installation of telegraphs and telephones was an important feature of the early phase of the industry. Next came cables, electric lighting and electric trams; then electric trains, power-generating stations and wireless. By the beginning of the twentieth century the two main branches of the industry had developed—'electrical engineering' (the manufacture of generators and other apparatus and the installation of electrical plant) and electricity (the electrification of railways, furnaces and machinery and the maintenance of power plants and power-transmission systems). In 1906–7 the industry employed 107,000 workpeople. A few years later (1913) half of the world's trade in electro-technical products was in German hands. 'Beyond question the creation of this industry was the greatest single industrial achievement of modern Germany.'

TEXTILE INDUSTRIES

German textile industries also made considerable progress. With the rapid growth of population she became increasingly dependent on imported wool, despite some increase in home production after 1850. In 1880 home-produced wool supplied two-thirds of the wool used, but by 1910 it represented a much smaller proportion. 'No great nation', it has been said, 'was so dependent on the outside world for the raw material of its warm clothing.'

Domestic workers in the textile industries declined rapidly, and by 1895 only 28,000 out of a total of 153,000 weavers were in this class, whilst four-fifths of the spinners were in large factories with an average of over 200 workers in each. The woollen industries were widely dispersed—in Saxony, Silesia, Thuringia, Alsace, Berlin, Aachen—but the production units increased in size and declined in numbers.

The linen and cotton industries displayed the same characteristics, dependence on imported raw material, the steady

Number of factories and workers in the German woollen industry, 1882–1925

	Factories	Workers
1882	48,200	206,400
1895	37,900	269,900
1907	17,300	227,700
1925*	10,900	215,000

* Frontiers of 1919.

Source: *Deutsche Wirtschaft*, 1928, p. 154 (issued by the *Statistisches Reichsamt*, Berlin, 1930).

elimination of domestic workers and the creation of large modern factories. The competition of the cotton industry acquired by the annexation of Alsace-Lorraine hastened the process. By 1895 there were 304 large cotton-spinning firms employing nearly 70,000 persons, whilst the consumption of raw cotton rose from 37,500 tons in 1878 to 370,000 tons in the early years of this century. The industry was concentrated mainly in the Rhineland, Westphalia, Saxony, Silesia and southern Germany, including Alsace.

GROWTH OF INDUSTRIAL ORGANIZATION

Two distinctive features of Germany's modern industrial development deserve notice—the growth of cartels and the unusually close connection between banks and industry.

Cartels are federations of businesses, 'the functions of which are to control the prices, the amounts produced and the methods of marketing of its various members; and in some cases to conduct their marketing for them'. Cartels may be either 'horizontal' or 'vertical'. The former is a federation of firms producing the same material or goods; the latter is an association of businesses engaged in different stages of the production from the raw material to the finished article. A union of firms operating steel works is a horizontal cartel; an association of firms owning collieries, iron and steel works, and machine-building plants is a vertical cartel.

Attempts to ascribe the development of cartels to uniform causes are unsatisfactory. Many factors promoted their establishment. Some combinations were formed when trade was bad, since a large production unit might weather the storm more successfully than several small firms. Others developed under the protection of a tariff, for joint action might enable a number of firms to utilize to the full (in the home market) the advantages conferred by import duties. The possession of a natural monopoly —such as the production of potash—might also favour industrial combination. In foreign as well as home markets this situation could best be exploited by large firms. In the new electrical and chemical industries adequate capital to meet the heavy initial expenditure on experimental research could be raised more easily by big concerns than by small firms.

Growth of cartels after 1873. There were some early industrial combinations in the Zollverein era, but it was after the crisis of 1873 that important cartels began to be established. Their development was fostered by the protective duties of 1879, and the Cartel Commission of 1905 enumerated 352 industrial combinations whilst, twenty years later, it was estimated that there were 3000 German cartels.

What is significant is that in all the manufactures connected with the extractive industries and trades depending upon mineral production a few great cartels achieved a dominant position. Among the monopolist combines were the Rhenish Westphalian Coal Syndicate, the Steel Union, the *I.G. Farben Industrie* and the *A.E.G.* In Germany cartels received legal protection, their agreements being treated by the law in the same way as other private contracts. Elsewhere monopolistic industrial combinations were often viewed with strong suspicion. In Britain agreements 'in restraint of trade' were not legally enforceable, and in the United States anti-trust laws were passed.

The banks and industry. The growth of the size of units of industrial production and the formation of cartels accentuated that unusually close relation between banking and industry which had already been a feature of Germany's economic development in the days of the Zollverein. By the early years of the twentieth century there were some twenty-five important business (non-issuing) banks. The four great 'D Banks'—the *Darmstädter Bank* (1853), *Diskontogesellschaft* (1856), *Deutsche Bank* (1870) and *Dresden Bank* (1872)—gradually absorbed many of their rivals. The joint-stock banks lent money on personal security and goods. Above all, they helped to float companies and gave such long credits that they were generally partners in the firms concerned. They had representatives on companies' boards of directors and so helped to mould industrial policy, and they encouraged the formation of cartels so as to protect from competition firms to which they had given credit.

German banks also played an important part in fostering

foreign trade. Branches of subsidiary banks were set up in important centres all over the world. The banks were also pioneers in promoting German economic expansion in backward areas—particularly in the Near East, South America and the Far East, and in all these activities were in close touch with the government. The financial side of Germany's *Drang nach Osten* was, in no small measure, in the hands of the *Deutsche Orientbank*, which had branches in Turkey, Egypt and Morocco. The *Deutsch-Asiatische Bank* (1889) promoted German interests in Shantung and elsewhere in China. The *Deutsche Übersee Bank* and the *Deutsch-Südamerikanische Bank* were active in Latin America. But it proved to be difficult to secure financial support from German banks for enterprises in Germany's own colonies.

FOREIGN TRADE

The vast development of Germany's industries was accompanied by a great increase in her foreign trade. Between 1872 and 1914 the value of her imports rose from £173,250,000 to £538,515,000 and of her exports from £124,600,000 to £504,825,000. She imported foodstuffs (e.g. meat, dairy produce, coffee) and raw materials (e.g. wool, cotton) and exported a great variety of manufactured goods. Three important changes in Germany's foreign trade in the years 1871–1914 deserve notice. First the export of finished industrial products held an increasingly

Value of Germany's foreign trade, 1860–1913 (£)
(excluding re-exports and the precious metals)

	Exports	Imports
1860	70,000,000	54,750,000
1872	124,600,000	173,250,000
1880	148,850,000	142,200,000
1890	170,500,000	213,650,000
1900	237,650,000	302,150,000
1910	373,735,000	446,705,000
1913	504,825,000	538,515,000

Sources: The figures for 1860 are taken from W. H. Dawson, *The Evolution of Modern Germany* (London, 1911), p. 64; the figures for 1872–1913 are from G. Stolper, *German Economy, 1870–1940* (London, 1940), p. 52.

important place in her foreign commerce. Between 1873 and 1913 they rose from 38 to 63 % of Germany's total exports. Secondly, Germany's trade outside Europe became increasingly important. In 1889 her trade with European countries accounted for nearly 80% of her exports and over 77 % of her imports. In 1912 trade with European countries still claimed nearly three-quarters of Germany's total exports, but her imports from Europe amounted to only 56·2 % of her total imports. Thirdly, the balance of payments of Germany's foreign trade became increasingly passive. At the beginning of the twentieth century the value of her exports was £60,000,000 a year less than her imports. This deficit was covered by payments received from foreigners for German shipping services and by interest paid on German investments abroad which amounted to between £1,000,000,000 and £1,250,000,000 in 1914. Germany's foreign investments, however, amounted to only one-tenth of her total investments in 1906–10, whereas Britain's foreign investments in those years were three-quarters of her total investments.

COMMUNICATIONS AND MERCANTILE MARINE

The great expansion of Germany's internal and external trade owed much to the development of communications. Bismarck failed in his effort to transfer the German railways to the Reich, but he gradually brought many private lines under the control of the Prussian state. Some of them—such as the *Ludwigsbahn* in Hesse-Darmstadt—lay outside Prussia. In 1910 there were 35,000 miles of railways in Germany, of which 23,350 miles belonged to Prussia and 10,625 to Bavaria and other large states. The railways were efficiently run at a profit. The Imperial Railway Office, established in 1873, unified railway rates throughout the country. It was a simple matter for the Weimar Republic to nationalize the whole railway system.

Between a fifth and a quarter of Germany's goods traffic was carried by the inland waterways. Among the more important commodities transported by water were grain and timber in eastern Germany and coal and iron in Westphalia and the

Rhineland. Two important new canals were constructed—the Kiel Canal, completed and opened by June 1895, and the Dortmund-Ems Canal (which gave the Ruhr industrial region access by water to the North Sea without crossing Dutch territory). These inland waterways were run at a loss and were subsidized by the state. In 1905 work was begun on the Mittelland Canal which was to join the Dortmund-Ems Canal to the River Elbe.

Growth of shipping. After 1871 an increasing proportion of Germany's overseas trade was carried in her own ships. When the Empire was founded Germany had 4519 merchant vessels (982,355 tons), nearly all of which were sailing ships. The growth of the German mercantile marine was particularly marked after Hamburg and Bremen joined the Imperial customs system in the 1880's. The steamships of Hamburg increased from 99,000 tons in 1880 to 746,000 in 1900, and those of Bremen from 59,000 to 375,000. By 1914 Germany, with 3,000,000 tons of shipping (four-fifths of which belonged to Hamburg and Bremen lines), had a larger mercantile marine than any other Power except Britain (11,700,000 tons). The three biggest shipping companies were the Hamburg-America Line, the North German Lloyd and the Hansa. In 1913 the Hamburg-America Line had a fleet of 172 steamships (1,028,762 tons), and a further nineteen steamships (268,766 tons) were being built. Profits in the years 1886–1913 had amounted to over £26,000,000, and the average divi-

Mercantile marines of Germany, Britain and the United States

		1870	1900	1910–12
Germany	*t*	982,000	1,942,000	3,000,000
	s	82,000	1,348,000	2,500,000
Britain	*t*	5,601,000	9,304,000	11,700,000
	s	1,113,000	7,208,000	10,700,000
United States	*t*	1,517,000	827,000	928,000
	s	193,000	341,000	618,000

t = total tonnage; *s* = steam tonnage.

Sources: Sir J. H. Clapham, *The Economic Development of France and Germany* (Cambridge, 1928), p. 356, which cites for the German figures the parliamentary return Cd 329 of 1902; and the *Statistisches Jahrbuch*, 1913 (Berlin, 1914), p. 46, which gives the figures for 1913.

dend had been 7% per annum. Two companies which were actively engaged in trade with the colonies were the Woermann Line and the German East Africa Company (both of Hamburg). Other important shipping lines were the German-Australia Steamship Company, the German Levant Line and the German-American Petroleum Company. A great shipbuilding industry developed in Germany, the Vulkan yard of Stettin and that of Blohm and Voss of Hamburg being of special significance.

THE GERMAN COLONIAL EMPIRE

The expansion of her manufactures, overseas commerce and shipping made it natural that Germany, like other great industrial states, should endeavour to consolidate her position as a World Power by establishing a colonial empire. But she was late in entering the field, and Bismarck's acquisitions (see pp. 98–101) remained the core of her colonial empire until she lost it in 1918. In 1914 Germany's colonies were rather more than a million square miles in area and had an estimated population of between twelve and fourteen millions.

Colonial ambitions. Germany held her colonies for only thirty years and so had hardly sufficient time to develop them successfully. The economic resources of the overseas territories and the purchasing power of their native inhabitants proved to be incon-

Colonial empires in 1913

	Area (sq. km.)	Population
Germany	2,950,000	12,000,000
Britain	33,000,000*	400,000,000
France	11,500,000	56,000,000
Holland	2,000,000	38,000,000
Belgium	2,400,000	15,500,000
Portugal	2,100,000	7,000,000
Japan	300,000†	17,000,000
U.S.A.	324,000	10,000,000
Italy	1,500,000	1,600,000
Spain	250,000	700,000

* Including Egypt and Sudan.   † Including Korea.

Source: P. Leutwein, *Dreissig Jahre deutsche Kolonial-politik* (Berlin, 1922), p. 399.

siderable. The rubber of the Cameroons, the sisal-hemp of East Africa, the diamonds of South-West Africa, the phosphates of Nauru and the copra of Samoa were no adequate return for the cost of conquering and maintaining the Empire. Attempts to encourage the large-scale production of cotton, cocoa and tobacco in the African colonies achieved only a very modest measure of success. None of the principal African colonies balanced its budget, and up to 1913 colonial budget deficits cost the German taxpayer about £50,000,000. Germany's colonial trade on the eve of the war of 1914–18 amounted to a mere half of 1 % of her total commerce. In 1914 there were less than 24,000 Germans in the colonies, and most of them were officials, soldiers and police and not permanent settlers. Yet the limited extent and relative poverty of the German colonial empire only increased the desire of many Germans for its extension, for a larger 'place in the sun.' Looking at Great Britain and France, with their great colonial empires, Germans felt that their country had been cheated in the race. The Colonial League, the Navy League, the Pan-Germans were all determined to make good the failures of the past. They had ambitions in the Near East and in Africa, and there is no doubt that a section of the most active propagandists for a great navy looked to the dissolution of the British and French empires after defeat in war as the means to provide satisfaction for German colonial ambitions.

These desires were fed both by the sense of dependence on other countries for raw materials as a result of the industrial developments already described and also by the increasing pressure of population on subsistence and the fear that, unable to provide work, Germany might be faced either with internal disorder from the rising Socialist and trade union movement, or with the necessity of resuming the export of men by emigration, which Caprivi described in 1891 as the only alternative to the export of goods.

The Germany of William II. Thus the Germany which William II had to rule was one in which sweeping changes resulting from the mechanization of industry were taking place. A group of great industrial magnates, controllers of the cartels which governed industry, was emerging and allying itself politically and through social intercourse with the older Junker-agrarian group. The Krupps, Stumms, Thyssens, and the rest sought to be as absolutely masters in their own industries as were the Prussian landed magnates on their estates. Despite the rapid growth of trade unionism the Central Union of German Industrialists was still refusing in 1905 to enter into a system of collective bargaining, and it was only on the eve of the war of 1914–18 that they were being forced to revise their attitude. Meanwhile the bulk

Growth of free (Socialist) trade unions in Germany (1891–1928)

	Membership
1891	277,600
1902	733,206
1906	1,689,709
1912	2,553,000
1928	4,841,000

Sources: Figures from 1891 and 1912 are from W. F. Bruck, *Social and Economic History of Germany from Wilhelm II to Hitler* (Cardiff, 1938), p. 130; figures for 1902 and 1906 are from W. H. Dawson, *The Evolution of Modern Germany* (London, 1911), p. 110; the figure for 1928 is from *Deutsche Wirtschaft*, 1928, p. 291 (issued by the *Statistisches Reichsamt*, Berlin, 1930).

of the middle class, unable to accept the Marxian doctrines of the Social-Democrats intellectually, and contemptuous of its members socially, accepted the ideas and followed the leadership of the Prussian aristocrats and entrepreneurs. The post-Bismarckian society, over which William II ruled, and to which he contributed his quota of braggadocio and restless ambition, was a society expanding with great rapidity both in wealth, numbers and productive capacity. It had many of the less pleasant characteristics of the *nouveau riche*. It was ambitious, increasingly materialist, and it worshipped power and success. The rapid changes and the movements of population incidental to modern industrialism were breaking down its old local loyalties and traditions. Yet the monarchical-feudal tradition of its people and the autocratic structure of the state made the Kaiser the centre of loyalty, and imposed upon him the heavy responsibility of guiding the desires of his people for expansion into channels of wisdom and moderation.

1. THE REIGN OF WILLIAM II

THE 'NEW COURSE'

The first four years of William II's reign showed few signs in public policy of the new expansionist tendencies in German life. On the contrary, like the first years of the reigns of Frederick William IV, of William I, and of Bismarck's rule after 1871, they gave promise of a more liberal regime, only to disappoint the hopes aroused.

Caprivi as Chancellor. For some time William and his advisers, and even some influential politicians, had agreed that preferably Bismarck should be succeeded by a General—if only because this would ensure him at least a modicum of the authority which Bismarck had wielded. The choice might well have fallen on General von Waldersee, Moltke's successor as Chief of the General Staff, had his name not been linked with the extreme right. Waldersee was consequently passed over in favour of the Commander of the Hanoverian Army Corps, General von Caprivi, a man of moderation and honesty of purpose, who had already shown administrative capacity of a high order and who was in sympathy with the programme of internal and external conciliation which the young Kaiser wished to pursue. Between 1890 and 1894, when Caprivi fell, the anti-Socialist law was allowed to lapse, the repressive character of the regime, both in Poland, where a Pole was made archbishop of Posen, and in Alsace-Lorraine, was considerably lightened and, after a reduction of the tariffs on foreign goods had been passed by the Reichstag, a series of commercial treaties with surrounding countries was negotiated (1892–4) which committed Germany to a policy of low protection for the next ten years. A very mild reduction of the powers of the Junkers in local government in the eastern provinces was also passed, in a much mutilated form, by the Prussian Landtag; laws creating courts of industrial arbitration and limiting the hours of labour of women and children in industry were enacted by the Reichstag, and the new Army Law of 1893 reduced the term of service in the infantry from three years to two. In foreign policy the decision was taken, in 1890, not to renew the secret Reinsurance Treaty with Russia, for the prolongation of which Bismarck was negotiating when he fell, on the grounds that it could not be reconciled with the terms of the Triple Alliance, but the Czar Alexander III thought highly of Caprivi, and the young Kaiser, who still trusted to the influence of dynastic relationships in foreign affairs, made every effort to keep on friendly terms with Russia, more especially when his admiring cousin Nicholas II succeeded to the throne in November 1894. Yet the exchange of visits between the Russian and French fleets in 1891 and 1893, which preceded the formal conclusion of the Dual Alliance between the two Powers, was a warning that a price might have to be paid for honesty.

Opposition to the Kaiser's policy. The effects of the Kaiser's 'new course' in internal affairs soon showed themselves to be unpleasant. The Prussian Junkers went into opposition; the *Kreuzzeitung*, their organ, wrote of the policy of lower tariffs that 'the German farmer will now be inclined to regard the Emperor as his political enemy'; in January 1893 the Landowners' Union (*Bund der Landwirte*) was formed to represent their agrarian demands and, in the same year, the Eastern Marches Association (*Ostmarkenverein*) was organized to protest against the Kaiser's pro-Polish policy. The Kaiser's social legislation entirely failed to wean the workers from the Social Democratic Party, now released from its legal fetters, and at the elections of 1893 the party gained over a third of a million votes and, with forty-four seats, became the fourth strongest party in the Reichstag.

At first the Kaiser met the opposition which his policy aroused in Conservative circles with brave words. 'To those, who increasingly express dissatisfaction with the new course, I reply quietly but with determination, "My course is right and I shall continue to follow it".' But, by the end of 1893, his own natural conservatism, combined with the ill-success of his measures, had conquered his superficial liberalism. The influence of the military circles in which he moved, the attractions of a more active foreign policy, which would satisfy his own desires for fame and those of his people for expansion, overcame his earlier wishes for social reconciliation. In October 1894 Caprivi, long since aware that he had lost his master's support, resigned and the 'new course' was at an end.

CONSERVATISM AND EXPANSIONISM

The years which followed Caprivi's fall were, in home policy, years of reaction. Under the next two Chancellors (Prince Hohenlohe 1894–1900, Prince Bülow 1900–9) there were a few extensions of the social insurance laws and, in 1899, an act permitting the federation of associations throughout Germany made possible a great development of trade union organizations. But German historians have not unjustly called these years 'the Stumm era', after Baron von Stumm-Halberg, autocrat of the Saar heavy industry, who refused to permit not only Social Democrat but even Christian Social agitation within his area. And the Kaiser's change of attitude is clearly marked by his withdrawal in 1894 of the instructions to Lutheran pastors, given in 1890, to concern themselves with social questions. He now directed that they should confine themselves to the spiritual welfare of their flocks.

Reaction in power. Whilst, therefore, the Social Democratic party and press and the trade union movement made great headway so that, in 1912, the Social Democrats polled 4,250,000 votes and became, with 110 members, the largest party in the Reichstag, the policy of the state made no concessions to this growth of radicalism. On the contrary, plans for a conservative 'revolution', such as Bismarck had suggested in 1890, were openly discussed in conservative circles in 1895, and the repressive action of the police was supplemented by a long series of prosecutions for *lèse-majesté*. And, in 1902, before the Caprivi commercial treaties expired, Bülow introduced a tariff law greatly increasing the duties on imported corn and granting further protection to German manufacturers against foreign manufactured goods. The Landowners' Union and the Central Union of German Industrialists triumphed at the expense of the working class. Imperial policy towards the national minorities in the Polish provinces and in Alsace-Lorraine also hardened.

Bismarck's policy of internal colonization in the Polish areas was taken up again, administrative decrees virtually banished the Polish language from the schools and, just before his fall in 1909, Bülow passed a law through the Prussian Landtag empowering the government to expropriate Polish landowners compulsorily. The effect of his measures was, as might have been expected, to increase the agitation of the Poles for their national aims.

Propaganda leagues and expansionism. The tone of German policy was largely set, and its aims defined, by the propaganda leagues which flourished after 1890. The Eastern Marches Association, the Colonial League, the Navy League, the Pan-German League, all conducted propaganda campaigns of an ultra-patriotic character. Their membership interlocked and their presidents and committees were drawn from the great landowners and industrialists who also supplied them with funds. The Navy League (*Deutsche Flottenverein*) was backed by the head of the shipping firm of Woermann, and by the great iron, steel and coal magnates, Krupp and Stumm, who contributed 800,000 marks between them to its funds, and put two newspapers at its disposal. In return they both made large profits out of the naval armament programme between 1898 and 1914. Similarly, the Pan-German League, the most violently expansionist of these propaganda leagues, received its financial backing from the leaders of heavy industry—Kirdorf, Stinnes, Borsig and Röchling. Amongst its foundation members was Alfred Hugenberg who became a director of Krupps and, after 1918, head of the Ufa-film combine and the greatest press magnate of Weimar Germany. In 1928 he became leader of the Conservative (*Deutsch-Nationale*) party, and his alliance with Hitler was largely responsible for bringing the Nazi party to power (see p. 175). Moreover, the Pan-Germans in the German Empire were stimulated by the movement in Austria where, in the nineties, a violent group of anti-Semitic Pan-Germans led by Schönerer exhibited both in the Austrian Parliament and outside it the character and temper of the later Nazis. Though these propaganda leagues varied in the closeness of their relation to the government, and were sometimes regarded as a nuisance both by the Kaiser and by Bülow himself, they represented and stimulated the expansionist, imperialist aggressiveness of large sections of the German military, bureaucratic, agrarian and industrialist upper and middle classes.

THE ISOLATION OF GERMANY

The foreign policy of Germany during the fifteen years after Caprivi's fall (1894–1909) corresponded to the expansionist tendency arising from Germany's rapid industrial growth expressed by the propaganda leagues. But it was so fitfully conducted, and the general situation was so unfavourable in itself, that, whilst Germany gained little territory, she acquired the suspicion and hostility of the Powers and fell into dependence on her one remaining ally, Austria.

The Kaiser's foreign policy. The lack of consistency in German foreign policy was due to the governmental system itself. The Kaiser sought to direct policy, but his ideas were incoherent and his intervention intermittent. His determination to build a great navy involved the alienation of Great Britain, yet he had no real desire to fight this—or indeed any other—country. He relied on his personal friendship with the Czar ('Nikki' in his letters to him), and he played with the idea of a great continental league. But the days when the foreign policy of states was decided by dynastic sympathies were over. The Russian rivalry with Austria in the Balkans and her alliance with France made a united continent impossible.

Moreover, the Kaiser's policy was crossed by that of Marschall (Under-Secretary for Foreign Affairs till 1897), of Bülow (Under-Secretary 1897–1900, Chancellor 1900–9) and of Holstein, the permanent Counsellor of the Foreign Office. Of these men Holstein was perhaps the most dangerous, for he exerted from behind the scenes a powerful and almost uniformly short-sighted influence until his dismissal in 1906. Though all were agreed that Germany must pursue a *Weltpolitik* and that she should, by diplomacy and veiled threats of force, acquire whatever territory might be obtainable in any part of the globe, the general effect of this policy of 'compensations' and of the lack of consistency with which it was conducted was to make all other Powers regard Germany as a dangerous potential enemy and an unreliable friend.

Anglo-German relations. An agreement was reached between Germany and England in 1890, by which the frontiers of German East Africa (Tanganyika) were defined in a sense favourable to Germany, and Heligoland was transferred to German sovereignty, whilst British predominance in Zanzibar and her sovereignty in Uganda were recognized. Relations between the two countries remained cordial for some time, but the agreement of 1890 was bitterly attacked by the Colonial League and the Pan-Germans and, even before Caprivi's fall, Marschall had concluded a frontier agreement (1894) with France in the Cameroons, which opened a path for the French to the Nile, had joined with the United States (1893) in thwarting Rhodes's ambition to gain control of the railway from Pretoria to Lourenço Marques, and had sent German warships to Delagoa Bay (1894) when England was seeking permission from Portugal to land troops there. The Kaiser's telegram to Kruger, the Boer President, at the time of the Jameson Raid (1896) congratulating him on having preserved 'the independence of his country against attacks from outside', was, it is now known, a milder alternative to far more serious steps proposed at the Wilhelmstrasse and it aroused intense hostility in England, and, since it could do no good to the Boers, was an act of tactless folly from the German point of view. It appeared to the British as an unwarranted interference in their imperial affairs and stirred up resentment against Germany as a trade rival; whilst the Triple Alliance itself was weakened when Salisbury, in 1897, refused to renew the Mediterranean agreement to maintain the *status quo*, which played a large part in making the alliance palatable to Italy.

Yet the Kaiser and his advisers remained obstinately convinced that the differences between England and the Dual Alliance went so deep that no permanent agreement between them was possible. Marschall's patronage of the *Deutsche Bank's* economic penetration of Turkey and of the Berlin-Baghdad railway was continued, and its possible threat to both British and

Russian interests in Perisa and India appeared clearly in Pan-German articles advocating German control of the Near East and the Persian Gulf. The Kaiser, whilst on a visit to Damascus in 1898, only two years after the Armenian massacres, toasted Abdul Hamid ('Abdul the damned') with the words, 'May the Sultan and the 300 million Mussulmans scattered over the earth be assured that the German Emperor will always be their friend.' And the British offer of an alliance in 1901 met no serious response in Berlin.

Yet, from 1898 to 1902, Anglo-German relations improved. In 1898 an Anglo-German convention was reached on the future of the Portuguese colonies, if that country found itself forced to sell them and, in 1899, the Samoan question was solved by the recognition of German sovereignty in the islands of Upolu and Sawai in return for compensations to England elsewhere. Throughout the South African War, too, German policy towards England was correct, and the Kaiser refused Kruger's request for diplomatic intervention, although German public opinion was violently hostile to England.

Anglo-German naval rivalry. From 1898 onwards, however, a new factor entered into Anglo-German relations—that of naval rivalry—though it was only towards the end of 1901 that British opinion began to be alarmed by it. Successive Navy Bills were passed by the Reichstag from 1898 onwards to 1914 which rapidly turned the German navy into a formidable weapon and imposed on England the necessity of meeting the German challenge. The cost of this shipbuilding on both sides of the North Sea imposed heavy burdens on both the British and German taxpayers and roused in England, especially after 1906 when the Liberal Government came into power, not only resentment at the postponement of social reforms which it involved but genuine fear lest the 'sure shield' of the British Navy, on which the world position of the country rested, should prove inadequate to its purpose.

The chief instigator of the programme of naval expansion in Germany was Tirpitz, who returned to Germany in 1897 as Secretary to the Navy Department (*Reichsmarineamt*). He was given the Kaiser's enthusiastic support, whilst the German Navy and Colonial Leagues conducted vigorous propaganda in favour of a great navy. What was more important, the Kaiser and Tirpitz refused to listen to any arguments from the British side for the mutual limitation of naval armaments and the efforts made to secure this at the Hague Conference of 1907, the warnings of the German Ambassador, Metternich, in London, and the conversations attempted during the visit of King Edward VII to Germany in 1908 all proved in vain. In 1901 the Kaiser had said 'Our future is on the water' and he regarded any attempt by another Power to restrict the German Navy as intolerable and insulting.

Even after Europe had been on the verge of general war in 1911, the Haldane Mission of 1912 produced no results and the German naval estimates for 1912–13 provided for a further increase in the navy, which would have given it by 1920 a fleet of forty-one battleships for home service and of eight large and eighteen smaller cruisers for service abroad. To this Great Britain was forced to reply by increasing her navy, and the tension between the two countries which necessarily resulted from this continuous naval rivalry continued until the outbreak of war in 1914.

England and the Dual Alliance. The future effects on Anglo-German relations of this rivalry at sea were not perceived by Bülow and Holstein when they received with cool indifference the renewed overtures made by England in 1901 for an alliance. Bülow remarked that the English threat to make terms with the Dual Alliance was 'a hideous spectre invented to terrify us'.[1] His folly was promptly exposed by the opening of negotiations between England and France, which led to formal agreements in 1904 settling all the outstanding colonial differences between the two Powers. Since Italy in 1902 had also made an agreement with France by which she gave France freedom of action in Morocco in return for the same freedom for herself in Tripoli, the Triple Alliance had been much weakened, and the phase of German-Austrian isolation had begun.

[1] Erich Brandenburg, *From Bismarck to the World War*, trans. A. E. Adams (Oxford University Press, 1927), p. 157.

Towards Russia, good relations with which Bismarck had always regarded as fundamentally important, the Kaiser and his advisers were equally unskilful. In 1897, after the murder of two German missionaries, Kiao-Chau was occupied by Germany although Russia had already negotiated for control of it with China. Germany's gain of an eastern base, while warmly applauded by all sections of opinion in Germany, was neutralized by the Russian occupation of Port Arthur and the British lease of Wei-hai-wei. On the eve of the Russo-Japanese war (1904–5) the Kaiser vehemently urged 'Nikki' to undertake a crusade against the Japanese, but he offered no military assistance, and the severe Russian defeat at the hands of Japan was used by anti-German influences at the Russian court to throw doubt on the Kaiser's disinterestedness in advising so disastrous a course. The Treaty of Björkö (July 1905), arranged between the Kaiser and the Czar at a private meeting in Finland, represented the Kaiser's last effort to build a continental league, which would bring the Triple and Dual Alliances together. But it broke down over the issue of Russian obligations to France and resulted in cooler relations between the two Powers. The increasing German influence at Constantinople, the rapid extension of the German economic penetration of Turkey, together with the wide concessions granted by the Turkish government in 1903 to the promoters of the Berlin-Baghdad railway, with its proposed network of lines to the Persian frontier and the Persian Gulf, were even more objectionable to the Russian than to the British government. For, after her defeat in the Far East, Russia turned her eyes back to the Balkans, to Constantinople, to Asia Minor and Persia, and was there confronted with the designs of Austria in the Balkans, and of Germany in Turkey.

Effects of isolation. 'By the end of the year 1905', writes Erich Brandenburg, 'Germany was almost completely isolated.'[1] Such was the result of the joint policy of the Kaiser, Bülow and Holstein since 1897. The effects of this fact were quick to show themselves. In Morocco the French, once the Anglo-French entente was signed, at once began to increase their control and at first

[1] Erich Brandenburg, *op. cit.* p. 243.

Germany made no resistance. But in March 1905, Bülow persuaded the Kaiser to land at Tangier, and the Moroccan question took on a new significance. Under German pressure a conference was held at Algeciras (1906), at which, apart from 'doubtful and reluctant' support from Austria, Germany found herself alone. The agreement finally reached formally recognized the Sultan's independence and the principle of the 'open door' for the trade of all nations. But the German demonstration at Tangier had proved a failure, and France now brought about a reconciliation between Russia and England, which led to a series of agreements in 1907, by which not only were all outstanding questions between Russia and England settled, but also Russia and France agreed with Japan to support the *status quo* in the Far East, whilst Spain was drawn into a similar agreement for the Mediterranean. Germany was now alone, except for Austria and the doubtful support of Italy and Roumania. Bülow, who was so largely responsible for this situation, now began to speak of Germany's 'encirclement', whilst the Pan-Germans were furious that the Kaiser and Bülow had failed to secure territorial gains in Morocco, where they coveted the Atlantic seaboard to provide the German navy with bases.

GERMAN DEPENDENCE ON AUSTRIA

Germany, faced by the Triple Entente between Russia, France and England, was now thrown back on the Triple Alliance as her only support and, therefore, on Austria, since Italy could not be relied on. Austria's relations with Russia, however, were rapidly deteriorating because she felt the integrity of her Empire threatened by the growth of a Pan-Serb movement in Serbia which received vigorous support from the Pan-Slav party in Russia. When, therefore, the Near Eastern question was reopened by the 'Young Turk' revolution of 1908, Aerenthal, the Austrian foreign minister, seized the opportunity of Russia's unreadiness for war to present her, and Europe, with a *fait accompli* by declaring Bosnia-Herzegovina annexed to the Austrian Empire (5 October 1908), whilst, at the same time, Ferdinand of Bulgaria, in concert with Aerenthal, declared the independence of Bulgaria from Turkish sovereignty. A violent reaction occurred in Serbia, and Russia was faced with the unpleasant alternatives either of forcing the Serbs to withdraw their claims for compensation, or of going to war with Austria. In the end Russia chose the first alternative and war was averted. But, during the crisis, German policy showed clearly her new dependence on Austria and, as clearly, foreshadowed the outbreak of war in 1914. Bülow, for fear of losing his last ally, gave Austria his unreserved support in the Serbian question and wrote to Aerenthal, 'I shall...regard the decision to which you may ultimately come as that demanded by circumstances', thereby offering, as Brandenburg says, 'an unlimited blank cheque for the future'.[1] Though the retreat of Russia in face of the threat of war gave Germany and Austria a resounding diplomatic success, it led to an immediate intensification of preparation for war both in Russia and France, and to an increased determination not to let such an event recur. During the crisis, too, Italy had been ignored by her allies and England's neutrality relied upon. In any repetition of the situation no reliance could be placed on the willingness of either Power to accept these silent roles, and, if they did not, war must result.

The dangers of the situation, in which Germany and Europe might be involved by the irresponsible controllers of Germany's foreign policy, were ludicrously illustrated by the publication whilst the Bosnian crisis was at its height, in the *Daily Telegraph* (28 October 1908), of an interview with the Kaiser. William had intended it as an olive branch to English opinion, but, in the course of it, contrived to exhibit his own vanity and incomprehension, to convince the English of the hostility felt in Germany to this country, and to threaten Japan, Russia and the United States by representing the German fleet as intended to act with the British in settling the great questions of the Pacific. The interview caused an immense sensation both at home and abroad. It even led the Conservative party in Germany to protest. But, though Bülow induced the Kaiser to promise greater circum-

[1] Erich Brandenburg, *op. cit.* p. 323.

spection in future, the futility of the parties in the Reichstag was shown by their total failure to secure, or attempt to secure, any advance towards responsible government. After a period of nervous breakdown the Kaiser recovered his composure and, having dismissed Bülow (1909), resumed his habits of oratory. The essential German system remained intact.

Bethmann Hollweg as Chancellor. The legacy to which Bethmann Hollweg succeeded was a grievous one, and he was ill fitted to deal with it, for, though a man of excellent intentions, he possessed insufficient force of character and no experience of foreign politics.[1] As a result the influence of Tirpitz on the Kaiser became even more powerful and dangerous, particularly since Kiderlen-Wächter, who became Under-Secretary for Foreign Affairs in 1910, was disliked by the Kaiser, who only reluctantly admitted him to office, at Bethmann Hollweg's insistence.

The division of Europe into two camps, arming strenuously against each other, for a while imposed the greatest caution upon all concerned, and, after the Bosnian crisis, efforts at appeasement were made on all hands. But in 1911 they were rudely interrupted by the second Moroccan crisis and by the Italian attack on Tripoli. The Moroccan crisis was provoked by the extension of French authority in that country, but was handled by Kiderlen in so *gauche* a fashion as to put Germany largely in the wrong. His despatch of the German gunboat *Panther* to Agadir, where the ship arrived on 1st July, was in line with his encouragement of the Pan-German agitation for the annexation of western Morocco, and was intended to force France to face war if she would not agree to large compensations to Germany —the whole of the French Congo was proposed—in return for German acceptance of French control in Morocco. The event created a European sensation and drew his first belligerent speech from Mr Lloyd George, an event in itself. But the Kaiser, as Kiderlen well knew, was firmly determined not to go to war over Morocco, and, in the event, to the great disgust of the Pan-Germans and the Colonial and Navy Leagues, Germany

---

[1] He was in fact a highly competent Prussian civil servant who had risen rapidly to the Under Secretaryship in the Reich Office of the Interior.

was forced to assent to French predominance in the last available portion of Africa, in return for two strips of territory in the French Congo. Throughout the crisis England stood firmly by France, whilst once again the isolation of Germany was brought home to her and, with it, a sense of increased dependence on Austria.

The Italian attack on Tripoli in September 1911 relied on promises previously given by her allies in the Triple Alliance and by Russia, as well as on a promise by France conditional on her acquisition of Morocco. Military operations ended in October 1912 when the Turks sought peace in order to cope with the new attack made on them in that month by the Balkan League with unexpectedly successful results, until quarrels over the spoil led to the second Balkan War (1913). During these wars the influence of Germany and England was exercised, on the whole consistently, to persuade Austria and Russia to moderation, and their joint efforts in the Balkan crisis, together with the imminent probability of the recurrence of the danger of war, led Sir Edward Grey to make further efforts for peace. But although, in 1913–14, colonial questions and the Baghdad railway dispute were in a fair way to settlement, the stubborn adherence of the Kaiser and Tirpitz to their naval programme prevented the development of any real understanding between the two countries. If, in Morocco, Kiderlen and Bethmann Hollweg had both been belligerent and the Kaiser pacific, on the naval issue the Kaiser and Tirpitz were adamant and must bear the major responsibility for rendering impossible that understanding with England which alone might have prevented war in 1914. The underlying hypothesis, or gamble, on which the German government and the Kaiser himself were relying was expressed by Jagow in a letter to the German ambassador in London, Lichnowsky, on 26 February 1914: 'I think you are inclined to look on the dark side of things, as when you express the view that no matter what happens, in the event of war, England will be on the side of France, against us. After all, we have not built our fleet in vain....'[1] The calculation is as revealing of the German incapacity to understand England as it proved false in the event.

[1] Erich Brandenburg, *op. cit.* p. 371.

SARAJEVO AND THE OUTBREAK OF WAR, 1914

The final crisis came in the summer of 1914. Austria was already alarmed by the results of the Balkan Wars. Russian influence in the Balkans had increased, most of all in Serbia, which had gained largely in population and territory. The Pan-Serb movement grew in intensity and threatened Austria's multi-national system not only in Bosnia-Herzegovina, of which the population was mainly Serb, but also amongst the large number of Serbs in southern Hungary and in Croatia and Dalmatia. The aged emperor, who had ascended his throne in 1848, was past control of events, and Conrad von Hoetzendorff, the Chief of the General Staff, was convinced that military action must be taken rapidly against Serbia before the forces of disruption became too strong in Austria, and before Russia was ready to fight. This view he pressed tirelessly and when, on 28 June 1914, the Crown Prince, Francis Ferdinand, was assassinated by a Bosnian Serb at Sarajevo, the Foreign Minister, Berchtold, at once accepted Conrad's point of view that Serbia must now, or never, be chastised and reduced in power and extent at whatever risk.

To that policy the Kaiser and Bethmann gave their assent. As in the crisis in 1908, they gave Austria a free hand in her dealings with Serbia, coupled with the assurance of their full support. They did this with the full knowledge that Russia would very probably take part in an Austro-Serbian war and that Germany's participation would certainly involve France and might involve England. Although, in the later stages of the negotiations, under pressure from Sir Edward Grey, they sought to moderate Austrian policy, they only did so when it was too late. The result of Germany's restless *Weltpolitik*, of the Kaiser's blind determination to build his Grand Fleet, and of his obstinate refusal to face the effects of that policy on England, had been Germany's isolation and her dependence on Austria. And, at the moment when the last reliable ally determined to adopt a warlike solution of the insoluble problem of her conflicting nationalities, the Kaiser and Bethmann Hollweg honoured the 'blank cheque' already given by Bülow in 1908. They were not bound to do this under the terms of the Triple Alliance and, in doing so, they made a general European war, probable enough in any event, an imminent certainty. That is the measure of their personal responsibility.

THE POLITICAL SITUATION IN GERMANY IN 1914

The outbreak of war found the German home front in a condition of strain. The growth of the Social Democratic party and of the trade unions had been accompanied by the growth of a left-wing section of the Centre, representing the Christian (Catholic) trade unions, so that the possibility of a majority in the Reichstag for the principle of Parliamentary government resting on the joint action of the Centre, the Left Liberals and the Social Democrats had emerged. This situation is clearly revealed in the election returns for 1912 as compared with those for the previous elections of the Kaiser's reign.

Strength of parties in the Reichstag during William II's reign

Date of General Election ...	1890	1893	1898	1903	1907	1912
Conservatives and Free Conservatives	93	100	79	75	84	57
National Liberals	42	53	46	51	54	45
Left Liberals	76	48	49	39	49	42
Centre	106	96	102	100	105	91
Social Democrats	35	44	56	81	43	110
Poles, Danes, Alsace-Lorrainers and Hanoverians	38	35	34	32	29	33
Anti-Semites	5	16	13	11	21	13

Table adapted from *Die deutschen Parteiprogramme*, vol. II, edited by W. Mommsen and G. Franz (Leipzig and Berlin, 1932).

It will be seen that a coalition of Left Liberals, Centre and Social Democrats could command a clear majority in the Reichstag of 1912, which continued in existence throughout the war and until the Revolution of 1918. The possibility of such a coalition was shown in the debates over the Zabern (Saverne in Alsace) affair in 1913, when the insolent behaviour of a young officer was followed by the illegal declaration of martial law by his commanding officer and by bayonet charges on the crowds who protested against the conduct of the officers. A vote of no confidence in the Chancellor was moved in the Reichstag and passed by 293 votes to 54—only the Conservatives voting in the minority. Yet, as in the case of the *Daily Telegraph* interview, the opposition parties did not press forward in a united effort to secure the responsibility of the government to the Reichstag. The vote of censure made no difference to Bethmann Hollweg's position, and the officer in command of the Zabern garrison was decorated by the Kaiser soon afterwards. Indeed, so little had the Prussian ruling class changed its attitude towards democratic government that, in 1909, a timid effort of the government to modify slightly the Three-Class system of voting was so mutilated by the Prussian Landtag that it had to be withdrawn. The classes in possession would yield none of their privileges, and the Pan-Germans and the supporters of the Navy and Colonial Leagues were ready to welcome a war in which they expected to realize their aims of German expansion. Their political opponents—Left Liberals, Centre and Social Democrats—were too divided amongst themselves to pursue a consistent policy, even for the attainment of the basic principle of democracy, the responsibility of the government to the elected chamber. And, when war came, the German politicians of the Left Centre and the Left showed that their patriotism was stronger than their desires for political reform. They joined with the Right in the political truce (*Burgfrieden*) for the duration of the war and in voting the necessary war credits. Poles, Alsatians and Danes might regard the war as their one chance of escape from the German Empire. But, so long as the Imperial autocracy could offer the prospect of swift success, the German political system would support it. And, even when hope deferred had begun to turn into dull despair, when the Left Centre and Left had become convinced that further obedience to their Kaiser and the High Command spelt disaster for the German state, the latent tension in the Prusso-German system of Bismarck's creation did not spontaneously turn into open conflict for the supersession of the old governing forces. The actual solvent of defeat itself was necessary to produce even the semblance of revolution in the disciplined society of Germany.

1. *THE WAR OF 1914–18*

THE WAR ON LAND

The mobilization of the German army in 1914 proceeded smoothly and swiftly, and the application of the Schlieffen plan, which involved the violation of Belgian neutrality, was decided

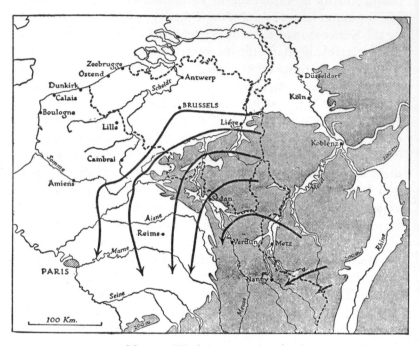

Map 13. The German attack, 1914

The arrows show the general direction followed by the seven invading armies. Land over 200 m. is shaded.

on. The military advantages of a swift decision, to be secured by rolling up the French left wing, were regarded as great enough to outweigh the disadvantages, even though these should include British participation in the war. For the German decision to invade Belgium Bethmann Hollweg presented an embarrassed apology to the Reichstag and the world, based on the grounds of military necessity.

The great wheeling movement of seven German armies
(Map 13) was brought to a halt only at the Marne (8–9 September) and might well have accomplished its purpose if Moltke,
Chief of the General Staff, had not been far from the front, in
Luxembourg, and had not sent two Army Corps to the eastern
front at the critical moment. They arrived in East Prussia to find

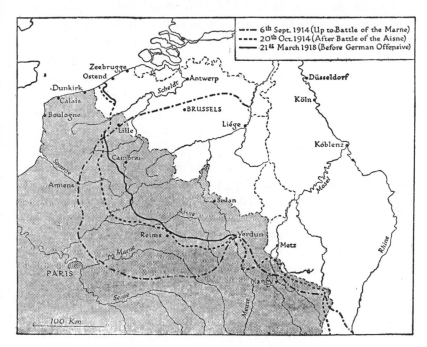

Map 14. The Western Front to 21 March 1918
The territory of France is shaded.

that Hindenburg and Ludendorff had already beaten the invading Russians decisively at Tannenberg and that the province
was rapidly being cleared of enemy forces. In the west, after
September 1914, the fighting settled down into trenches and
for four years the *guerre d'usure* went on with fluctuating fortunes, immense losses in human life and material but, until
August 1918, with no decisive result (Map 14). The first and
second battles of Ypres (October/November 1914 and April

1915), the Franco-British offensives in September 1915 in Champagne and at Loos, the great German assault on Verdun (February 1916), the battle of the Somme (July 1916), which ultimately forced the Germans to retreat to the Hindenburg line (March 1917), were all alike indecisive, except as contributing to the exhaustion of the combatants. The costly failure of Nivelle's attack on the Chemin des Dames in April 1917, followed by serious mutinies in the French army, suggested that it might well be France which would first lay down its arms. Already (August 1916) the famous pair of generals, Hindenburg and Ludendorff, had taken over control of the High Command from Falkenhayn, who had replaced Moltke after the battle of the Marne. It was certain that what could be done by ruthless determination and superb organization they would do.

Moreover, despite early Austrian reverses in Serbia in 1914, that country was overrun in November 1915, and Bulgaria (October 1915) joined the Central Powers to counterbalance the loss of Italy, which had declared war on Austria in May 1915. In 1916, although a successful Russian offensive was made by Brussilov in Galicia and Roumania joined the Allies, the German-Austrian forces more than held their own in the east and, indeed, had conquered Roumania before the year was out.

By the beginning of 1917 both sides were desperate, for the German successes in the east were counterbalanced by their severe losses in the Somme and Ancre battles, and at one moment in the autumn of 1916 they had only five divisions in reserve on the western front. The failure of President Wilson's peace note, in December 1916, to arouse any response in the Entente countries determined Hindenburg and Ludendorff to press for the unrestricted submarine campaign which the German Admiralty also desired but which, in February 1916, Bethmann Hollweg had firmly refused to adopt.

America enters the war. The decision was made to open the U-boat campaign on 1 February 1917, and was based on a German Admiralty memorandum, which implied that victory would result within the year. But, although the new submarine attack brought England dangerously near starvation, it also

brought the United States into the war (6 April 1917) and thus
provided a vast reserve of first-rate fighting men, when once
trained, and a great supply of munitions and shipping for the
Allied side. Moreover, it greatly strengthened the confidence of
the Allied peoples, especially the French, in victory, and as
greatly depressed the Germans, already suffering severely from

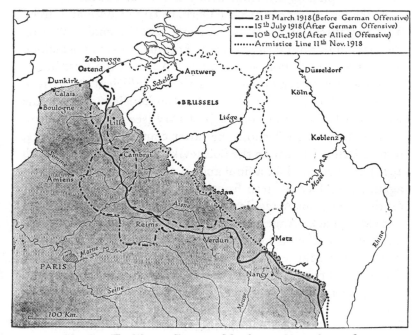

Map 15. The Western Front, 21 March to 11 November 1918
The territory of France is shaded.

the British blockade. Not even the disorganization of Russia by
the revolutions of March and October 1917, in the second of
which the Bolsheviks, determined on immediate peace, seized
power, could compensate Germany for the aid given by America
to the Allied cause.

Yet, in 1917, American land forces were not yet ready to take
a serious part in the struggle and the long-drawn-out misery and
loss of the third battle of Ypres (Passchendaele) was only very

partially compensated for the British by the limited success won at Cambrai (November 1917) when tanks were used on a large scale for the first time. The rout of the Italians at Caporetto (October 1917) compelled the Allies to send Franco-British troops to her support, and a further blow to Allied hopes came in December 1917, when the new Bolshevik government in Russia accepted an armistice with the Central Powers.

At the beginning of 1918 the German High Command, freed from any threat on the Russian front, had the choice of using their favourable military position to negotiate peace or of making one last supreme effort to defeat the Allies in the west before American reinforcements could arrive in sufficient strength to make any German attempt at a decision hopeless. Despite the Reichstag Peace Resolution of July 1917 (see p. 145), Hindenburg and Ludendorff chose the latter course. They, therefore, imposed a harsh treaty on the Bolsheviks at Brest-Litovsk (March 1918) and prepared for a final and, as they hoped, decisive blow against the Allied western front. The blow fell in March 1918, on the front from Arras down to Rheims. The Allied line was pushed far back. Amiens was threatened, Montdidier captured and, though Rheims held, a great German salient was thrust down to the Marne at Château-Thierry. Yet, once again, no decision was reached, and a secondary attack in Flanders similarly gained ground, at heavy expense, but did not achieve the break-through, which alone could bring victory. Ludendorff had expended the last German reserves in vain. The crisis had at last overcome inter-allied jealousies, and, in Foch, supplied the supreme commander so long lacking. American reinforcements were beginning to pour in. The submarine menace was being rapidly overcome. As a Swiss military critic said at this time the German situation was 'brilliant but hopeless'. Ludendorff made one last large-scale attack on the Marne near Château-Thierry (15–17 July) but, when that failed, the initiative had finally passed to the Allies.

On 8 August 1918 the Allied counter-offensive began near Amiens, and was taken up on the other sectors of the front. It was successful from the outset and went on continuously in one sector or another until the armistice (Map 15). Meanwhile the Austrian Empire was breaking up, and the door into Hungary was opened to the Allies by the collapse of Bulgaria in September. By 29 September even Ludendorff had become convinced that the war was lost and that an armistice must be asked for. He was equally convinced that, to obtain the best terms for Germany, responsible Parliamentary government must be introduced, and the liberal-minded Prince Max of Baden was made Chancellor to carry through the change. Before the armistice negotiations were completed revolution had broken out in Germany, the Kaiser had abdicated, and it was a Republic, under the saddler's son, Ebert, as Chancellor which accepted the armistice terms on 11 November 1918.

THE NAVAL WAR AND THE BLOCKADE

It was in the German navy that the revolution of 1918 began with mutinies (29–30 October) in the ships at Kiel, and the disaffection in the navy owed much of its force to the inaction to which the German fleet had been condemned ever since the outbreak of war. From the first the Kaiser and Pohl, the Chief of Staff, ignored Tirpitz and pursued a policy of conserving their main battle fleet. But their forces outside the North Sea remained to be dealt with by the British navy.

In August 1914 the first task facing the Anglo-French forces in the Mediterranean was to destroy or put out of action the German battle-cruiser *Goeben* and the light cruiser *Breslau*. By a series of mischances or misjudgments they were allowed to escape from Italian waters and they entered the Dardanelles on 10 August 1914, by permission of Enver, leader of the war party amongst the Young Turks. Their guns, dominating Constantinople, strengthened Enver's arguments for joining the Central Powers, and the Turkish declaration of war on the Allies followed in November 1914.

At that moment Admiral Cradock, commanding the South American station, attacked Admiral von Spee's much stronger China squadron off Coronel (1 November 1914), with the result that Cradock's flagship, *Good Hope*, and the cruiser *Monmouth* were both sunk. But the position in these waters was restored by Admiral Sturdee's victory at the Falkland Islands (8 December 1914) when the *Gneisenau*, von Spee's flagship, the *Scharnhorst*, *Leipzig*, and *Nürnberg* were all destroyed and only the *Dresden* escaped. Though she survived 'by persistent disregard of the neutrality of remote Chilean possessions' until March 1915 she did little damage, and the most dangerous commerce raider, *Emden*, met her end at the Cocos Islands on 9 November 1914. From that time onwards the high seas were dominated by the British and French navies, and the expeditions which successfully captured the German colonies in Africa and the Pacific were the fruits of that fact.

Though the Allied fleets failed to force the Dardanelles in March 1915, the campaign which followed (March 1915–January 1916) depended wholly on Allied sea power, as did the Allied armies based on Salonica and those which operated in Mesopotamia, Palestine and Syria. Not only were the supply routes to and from India kept intact but, after initial failures, Allied armies were able to conquer Baghdad (March 1917), to overrun Palestine and enter Jerusalem (December 1917) and, in 1918, to deliver a heavy and successful attack on Bulgaria, which resulted in her surrender (10 September). The fact that, with the German submarine menace at its worst, the Allied navies were able to maintain these widely separated fronts was a vitally important factor in the ultimate victory.

Still more important for the issue of the war was the enforcement of the blockade on Germany, which became much more stringent after the first German submarine campaign opened in February 1915. During the remainder of that year and throughout 1916 the Germans were restricted in their activities both by their limited number of submarines and by the determination of Bethmann not to strain American patience too far. The battle of Jutland (31 May–1 June 1916) could not be regarded with much satisfaction by the British fleet, and, in particular, showed the German ships to be superior in construction, their range-finding more accurate, and their armour-piercing shells more effective than our own. Yet, within a month, Scheer, the German Commander-in-Chief, reported to the Kaiser that 'there can be no doubt that even the most successful result from a high sea battle will not compel England to make peace.... A victorious end to the war at not too distant a date can only be looked for by the crushing of English economic life through U-boat action against English commerce.' Jutland had not been fought in vain, and the British superiority in battleships kept the German High Seas fleet in harbour for the rest of the war except for occasional sallies. This, and the withdrawal of many of the best officers and petty officers for the U-boats, lowered its general morale and, as early as June–July 1917, mutinies occurred which revealed not only discontent with living conditions but sympathy with the policy of a negotiated peace. Yet the unrestricted U-boat warfare in 1917 proved at first a deadly threat to Allied supplies. The German navy had constructed many more submarines, and in the quarter April–June 1917 over two million tons of Allied shipping were lost. But the adoption of the convoy system (April 1917), made still more effective later by the assistance of both American and Japanese destroyers, greatly lowered the rate of sinkings and the total for the year 1918 (January to November) was only 600,000 tons more than that for the April–June quarter of 1917. The submarine menace remained serious, but German hopes of victory founded upon it proved delusive, and the number of submarines sunk during the war, estimated at about 180 out of a total of 360, began to break the morale of their crews.

By 1918, therefore, the morale of the lower-deck in the German navy was very low, and the rumour that Admiral Scheer intended to take the whole fleet to sea in October to strike a desperate blow at the British, thus perhaps bringing the negotiations for an armistice to an end, resulted in mutinies which began in the *Thüringen* and *Helgoland* at Kiel (29–30 October) and rapidly spread through the fleet. At Hamburg the sailors were joined by the army reservists, and the movement for Soldiers', Sailors' and Workers' Councils spread rapidly through Germany. It is not without historic justice that the breakdown of German discipline should have begun in the service so painfully built up by the Kaiser and Tirpitz and for which they had forfeited English friendship with such light hearts.

GERMAN SUCCESS AND FAILURE

The German military effort during these four years of war had been one of the most remarkable in history. Aided by the revolutions of 1917 and by their superior equipment and supply services, they had secured the dissolution of the armies of Russia and, after Brest-Litovsk, were masters of the whole of her western borders. Finland, the Baltic provinces, Poland, the Ukraine to the gates of the Caucasus, were all, for the moment, under German control, and Turkey was their ally (Map 16). The Pan-German dream of a Greater Germany ruling over millions of dependent Slavs, but with *Lebensraum* for the indefinite expansion of the German master race, had been realized. But, at the moment of its establishment, the deadly pressure of the blockade and the exhaustion both of the German people and of the German armies on the west, together with the break-up of the hetero-geneous territories which composed the Austrian empire, shat-tered the fabric so painfully created. Germany had 'killed herself by victories' (*Wir siegen uns zum Tod*), but had also been killed by Allied sea power, which enforced the blockade, and brought the supplies to the land forces. These French and British forces, which had borne the brunt of the fighting during four years and now supported by their American allies were at last rewarded by being able to deal the final blow to German hopes. Germany, without Austria, had lost over 1,800,000 killed and 4,200,000 wounded. The deaths from disease amongst her civilian popu-lation are not accurately known, but must have been very heavy, and, in November 1918, she lay prostrate and helpless in defeat. Yet she had been within sight of a victory which, in the modern technical age, would have made her undisputed mistress of Europe. Supplied with the corn and mineral wealth of the Ukraine and the oil of the Caucasus, able to command both the Adriatic and the Aegean, her influence predominant in Turkey and penetrating to the Persian Gulf and to Suez; controlling the Baltic, with inexhaustible supplies of high-grade iron ore from Sweden, and with the heavy industry of Lorraine, the Saar, the Liége district, as well as that of Bohemia and Styria at her disposal, she would soon have been in a position to break the

Map 16. The Treaty of Brest-Litovsk

British naval stranglehold and to conquer Egypt and North Africa. The dream, so near realization in the first months of 1918, collapsed in defeat. But it remained in many German minds an ideal yet to be realized. The history of the German Republic is largely that of the failure of the German 'Left' to replace these dreams of conquest and exploitation by any satisfactory substitute, so that in 1933 Hitler and his Nazi Pan-Germanists were able to attempt their renewal in grim earnest.

THE DICTATORSHIP OF LUDENDORFF AND THE GERMAN REVOLUTION

Although all the political parties in the Reichstag, including the Social Democrats, had accepted the *Burgfrieden* (political truce) in 1914, and although a strict censorship of the press and the prohibition of political meetings were imposed by the government, the long-drawn-out war, the need to define German war aims, the shortage of food owing to the blockade, and the Russian revolutions of 1917, all contributed to assist the development of a demand for more responsible government as the war dragged on. The very basis of the Prusso-German empire, the power of the Kaiser as War Lord, disappeared as soon as war broke out for, as though distrustful of his own capacity to command, William II made little effort to control military policy and, as time went on, exercised less and less influence on the decisions of the High Command. Of this he was himself aware and wrote bitter marginal comments on the virtual extinction of his own authority.

When Hindenburg and Ludendorff took over the general staff in August 1916, they rapidly established a joint dictatorship in political as well as in military affairs. In this Ludendorff took the lead, and when he disagreed with Bethmann Hollweg's policy, he refused to accept 'responsibility' for measures which he regarded as injurious to the conduct of the war and threatened resignation. By this form of blackmail, similar to that practised by Bismarck on William I, he obtained a complete ascendancy over the Kaiser and established a hitherto unparalleled control of political as well as military policy in the hands of the High Command, that is, of Hindenburg and himself.

From 1916 to 1918, then, Germany was ruled by a military dictatorship. In July 1917 Ludendorff secured the dismissal of Bethmann Hollweg, who had opposed the unrestricted U-boat campaign and had been too inclined to listen to the Reichstag parties of the Centre and Left for Ludendorff's taste. Both

Michaelis, who replaced Bethmann Hollweg, and Hertling, who succeeded him in the autumn, were chosen with the approval of Ludendorff and both regarded it as their first duty to carry out Ludendorff's policy.

Criticism of war policy. Yet there grew up amongst both the German working and middle classes an increasingly critical attitude towards the existing imperial system as the war went on. As early as December 1915 twenty members of the Social Democrat party voted against a war credit and, in 1916, formed the Independent Social Democratic Party (*Unabhängige Sozial-Demokratische Partei* or *U.S.D.P.*), whilst a still more radical group, the Spartacus League, was founded and led by the fiery Rosa Luxemburg. These two groups, though small in numbers, represented the widespread longing for peace which was felt by the masses of the population, and which led in 1917 to the naval agitation already mentioned and to a series of strikes in Berlin, Leipzig and other towns which had a definitely political programme. At Leipzig the workers demanded not only better rations but an immediate peace without annexations, restoration of full civil liberty, and 'the introduction of universal, equal, secret and direct suffrage in elections to all public bodies in the Empire, in the federal states, and in the municipalities'.

Under the influence of these manifestations of public opinion and of his own conviction that, the submarine campaign having failed to win the war, Germany's position was growing desperate, Erzberger, of the Centre party, proposed in the Reichstag a resolution in favour of a 'peace without annexations' in July 1917. It was passed by the votes of a section of the National Liberals, the Left Liberals, the Centre and the Social Democrats and was accepted by the new Chancellor, Michaelis, though with the significant qualification 'as I interpret it'. The democratic coalition, always possible in the Reichstag since 1912 (see pp. 132–33), appeared at last to have come into being.

In fact, however, Ludendorff, the Conservatives and the Right-wing National Liberals had no intention of basing their policy upon the Reichstag resolution. Conservatives and National Liberals combined to form the Fatherland Party,

Pan-Germanism under a new name, and sought to whip up patriotic feeling in the country. And although, on Michaelis's fall, the government seemed superficially to be widened when Payer, a Left Liberal, became Vice-Chancellor to Hertling, the Reichstag majority parties made no serious effort throughout the winter and spring of 1917–18 to gain effective control of the government or even to enforce their policy of peace without annexations. On the contrary when, after the Bolshevik revolution (October 1917), Russia sued for peace, and the tide of war appeared to set once again in Germany's favour, the Reichstag accepted the 'annexationist' terms of the Treaty of Brest-Litovsk, even the Social Democrats doing no more than to abstain from voting for it.

During the first nine months of 1918, indeed, Ludendorff pursued the policy of victory with annexations, endorsed by the Prussian Conservatives, agrarians and industrialists alike. He suppressed the strikes which broke out in Berlin in January by proclaiming martial law. He forced the Kaiser to dismiss the head of his civil cabinet. With his approval the Prussian Landtag defeated the government's bill for equal suffrage by a majority of over 50 votes. If the temper of the people was growing more radical, it was a despairing radicalism, and they were too cowed to show it. Right up to the moment when military defeat had to be acknowledged by Ludendorff himself the old conservative Prusso-German structure was maintained intact—except that the dominating figure of Ludendorff dwarfed the Kaiser into insignificance.

Passivity of democratic parties. The extreme passivity of the more democratic Reichstag parties was exhibited most clearly in the hour of defeat. For it was Ludendorff who, on 2 October, sent one of his staff to Berlin to explain that the position of Germany was hopeless and that a new, more democratic, government responsible to the Reichstag must be formed in order to secure the best possible terms for Germany. It was the German High Command which, without any pressure from the political parties, admitted the failure of its policy and demanded that the Imperial system should be turned into a parliamentary democracy.

Even at this stage the democratic parties made no effort to take over effective control of power. Prince Max of Baden became Chancellor and included as Ministers in his government not only Centre Party members (Erzberger, Trimborn) and Left Liberals (Payer, Haussmann), but also Social Democrats (Bauer, Scheidemann). Yet, after meeting on 5 October to approve in principle the change to a parliamentary system of government, the Reichstag meekly went into recess until 22 October, whilst the necessary bills were being prepared and, when they had been passed (26 October), again adjourned until 9 November. Even the sudden acceptance of the principle of equal suffrage in Prussia (15 October) was largely due to Ludendorff's influence. And, although Ludendorff himself resigned on 26 October, the first German revolution in 1918—the adoption of the Parliamentary system—was his handiwork.

Character of the second 'revolution'. The second German revolution of 1918 broke out with mutinies in the fleet from 29 October onwards, but it was a movement against the idea of a desperate sortie to attack the British fleet and for the redress of service grievances rather than for constitutional change. How little revolutionary its character was is shown by the demand of the sailors that they should only be compelled to address their officers as 'Sir' once at the beginning of each interview. But, as the movement spread from the sailors at Kiel to the soldiers at Hamburg, it took on a more revolutionary form. Workers' and Soldiers' Councils on the Soviet model were set up, the abdication of the Kaiser and the Princes was demanded, and the Spartacus League urged a programme of full socialization. Yet, though the Majority Socialists responded to the revolutionary current sufficiently to secure the Kaiser's abdication, their leader, Ebert, only accepted the proclamation of the Republic because Scheidemann had forced his hand. Ebert's attitude to the extreme Left was shown by his words at this time: 'The social revolution, I hate it like sin.' His government, though representing the Berlin Soldiers' and Workers' Councils and formed of Social Democrats and members of the *U.S.D.P.*, retained Erzberger and some Liberals in office and at once made clear its intention that no revolution on the Russian model would, if they could avert it, be permitted in Germany. The German 'revolution' of 1918—the second revolution of November—was, in fact, far more a collapse than a revolution. It was the result of defeat and of hunger rather than of any genuine revolutionary spirit in the broad masses of the German people. The lack of violence against the Princes of Germany, whose abdications followed on that of the Kaiser, was evidence of this. And the Majority Social Democrats under Ebert, deeply imbued with the German love of order, were certainly interpreting aright the wishes of most of their fellow-countrymen when they rejected social revolution, however little their actions corresponded to their radical party programme.

Yet for a few months after 9 November the threat of a more radical revolution, led by the Spartacus League and some of the Independent Socialists, existed. But, after the failure of his attempt to enlist a republican volunteer force, Noske, the Social Democrat Minister of War, used the counter-revolutionary bands of young reactionaries, the Free Corps, financed by the great industrialists and landowners, against the sympathizers with Russian Communism. In Berlin Rosa Luxemburg and Liebknecht, and many of their working-class followers, were killed. In Bavaria, Eisner, under whom a Left-wing Socialist regime was set up, was murdered and the Free Corps removed any danger of Bolshevism with ruthless brutality (1–2 May 1919), shooting, amongst others, twenty harmless Catholic journeymen whom they mistook for Spartacists.

The anti-Communist activity of Ebert's Social Democratic government represented the docility and conservatism which had gradually made the party's programme largely meaningless. A great party bureaucracy, closely allied with the trade unions, had been built up and was ruled by a committee of elderly men, of mediocre ability, whose main idea was to keep their party machine intact and to score small tactical successes as occasion offered. Representing the skilled artisans, they were, in some respects, as deeply conservative as any class in Germany, and when a revolutionary situation arose, they desired to enforce order at whatever cost and by whatever means were available. In doing so they inevitably split the German working class into two irreconcilable groups and excluded the younger and more active men from their party. Their genuine devotion to the democratic principle was an inadequate substitute for the social revolution in the eyes of the younger generation.[1]

[1] The above account of the internal political developments in Germany from 1914 to 1919 is based mainly on two books by Dr Arthur (Artur) Rosenberg: *The Birth of the German Republic* and *A History of the German Republic* (see Bibliographical Note, pp. 241–2, below).

CHAPTER III

THE WEIMAR REPUBLIC, 1918–33, AND NATIONAL-SOCIALIST GERMANY, 1933–9

1. THE WEIMAR REPUBLIC

THE DEMOCRATIC CONSTITUTION AND THE VERSAILLES TREATY

As soon as power was in his hands, in November 1918, Ebert had announced that a National Assembly would be elected on the basis of universal suffrage to decide the political fate of Germany. The elections took place on 19 January 1919 and, before that date, the parties of the old Reichstag reconstituted, and in some cases renamed, themselves. The old Conservative and Free Conservative parties, with some National-Liberals, formed the German National People's party (*Deutsch-Nationale Volkspartei*), the remaining National-Liberals became the German People's party (*Deutsche Volkspartei*), the earlier Left-Liberals (Progressives) now called themselves the German Democratic party (*Deutsche Demokratische Partei*). The Centre and Social Democrats retained their party names, whilst the Independent Socialists formed a separate group to the left of the Social Democrats. The results of the elections to the National Assembly, which took place before such revolutionary fervour as there had been had died down, and before the terms of the Treaty of Versailles were known, deserve careful comparison with the returns to the Reichstag of 1912 and with the figures of later elections during the Weimar Republic.

A glance at the results of 1919 shows that the Social Democrats, at the moment of their greatest expansion, had no hope of forming a homogeneous majority government, and that a Socialist Germany could not be created by democratic methods. From the first, therefore, the Social Democrats were dependent on their 'bourgeois' allies of the Centre and Democratic parties, and

150

Germany as a whole was faced, under a parliamentary regime, with a series of coalition governments.

	1912	1919	1920	Mar. 1924	Dec. 1924	1928	1930
Conservative and Free Conservative (*Deutsch-Nationale Volkspartei*)*	57	44	71	95	103	78	41
National Liberals (*Deutsche Volkspartei*)	45	19	65	45	51	45	30
Centre	91	91	64	65	69	62	68
Bavarian People's party (*Bayrische Volkspartei, separated from Centre after* 1919)	—	—	21	16	19	16	19
Left Liberals (*Deutsche Demokratische Partei*)	42	75	39	28	32	25	20
Social Democrats	110	165	102 }	100	131	153	143
Independent Social Democrats	—	22	84 }				
Communists	—	—	4	62	45	54	77
National-Socialists	—	—	—	32	14	12	107

* *Titles in German are those adopted in* 1918–19.

Sources: Adapted from *Die deutschen Parteiprogramme, 1918–30*, edited by W. Mommsen and G. Franz, p. 139 (Leipzig and Berlin, *1931*).

The nature of the new constitution. The adoption of the Weimar constitution on 31 July 1919 turned the Prusso-German Empire, formally at least, into a fully democratic, though still semifederal, state. The President was to be elected by a plebiscite of the whole people. The Chancellor and the Ministers were responsible to the Reichstag, itself elected on the basis of universal suffrage. All the basic rights of other democratic countries— freedom of speech, the press and association, freedom from arbitrary arrest, even the right of the electorate to initiate and, in certain cases, to decide by referendum on legislation—were secured in the constitution. The old particularism of the states, now called 'Lands' (*Länder*), was greatly reduced by the provision that Reich law was to override the law of a *Land*; and, in particular, the predominance of Prussia was carefully reduced by the remodelling of the old *Bundesrath* into a *Reichsrat*, with much reduced powers. In addition, though the principle of private property was recognized, powers were taken for nationalization with compensation, and for the creation of central and local economic councils so that some degree of state control over industry and the land seemed assured. The boast that Germany now had 'the most free constitution in the world' was not unjustified.

The test of every constitution is the way it works and the perfection of the Weimar constitution from the point of view of democratic theory had its dangers in a country sharply divided in political opinion and quite unaccustomed to the 'give-and-take' of democratic politics. The old unity provided by the person of the Kaiser and the personality and office of the Chancellor, as Bismarck devised it, had worked badly enough under William II and Bülow. But now the German people were not only asked to transfer their allegiance from a royal figure standing above parties, they were asked to give it to a Social Democratic president or to a chancellor who might represent a *Weltanschauung*— a philosophy of life—with which they profoundly disagreed. Further, the democratization of the individual states (*Länder*) meant that, at the same time, a Social-Democratic-Centre coalition might be in power in Prussia, a mainly 'bourgeois' nationalist government in the Reich, a semi-Communist government in Saxony, and an extreme Right, reactionary government in Bavaria. Such a situation, which actually occurred in 1923, involved a serious threat to national unity. Finally, at a time when external pressure from the victorious Allied Powers called, above all, for strong and united government in Germany itself, the German people, long used to such government, had to suffer the spectacle, at each new crisis of their affairs, of long inter-party negotiations before a new government could be formed. This *Kuhhandel* ('cow-bargaining' or, as we might say, 'horse coping'), as the enemies of the democratic system called it, was enhanced by the lack of responsibility engendered in the various party leaders by the Bismarckian system (pp. 94–5) and by the rigidity of outlook which is so deeply characteristic of the German people as a whole.

It was a still greater handicap to the new democratic republic that its constitution was adopted only a few weeks after Germany had been compelled (28 June 1919) to sign the Treaty of Versailles. One of the strongest reasons for accepting democratic institutions with many patriotic Germans had been the hope of a 'good' peace based on President Wilson's Fourteen Points. This hope proved ill-founded. The armistice was not based upon the Fourteen Points and the peace treaty had to be concluded with Great Britain and France, who had borne the brunt of the fighting, and with their other Allies, as well as with the United States. Yet the hope remained and many Germans felt that a

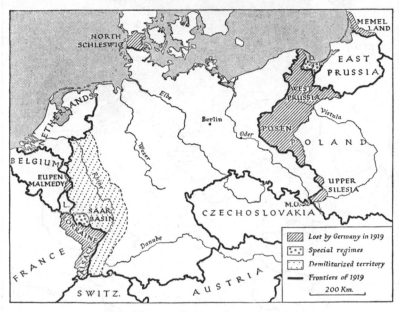

Map 17. Germany in 1919

M.O. = Morava Ostrava (Mährische-Ostrau).

moral obligation lay on the Allies to carry out President Wilson's programme.

The terms of the Versailles treaty. The territorial clauses of the Treaty of Versailles (Map 17) were, on the whole, in consonance with the President's principles, though they went much further than Germans had hoped. The return of Alsace-Lorraine to France (Point 8); the creation of an independent Polish state with 'a free and secure access to the sea'; the restoration of Belgium, Roumania, Serbia (Points 7, 11); the recognition of a Czechoslovak state (Point 10), could all be regarded as the

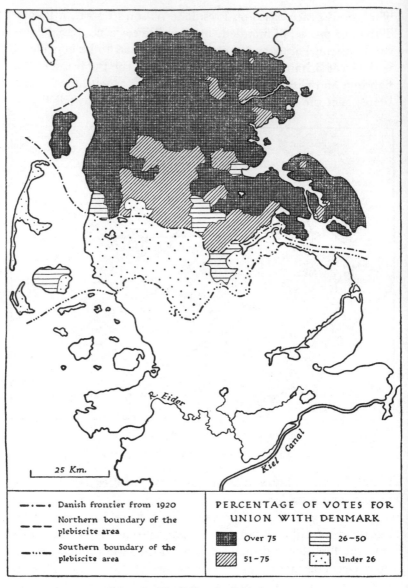

- —·—· Danish frontier from 1920
- — — — Northern boundary of the plebiscite area
- —··— Southern boundary of the plebiscite area

PERCENTAGE OF VOTES FOR
UNION WITH DENMARK

Over 75   26 – 50
51 – 75   Under 26

Map 18. The Schleswig plebiscite, 1920

logical outcome of the Fourteen Points, as could the decision to hold a plebiscite in North Schleswig (Map 18) to determine a new frontier between Denmark and the Reich. But the extent of the territories allotted to revived Poland, and especially the separation of Danzig and East Prussia from the body of the Reich (Map 19), aroused bitter German resentment, which was

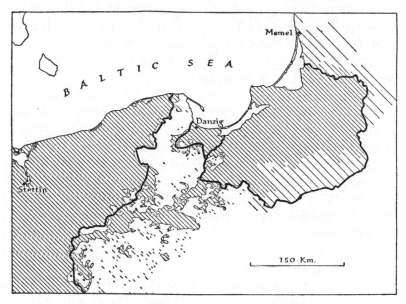

Map 19. Linguistic map of the Polish Corridor (1918)
Areas predominantly German-speaking are shaded. The boundaries are those of 1919.

increased by the subsequent division of Upper Silesia after a plebiscite (November 1921) in which the majority of the inhabitants voted for Germany. And the clause explicitly forbidding the union of Germany and Austria appeared to many Germans to deny them the right of self-determination ruthlessly applied by the Allies when it worked against Germany. Besides these grievances the cession of the Eupen and Malmédy districts to Belgium and the provision by which the Saar district was transferred to French control under a League of Nations Commission for fifteen years were comparatively small aggravations. But, as the direct result of the territorial provisions of the treaty, Germany lost 14·6 % of her arable land, 74·5 % of her iron ore, 68·1 % of her zinc and 26 % of her coal resources.

The Versailles treaty, however, contained much else that, as might have been expected, had found no place in President Wilson's liberal, and somewhat unrealistic, programme. Where the Fourteen Points spoke of 'a free, open-minded, and absolutely impartial adjustment of all colonial claims' (Point 5), the treaty provided for the detachment of her colonies from Germany and the creation of mandates for them, allotted to her enemies. The reduction of national armaments (Point 4) became a unilateral obligation imposed on Germany, by which her system of conscription was abolished and the great Prusso-German army was reduced to a force of 100,000 men, whose arms were to be controlled by a Disarmament Commission, whilst a large part of the German fleet was to be surrendered and in fact found a not ignoble end in Scapa Flow. By Article 231 of the treaty (the so-called 'War Guilt' clause) 'the Allied Governments affirm and Germany accepts the responsibility of Germany and her allies for causing all the loss and damage' which the Allies and their subjects had suffered 'as a consequence of the war imposed upon them by the aggression of Germany and her allies'. The obligation to pay reparations of enormous and unspecified amount was to German minds bad enough. The admission that the sole responsibility for the war rested on Germany and Austria was far worse. Finally, to enforce the treaty, Allied armies were to stand upon the Rhine for fifteen years and the Rhineland was to be permanently demilitarized (Map 20).

The effects of the treaty in Germany. The terms of the Treaty of Versailles came as a shattering blow to Germany as a whole and to the Republican parties in particular. Though the army leaders, including Hindenburg, advised that resistance was impossible, and though Hermann Müller, the Social Democrat, and Johannes Bell, the Centrist, deserved honour rather than obloquy for taking the responsibility of signature on their shoulders, the Right used the acceptance of the treaty by the

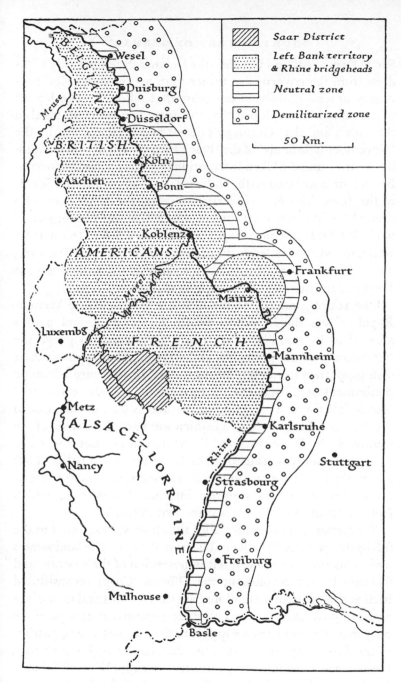

Map 20. Western Germany in 1919

The areas on the left bank of the Rhine held by the various
armies of occupation are indicated.

Social Democrats and Centre—the Democrats temporarily withdrew from the government rather than accept responsibility—utterly unscrupulously in the years that followed. The legend was assiduously developed that the army had been 'stabbed in the back', and that Germany's defeat had been ensured by the 'November Criminals' of the 'Black International'—the Catholic Centre—and the 'Red International'—the Social Democrats. Behind, or associated with, both was the 'Yellow International' of the Jews. The fact that Hugo Preuss, the Democrat, who drafted the Weimar constitution, was a Jew was not forgotten, whilst Walter Rathenau, the Jewish director of *A.E.G.* (see p. 108), who had, with Moellendorff, organized German war industry, and did fine work as Minister of Reconstruction, and, finally, as Foreign Minister after the war, was assassinated (1922).

One reason, indeed, of the ultimate failure of the Weimar Republic was the impunity which the constitutional parties allowed to its enemies. They made no attempt to purge the bureaucracy or the judiciary, and were unable to protect their own supporters from reactionary judges, or to secure adequate punishment of the violent young nationalists who committed 'patriotic' crimes. This attitude of weakness was, in part, due to the strict adherence to legality which was part of the creed of the Centre, Social Democrats and Democrats alike. But it was also due to the deeply ingrained desire for order on the political left and to their reliance on 'national' elements, including the new army (*Reichswehr*), to suppress internal disorders, of which Noske's use of the *Freikorps* was the first example.

The enemies of the Republic. This situation was exploited to the full by the enemies of the Republic from the first. The landowners and industrialists had been left in possession of their estates and factories by the revolution, the Officers' Corps reconstituted itself and chose with meticulous care the N.C.O.s and men of the new army (*Reichswehr*), and all alike regarded it as a patriotic duty to give tacit or open support to the militant young patriots of the Free Corps organizations. As early as 15 January 1919 the leaders of German heavy industry—Krupp, Kirdorf, Stinnes, Vögler, Röchling and others—formed an Anti-Bolshevik League, to which they subscribed many millions of marks. These funds were used to finance the Free Corps and other extreme nationalist and anti-republican groups. From the first the leaders of heavy industry were aware that their great plants, largely extended during the four years of war, could not be kept going profitably under a pacific regime. Through the German National People's party they, and the Prussian landowning class, interested in securing posts as officers and bureaucrats for their sons, fought their old battle for political, as well as social, predominance in the Reichstag. And, since they needed wider popular support to give strength to their claims, they encouraged all the ultra-nationalist political movements which were stimulated by the terms of the Versailles treaty.

Inflation and international crises. From 1919 to 1924 the history of the German Republic is that of a series of crises over the Allies' demands for the fulfilment of the treaty. At each crisis the German government offers what resistance it can, and then, faced by an ultimatum, resigns, is painfully reconstructed—and gives way. International conferences in Paris and London (1921), in Cannes and Genoa (1922), followed in swift succession. By 1922 the German mark (the normal rate of which was 4 marks = 1 dollar) was already losing value, and the failure of yet another conference in London (December 1922) was followed by the decision of the Reparations Commission that Germany was in default (28 December 1922) and by the French occupation of the Ruhr (January 1923). From that moment the inflation of the mark became catastrophic. Even by January 1922 a dollar could buy 191·8 marks; by January 1923 the dollar rate was 17,972·0, after which it raced towards infinity so that in November 1923 it had become virtually worthless, since one dollar could then buy 4,200,000,000 marks.

Meanwhile the internal enemies of the Republic had been active. As early as March 1920 a Pan-German agrarian official, Kapp, had led a rising in Berlin with the support of Ehrhardt's Marine Brigade, a Free Corps organization, whose suppression was demanded by the Allies. The government moved first to Dresden and then to Stuttgart. The new Reichswehr stood neutral in the conflict, but the civil servants in the ministries refused to take Kapp's orders. When a general strike of the workers took place Kapp's position became impossible and his movement collapsed. But the events which followed showed clearly the weakness of the democratic Republic. For, whilst the 'red' workers of the Ruhr district, who had broken out in revolt against Kapp's supporters, were bloodily suppressed by the Reichswehr and by some of the Free Corps troops who had supported Kapp, Ehrhardt's brigade received no punishment. The trade unions, whose intervention had been decisive in saving the Republic, received promises of further democratization of the army, police and civil service, and of measures for socializing industry. But none of these promises were carried out, and the elections of 1920 (p. 151) showed that the credit of the republican parties had suffered severely and that the gainers from the Kapp *Putsch* were the parties of the Right. One of the results of the affair was that Noske lost the office of Reichswehr Minister, and was relegated to be *Oberpräsident* of Hanover. But, since his place was taken by Gessler, a Democrat politician, who gave the Reichswehr generals a very free hand and spared them inconvenient inquiries into their activities (see below), the cause of the Republic was not strengthened.

The Kapp *Putsch* showed, then, that radical republicans could expect little protection from the Republic, and that 'national' groups had little to fear. For the next two years these groups of militant young patriots, estimated to have numbered 300,000 men at one stage, based themselves on Bavaria, where a very reactionary government held office. A series of assassinations of republican leaders took place. That of Rathenau has already been mentioned, but Erzberger, the leader of the armistice delegation, was murdered in 1921, threats were made against Ebert's life and an attempt made on Scheidemann. And when, after Erzberger's murder, the government sought (September 1921) to take stronger powers against the perpetrators of these outrages, they were met by fierce opposition from the Right, and by threats of secession from Bavaria.

Throughout 1921–2, especially after the Allied decision to

partition Upper Silesia, this internal tension continued and the occupation of the Ruhr (January 1923), followed by the hopeless inflation of the mark, brought the Republic to the verge of chaos. In the Rhineland the French were attempting to set up separatist states, in the Ruhr the workers carried on passive resistance against the occupying forces, in Saxony and Thuringia militant Socialist-Communist governments came into power, whilst in Bavaria, Kahr and General von Lossow played with the idea of nationalist counter-revolution at the moment of their country's greatest need for unity. The crisis was so profound that at length counsels of moderation gained a hearing in France, and, in Germany, Gustav Stresemann, of the German People's party, showed the wisdom and courage which differentiate the statesman from the politician. On 13 August 1923 Stresemann took office as Chancellor and Foreign Minister[1] and, having called off passive resistance and entered into negotiations with the Allies —themselves frightened by the results of their policy—prepared to deal with the extremists of Right and Left in Germany itself.

THE STRESEMANN PERIOD, 1923–9

Stresemann's first task was to assert the authority of the central government. In October the Bavarian reactionary Prime Minister Kahr virtually declared war on the Reich by taking over the Reichswehr in Bavaria, with General von Lossow at its head, as 'trustee for the German people'. At the same time this treasonable attitude was made worse by the concentration in and around Bavaria of racial-nationalist bands, with which Kahr was in touch, amongst them Hitler's group of National-Socialists,[2] to which Ludendorff gave the authority of his great reputation.

Hitler's Munich Putsch. Possibly to make intervention against the Bavarian nationalists more palatable the Reichswehr was ordered by Stresemann to suppress the Socialist-Communist

---

[1] He ceased to be Chancellor on 23 November 1923, but remained Foreign Minister until his death in 1929.
[2] See below pp. 171–5.

governments in Saxony and Thuringia (29 October)—an entirely unconstitutional action. It was still possible, however, that the Bavarian government and the extreme nationalist bands might attempt a coup against the Reich, and Hitler sought to secure this by bursting into a meeting addressed by Kahr in the Bürgerbräu Cellar at Munich on the evening of 8 November and forcing Kahr and Lossow at the pistol's point to declare for a march on Berlin. Once freed from compulsion, however, the Bavarian leaders withdrew their support and Hitler's demonstration on the morning of 9 November was met by the armed force of the Bavarian police. A few volleys decided the issue. After a dozen of his followers had been killed Hitler fled for his life and the demonstration dispersed. Hitler's first bid for power had failed ignominiously. But, as in the case of the Kapp *Putsch*, republican justice proved miserably weak against the counter-revolutionaries of the Right. Kahr and Lossow were not even charged—indeed they appeared as prosecution witnesses—and Hitler's sentence of detention in a fortress nominally for five years, reduced in fact to less than a year, was justly described by Heiden as 'virtually judicial praise' of his *Putsch*.

Nevertheless, Stresemann had accomplished his purpose. Both Right and Left extremists were, for the moment, subdued, and he was able to turn to the task of stabilizing the mark, of treating with the Allies for a settlement of the reparations question, and of recovering for Germany her place among the Great Powers of Europe. His task was made possible by the fact that the United States, though still unwilling to join the League of Nations, was ready to take part in the economic rehabilitation of Germany, in order to find some outlet for her own excessive gold reserves, and markets in Europe for her industrial production. By April 1924 the Dawes Plan was published, the German government was promised an immediate loan of 800 million gold marks, and, though the final reparations total remained unsettled, annual payments of a size within Germany's capacity to pay—so long as American support continued—were fixed. A price, it is true, had to be paid for this assistance. The German railways and the Reichsbank were removed from Reich control, and the Reparations Commission, under an American financier, Parker Gilbert, exercised a considerable degree of supervision over the finances of the Republic. But at least an air of financial stability was given to German economic life, and for the next five years (1924–9), the country enjoyed a somewhat spurious prosperity, marred only by scandals in the public administration, the ultimate disclosure of which did much to undermine the Weimar Republic.

Yet the relatively peaceful years of Stresemann's period of office as Foreign Minister owed their tranquility largely to the exhaustion of the whole of German society after the inflation period, and to the fact that the great industrialists themselves moderated their hostility to the Republic whilst it was in the hands of a nationalist leader. For, so long as American loans poured in, they were busy in exploiting the situation, and the continuance of the loans depended upon internal tranquility in Germany.

The effects of the inflation. But the effects of the inflation did not quickly disappear. Whether it was in fact engineered by the great agrarians and industrialists for their own ends it is not possible to say certainly. But it is certain that they profited from it, whereas the middle and working classes suffered severely. The landowners and peasants could discharge their debts and mortgages in worthless marks, and the great cartels and banks did the same for the big industrial plants. But the small capitalist lost his savings, the trade unions their funds, and the wages of the working class never kept pace with the decline of the currency. The social effect of the inflation was catastrophic, especially in reducing the middle class to a 'proletarian' condition. And it lowered the tone of all German social and commercial life by creating a condition of affairs in which the clever speculator prospered. It also strengthened greatly the control of the highly concentrated heavy and chemical industries over the German economy. As early as December 1923, in a lecture before London University, Brig.-Gen. J. H. Morgan, who had served on the Disarmament Commission for four years, said of the inflation: 'It has destroyed the equipoise of society. It has ruined the middle classes and impoverished the workers....It has been a tremendous solvent of society. It is not merely that thrift...has disappeared.... The thrifty themselves have gone under.' And he added that the inflation had 'undermined the political basis of the Republic and concentrated all real power in the hands of a few—namely, the great industrialists...in no country in the world is capital so strong or politically so despotic. The economic form of society fails to correspond to the political theory: a republic in name, it is a capitalist despotism in fact.' Such a situation, especially where a people is politically inexperienced, provides the ideal opportunity for a demagogue lavish in promises and willing to arouse primitive emotions.

For the time being, however, the parties of the Right, among which the Bavarian People's party and a section of the Centre party must be counted in Reich politics after 1924, were content to rule by constitutional methods and even to make considerable concessions to the workers. If, in 1925, *I.G. Farbenindustrie* incorporated several rival dye corporations into itself, and, in 1926, heavy industry concentrated its power still further by forming the *Vereinigte Stahlwerke*, a merger of four large steel concerns in western Germany, the level of workers' wages also rose steadily during these years, the trade unions revived and began to build up their funds and, in 1926, the Social Democratic party was able to secure the passage of a law providing for unemployment insurance.

Secret rearmament. From the coming into force of the Versailles treaty on 1 January 1920—if not, indeed, from the signing of the Armistice on 11 November 1918—the army leaders had done everything within their power to circumvent the disarmament provisions. Although the treaty banned the General Staff in its traditional form, the Commander-in-Chief of the Reichswehr, Colonel-General Hans von Seeckt, succeeded in creating an equivalent *Truppenamt*, under his own immediate supervision, to carry on its work. He also contrived to add surreptitiously to the strength of the standing army. Taking advantage of the chauvinism displayed by the Poles in 1920 and 1921, he claimed that it was impossible to defend Germany's eastern frontiers with the 100,000-man army permitted by the treaty and that the Reichswehr must consequently be supplemented by secret formations disguised as labour battalions. Thus was formed, within the Berlin-Brandenburg Military District, the 20,000-strong force of *Arbeits-Kommandos*—later to become known as the 'Black Reichswehr'—in which the future Chancellor Kurt von Schleicher had a hand, and of which Fedor von Bock (later Hitler's Field Marshal in Russia) became Chief of Staff. Nor was Seeckt solely concerned to preserve the best of what had been and to attain, by training and reorganization, the highest standards for what remained. The preparation for future military expansion—to which he also looked—necessitated planning for economic mobilization. In November 1924 he accordingly established a highly secret 'Armament Office' (*Rüstungsamt*—commonly shortened to *Rüstamt*) with the task of ascertaining the requirements in munitions and equipment and other essential services of an army of sixty-three divisions,[1] and of enlisting the clandestine co-operation of heavy industry, not only in Germany but in certain foreign countries.

Collaboration with the Soviet Union. Much of Seeckt's secret planning to circumvent Versailles must necessarily have remained ephemeral but for the collaboration which he received from the Soviet Union—the other major European 'outcast' of the post-war period. As early as August 1918 a German group, which included Stresemann, had discussed with Joffe (the Soviet Ambassador in Berlin) and Krassin (the Soviet Commissar for Foreign Trade) a series of economic agreements supplementing the treaty of Brest-Litovsk and looking to some form of future military understanding. Karl Radek, the Soviet agitator, gaoled after the second Spartakist rising of March 1919, had, from his cell in the Moabit prison, propagated the idea of an alliance between Bolshevik Russia and Nationalist Germany against the Western capitalists. He was later in touch with Seeckt, and, by the spring of 1921, when Lenin asked for German assistance in reorganizing the Red Army after the Russo-Polish war, firm contact had been established between the Reichswehr and

[1] The goal was later scaled down to twenty-one divisions.

Moscow. Thanks to the ever-present danger of the Poles repeating against East Prussia or Pomerania the *coup* which in September 1920 General Zeligowski had carried out against the Lithuanian capital, Vilna, Seeckt was able to induce the Reich and Prussian governments to turn a blind eye to his schemes and to set up the secret 'Special Group R' (*Sondergruppe-R*) to co-operate with the Red Army General Staff.

From this point military collaboration proceeded along two parallel lines: the 'Special Group R', in which Schleicher again played an important part, helped to develop tank and aviation schools in the Soviet Union; while, also on Russian territory, a so-called 'Society for the Encouragement of Industrial Undertakings'—known by its German initials as *Gefu*—organized the production of war materials, including poison gas. Although some of the *Gefu* projects got little further than the drawing boards, there continued to be close contact between the Bendler-strasse (where, since the war, the War Ministry (*Kriegsministerium*) had been situated) and Moscow, thanks to the German military and technical mission which was established in the Soviet capital and to the visits which Schleicher, von Hammerstein (C.-in-C. of the Reichswehr, 1930–4) and von Blomberg (Reich Minister of Defence, 1933–8) subsequently paid to Russia.

Meanwhile the groundwork had been laid for a political *rapprochement* between Berlin and Moscow in the best Bismarckian tradition. In Freiherr Ago von Maltzan, the head of the Eastern European Division and subsequently Under-Secretary (*Staatssekretär*) in the Foreign Ministry, Seeckt found a diplomat after his own heart, and the first tangible result of von Maltzan's endeavours was the German-Russian Commercial Agreement of 6 May 1921. For von Maltzan and his chief, Walter Rathenau, this was, however, only a beginning, and within the next twelve months they were able, with the approval of the German Chancellor, Wirth, to negotiate the treaty of Rapallo (17 April 1922), which disclosed the long-suspected and (in France, at least) greatly-feared *entente* between Germany and the Soviet Union as a reality. The close understanding now reached between Berlin and Moscow was soon to be strengthened by the appointment of the bitterly anti-French Count Ulrich von Brock-dorff-Rantzau as German Ambassador to the Soviet Union. *Stresemann's policy.* Although it was as the foremost exponent of the policy of 'fulfilment' (i.e. of Germany's obligations under the Versailles treaty) that he established his place in history, and although Seeckt regarded him as a 'defeatist' (*Flaumacher*), Stresemann is now known to have been sympathetic towards the Reichswehr's schemes of secret rearmament, of which he was often cognizant.[1] Indeed, it was partly this sympathy which induced him to work so assiduously to get the Inter-Allied Control Commission withdrawn—a task in which he finally succeeded in January 1927. Although he resented the way in which Seeckt and the Reichswehr had tried to place themselves beyond the civil power, he more than once regretted the absence of a strong army as 'the main factor in a successful foreign policy'. There is reason to believe that he was aware of some of Seeckt's transactions with the Russians—in fact, he once admitted that, as far back as 1923, he knew that there were secret military ties with Moscow, but claimed that he had insisted upon their being severed. Nor could it be truthfully said that the role which he played in the diplomacy of the West weakened the link which Rapallo had forged with the East. Indeed, Seeckt's criticism that the Locarno Agreement (see below) jeopardized the Russian connection was effectively answered by the signing at Berlin on 24 April 1926 of the German-Soviet Treaty of Neutrality and Non-Aggression, extending Rapallo.

As Stresemann himself defined it, his aim was to make Germany 'the bridge which would bring East and West together in the development of Europe'. If he was not able to accomplish quite this, he at least established a tight-rope along which German policy could move, as necessity dictated, between the West and Moscow. Broadly speaking his policy aimed at breaking the encirclement of Germany, which had resulted from her defeat, by securing the friendship of England and, if possible, of France,

[1] Much new light has been thrown on Stresemann's policy by his collected papers (of which a microfilm copy is in the Public Record Office) which have been used by Professor Hans W. Gatzke in the preparation of his monograph, *Stresemann and the Rearmament of Germany* (Baltimore, 1954).

as the necessary preliminary to the evacuation of the Rhineland at the earliest possible date, and to a reasonable and final settlement of the reparations problem. Only when that had been done, and when Germany had resumed her place in the councils of Europe, could the problems of revision of the eastern (Polish) frontier be approached with hope of success. The pacts of Locarno (October 1925) by which England, France, Italy and Germany all guaranteed the Franco-German and Belgian-German frontiers represented the first part of his aims and were followed, though after an unfortunate delay due to rival claims, by Germany's entry into the League with a permanent seat upon the Council (September 1926). The agreement at Locarno also brought with it a reduction in the number, and cost to Germany, of the occupation forces in the Rhineland and the evacuation of Cologne by the British (30 January 1926), and, as already noted, at the beginning of 1927 the Inter-Allied Commission of control of German armaments was withdrawn.

But, though these were successes of real importance for Germany, Stresemann was unable to follow them up. The French, prevented from gaining permanent control of the Rhine, and deeply conscious of their inferiority in population and productive capacity to the Germans, had only temporarily accepted the conciliatory policy cautiously expressed by Herriot at Geneva in 1924. To them the Locarno pacts, with their free acceptance of the restoration of Alsace-Lorraine to France, and the joint guarantee by England, Italy and Germany herself of the French eastern frontier, represented the minimum which France could justly be expected to claim and, if there were many, like Seeckt, in Germany who thought that Stresemann had conceded too much at Locarno, there were those in France who thought that Briand had claimed too little. In July 1926 Poincaré, who had been largely responsible for the occupation of the Ruhr, again became Prime Minister in France, and throughout 1927 German relations with both France and England became cooler, so that Locarno produced no further fruits. By the beginning of 1928 Stresemann was complaining bitterly of the failure of the Allies to provide the further concessions to which he felt that his policy of fulfilment entitled him, and, under the pressure of ill-health, his impatience for results led him, on 30 October, to send a demand for a new and final settlement of the reparations issue. In December the Allied Powers agreed, and a committee of experts was appointed which produced the Young Plan on 7 June 1929. In August, at the Hague Conference, Stresemann accepted the proposals and secured also the immediate evacuation of the Rhineland by the British and Belgian contingents, and the withdrawal of the French forces, 'if it is physically possible', by the end of June 1930. Desperately ill, Stresemann forced himself to Geneva for the League Assembly in September, but on 2 October 1929 he died.

With the perspective we have acquired from later events it is reasonable to hold that Stresemann was 'happy in the hour of his death', for it is more than possible that not even his personality could have held in check the forces which, in the next four years, overwhelmed the Republic. It is clear, also, that his policy of conditional fulfilment, mixed with a subtle measure of treaty evasion, was misundertsood by many Germans from Seeckt downwards. It was based on a long-term view of a gradual and peaceful rehabilitation of Germany as a member of the European community, but there were few of his countrymen capable of a long-term view at the best of times, and almost none during the economic crisis into which the world was soon to be plunged. Yet there can be little doubt that Stresemann's death in 1929, and the loss of his great personal influence in international affairs, were a disaster not only for Germany but for Europe and the world.

THE YOUNG PLAN AND ITS OPPONENTS

Superficially, one of the more hopeful signs of greater stability in Germany during the Stresemann period was that, under the pressure of his personality, the German National People's party had temporarily abandoned its purely anti-republican attitude and had formed part of a government coalition in 1925 and in 1927. Both Hugenberg and Seldte, the leader of the semi-military *Stahlhelm*, had opposed this policy, however, and the party had withdrawn from the government rather than share in the responsibility for the Locarno pacts. But the mere fact of participating in a republican government appeared to show that even the extreme Right had come to the conclusion that the Republic had come to stay. The election of Hindenburg as President in succession to Ebert, who died in 1925, had assisted the Nationalists to take this decision, for, if the aged field-marshal found it compatible with his conscience to serve the Republic in serving Germany, it was somewhat ridiculous for other National-ists to be *plus royaliste que le roi*.

The relative economic prosperity of Germany during these years was another vital factor in this apparent stability. Germany received loans from abroad between 1924 and 1929 to the tune of 25,000 million gold marks, whilst the total of her reparations payments under the Dawes Plan for the same period was under 8,000 million. With the surplus she was able to re-equip her industries, to indulge in large public works and municipal enter-prises, to subsidize her agriculture, and to rebuild her export trade. In 1930 the value of her exports was a third greater than in 1914 and, despite her territorial losses, she produced consider-ably more pig iron and steel in 1929 than in 1913. Under these circumstances the great agrarians and the industrial magnates, rationalizing and re-equipping their plants, had good reason to be satisfied with the Republic. They could not reasonably com-plain because their workpeople shared in this flow of gold from abroad through better wages, better municipal services, and the new unemployment insurance payments in times of slack trade, or because the trade union movement was also recuperating.

Nationalist opposition to the Young Plan. Yet many of the Nationalists, and Hugenberg in particular, were dissatisfied. To them Stresemann's policy of fulfilment meant betrayal of the national cause. The Locarno guarantee of the western frontier sealed the loss of Alsace-Lorraine; membership of the League implied acceptance of the idea of an international order repug-nant to their belief in militarist expansionism and, what was worse, it involved acceptance of the Treaty of Versailles. So strong was their section that, before Stresemann's death, the division in the German Nationalist party had enabled Hugenberg, now in command of a great press organization, to become the official leader of the party (1928), and the first use this irreconcilable old Pan-German extremist made of his victory was to link hands with Hitler in a campaign for a referendum against the Young Plan. The measure they put forward was entitled, 'Bill against the Young Plan and the War-Guilt Lie'. Its fourth clause denounced Stresemann and those who had negotiated the Young Plan as guilty of treason. And the campaign itself was conducted both by Hugenberg and by Hitler and his followers with an unscrupulous bitterness and violence against the dying Stresemann and all who had supported him, which promised ill for Germany and Europe if once the 'national alliance' obtained effective power. Less than six million voters supported the Hugenberg-Hitler referendum—hardly more than one-third of the votes necessary to pass it. Yet the alliance of the German Nationalists with the National Socialists on this issue marks the turning point in Hitler's fortunes and the first stage in the final downfall of the German Republic.

NATIONAL SOCIALISM BEFORE 1929

The German Workers' party, which later (1920) became the National Socialist German Workers' party (*National-Sozialist-ische-Deutsche-Arbeiter-Partei*), known by its initials as *N.S.D.A.P.*, was founded by an independent craftsman Anton Drexler (or Drechsler), whose political ideas were a mixture of naïve nationalism and a desire to protect the small man. But Drexler's little group would have had no importance if it had not been captured by Hitler, for there were many similar small groups and, to be successful in the competition between them, a man of political genius was required.

Hitler's early career. Hitler was born on 20 April 1889, at Braunau on the Austrian-Bavarian frontier. His father, Alois Schicklgrüber, who assumed the surname Hitler in 1876, was illegitimate, but it is not unimportant that, brought up as a shoemaker, he managed to become a customs official under the

Austrian government, or that Hitler was educated in Linz under a teacher of history who, though Austrian, shared the Pan-German outlook of Schönerer and his party (see p. 121). Born into the lower middle class, bred in ideas of extreme nationalism, the death of first his father (1903) and then his mother (1908) left him, at the age of nineteen, faced with the problem of earning a living though, having been idle at school, without any qualifications for doing so.

For three years Hitler lived in Vienna as a proletarian in a 'men's hostel' or doss-house, earning a scanty living by odd jobs, including painting postcards, but always, if his own account may be accepted, deeply concerned with politics. He learned to hate, but to understand, both the working class, whose trade unions he refused to join, and the Jews. And from Lueger, the burgomaster of Vienna, he learnt most of the tactics and principles of politics which he was later to put into effect. In Lueger's Christian Social (*Christlich-Sozial*) party, 'Christlich' was synonymous with anti-semitic, and 'Sozial' with protection of the lower-middle class and peasantry against capitalists and proletarians alike. Thus, in Vienna, Hitler learnt to reject internationalism as represented by the hotch-potch of races in the old Austria, to despise the Hapsburgs, to adopt Pan-Germanism, and, above all, to hate the Jews with deep loathing and to regard them as the real force behind the Social-Democratic movement, and as, in his own words, 'the eternal fissure-fungus of humanity'.

In 1913 Hitler moved to Munich[1] and managed to live a somewhat more tolerable life until war broke out in 1914, when, though an Austrian citizen, he was permitted to join a Bavarian regiment, the List Regiment, and saw service at the first battle of Ypres. He was made a lance-corporal, wounded once and gassed, and received the Iron Cross, First and Second class. In 1918–19 he was still in a reserve battalion of his regiment, and it was the Reichswehr which sent him to effect a political liaison with the little German Workers' party, and supported

[1] In *Mein Kampf* he speaks of leaving Vienna in 1912, but the police records of that city suggest that he did not move until May 1913.

him financially as a propagandist of nationalist views amongst the working class. In September 1919 Drexler invited him to become a member of the party executive and he became no. 7 in that body.

The new member brought with him not only the fixed ideas of Pan-Germanism, anti-semitism and hatred of social democracy, but also an unlimited ambition, an intense propagandist energy, a hypnotic power of mass oratory, and a profound understanding of political tactics which was combined with a gambler's readiness to dare everything to attain his ends. What was equally important, he brought the promise of Reichswehr backing, and later of the Bavarian reactionary government under Kahr, as well as subsidies from the Munich nationalists and from other sources such as the Anti-Bolshevik League. By 1921 he had established his mastery and had become Führer, with Drexler relegated to an honorary presidency, and had already begun to knit connection with similiar groups, and to establish branch organizations outside Bavaria. He was able to secure assistance from wealthy families like the Hanfstaengl's and from intellectuals and ex-officers like Dietrich Eckart and Captain Röhm, who moved in circles far more influential than any in which Drexler had influence, and, by his untiring energy as a propagandist and the ruthlessness of his methods, he became the indispensable leader of the group.

From the first the *N.S.D.A.P.* under Hitler distinguished itself from the many similar groups by the ruthlessness of its methods. After a Munich Rabbi had appeared on Hitler's platform to protest against his grotesque slanders of the Jews the Nazi meetings displayed a notice 'Jews not admitted' and, from ejecting opponents forcibly from their own meetings, the party soon passed to breaking up forcibly the meetings of their rivals. The semi-military *S.A.*, an organization of young men ready for any violence required, might begin as a *Schutz-Abteilung* (Protective Detachment), but soon earned the right to be regarded as a *Sturm-Abteilung* (Assault Detachment). In the hands of Captain Röhm it aspired to be more—the vanguard of a military organization, closely allied with the Reichswehr and the other Free

Corps bodies, and to fill the role of the troops of the counter-revolution.

After the Munich Putsch. The fiasco of 1923 (see pp. 161–2) cured Hitler, though not Röhm, of this dream. Despite the countenance of Ludendorff he had failed. But, as was his wont, he turned failure into success by his persistence and propagandist genius. He set to work, with the assistance of Hess, to formulate his political ideas in *Mein Kampf,* and he emerged from the Landsberg fortress more mature, more patient, but also more fundamentally ruthless and determined than before. The *Putsch* had taught him that the time for open violence was not yet, and that the Reichswehr itself would not engage in open opposition to the legally established state. He would, therefore, accept the situation and the jeers of his less intelligent supporters against *Adolf Légalité,* but he was all the more determined to attain power in the end and to use it, in the hour of his triumph, with utter ruthlessness against all his opponents.

Yet, when Hitler was released in December 1924, his position was precarious. The 'unalterable programme' of February 1920, though it contained a *Grossdeutsch* demand for the unity of all Germans in one state, an anti-semitic clause promising exclusion of Jews from full citizenship, and a denunciation of the parliamentary party system of the Republic—all points with which the German Nationalist party agreed—also contained a rather confused socialism which was borne out in practice by the fact that, within the *S.S.* and *S.A.,* and in the party organization in general, the sharp social divisions, inherited from imperial Germany, were largely ignored. Moreover, the best organizer of the small party, Gregor Strasser, had already begun to build up in Berlin and north Germany a party machine and a following which took the socialist aspects of the party programme seriously.

Between 1925 and 1928 Hitler triumphed over these difficulties. He established himself as sole leader to whose decisions all members of the party were subordinate. He captured Goebbels, whom Strasser had put in charge of the Berlin movement, for himself. He got rid of Röhm temporarily, because he recognized that the Reichswehr would not, after 1923, tolerate a rival military organization. He created the *S.S.* (*Schutzstaffel*) as a special Body of Guards bound by an oath of loyalty to his person. By the end of 1926 the party organization was firmly in his hand.

Yet, though both the party and its organizations were growing, it was still a tiny minority in Germany. By 1928 Nazi Lawyers', Teachers' and Physicians' Associations had been created, and there was also a Hitler Youth organization. But the party membership in 1927 was a mere 40,000, and the difficulties of developing its hold by propagandist activities were increased by the reluctance both of the Reichswehr and the great capitalists to disturb the peace of the Republic, upon which the flow of foreign loans and the conditions favourable to large profits depended. When, therefore, in 1929, Hugenberg offered him alliance and the support of his syndicated press for a campaign against the Young Plan, Hitler was at once ready to grasp the proffered hand. His Left-wing supporters, Gregor and Otto Strasser, and their following, might look askance at an alliance with a peculiarly ruthless capitalist and his associates. But, for Hitler, the socialist side of his movement meant nothing—except as a drug for the masses. His heart and soul were in the pursuit of power, in the creation of a Great Germany, in the ruthless elimination of all opponents, beginning with the Jews. The referendum against the Young Plan satisfied all his desires. He could denounce the Versailles *Diktat*; the 'November criminals', who had 'betrayed' Germany; the Weimar system, which enabled these 'betrayers' of Germany to exploit their country and to sacrifice its interests to the foreign capitalists—again represented as mainly Jews—who sought to place the German people under permanent 'interest slavery' in the form of reparations. And, in all this, he could rely on Hugenberg's press to report his speeches and on the funds of Hugenberg and the heavy industrialists to pay his party's expenses. It is small wonder that he welcomed and accepted Hugenberg's proposal.

NAZIS, NATIONALISTS AND THE
ECONOMIC CRISIS

The result of the Young Plan referendum was to convert the Nazi party from a small group into a nation-wide organization of the first importance. This result was, in part, due to the support which Hugenberg's national press was bound to give to its allies during the campaign, in part to the new sources of financial assistance which that campaign brought with it. In 1928–9 Hitler had broken up Strasser's semi-socialist organization in the Ruhr district. He had got into touch with the great iron and steel magnate, Emil Kirdorf, through Dr Otto Dietrich, and, in 1929, Kirdorf attended the Nuremberg Congress of the party as a guest of honour. From that moment funds from heavy industry began to flow into Hitler's coffers, for the coal and iron magnates learnt to recognize that the socialism in the *N.S.D.A.P.* programme did not interest its leader, and that Hitler was, in fact, as 'pure' a patriot as themselves.

But it was not mainly the support of heavy industry which changed the position of the Nazi party in Germany. It was the collapse of the Streseman system, owing to the economic crisis of 1929–30, which seemed to show that, in their contention that Germany could not pay the reparations provided for under the Young Plan, Hitler and Hugenberg were right and Stresemann and his supporters wrong. Even before the Young Plan was passed by the Reichstag the flow of foreign capital to Germany had begun to diminish. But, in the autumn of 1929, a world economic crisis of the most severe kind began to develop after a crash in values in Wall Street. Germany's import of foreign capital in 1928 was still over 5000 million Rm., but in 1929 that sum was halved and, in 1930, reached only 700 million Rm. Not only did foreign investment in Germany fall away but many of the short-term American loans, which had been taken up and used with equal recklessness by industrialists and municipalities for long-term purposes, began to be called in. As a result a state of economic instability developed in Germany, so that unemployment rose sharply, confidence in the banks and the currency was shaken and, by the end of 1930, the whole German economic system seemed threatened with breakdown.

	Percentage of trade union members	
	Wholly unemployed	On short time
1929	14·6	9·4
1930	24·4	16·2
1931	37·0	21·7
1932 (first half)	48·0	24·2

Source: Erich Roll, *Spotlight on Germany* (London, 1933), p. 187.

In this situation it was not surprising that fears of a second inflation should be widespread, nor that an over-simplified explanation, which cast all the blame on the bourgeois-socialist Republic, should have been accepted, particularly by the young and by those who had previously been indifferent to politics. Already aroused by the burning patriotic eloquence of Hitler and Goebbels against the Young Plan, these elements poured into the ranks of the party and the *S.A.* in the winter of 1929–30. When the Centre Party Chancellor, Brüning, who had taken office without a majority to deal with the crisis and had already begun to rule by presidential decree under Article 48 of the Constitution, appealed to the country in September 1930, the Nazis who, in 1928, had secured only twelve seats in the Reichstag with 810,000 votes were now supported by over six million voters and became a party of 107 members, second only in size to the Social Democrats.

Brüning and the depression. After the elections of 1930 it is doubtful if anything could have saved the German Republic, except a great economic revival, which did not come. In the Reichstag three parties, on principle opposed to parliamentary government, Hugenberg's Nationalists, the Nazis and the Communists, who had grown to seventy-seven members, came near to forming a majority of the whole body. Brüning, a noble if rigid character, who had originally been called to office at the suggestion of Schleicher and the other army leaders, pursued a policy of stiff deflation, which involved the drastic reduction of all social services, including the cutting down of unemployment benefit

177

at the time when it was most needed. The Social Democrats were without any policy at all, except that of supporting Brüning, lest worse should befall. The Communists, loudly revolutionary in speech, were, and their leaders knew it, too few, too ill-organized and too badly armed to have any chance of carrying through a revolution of their own. On the other side, as the economic crisis deepened, the old Nationalists were divided. The aged President and the Reichswehr generals feared the effects of Nazi radicalism in the army. One wing of the Nationalist party, under Count Westarp, broke with Hugenberg, and many more feared the violence of Hitler and his followers. But others, some of the great landowners and many of the industrialists among them, saw in the rise of the Nazis the heaven-sent opportunity of over-throwing the Republic itself and of capturing for reaction a great party which could give the cause of Nationalism what it had always lacked—the support of the masses.

It was this division in the governing class, more than any other single factor, which at once facilitated and delayed Hitler's accession to power. From 1930 to 1932 Brüning, whose Cabinet was at least united and disciplined, continued to rule by decree and to cut down the expenses of the state in every direction, whilst unemployment grew with menacing rapidity from 4,500,000 at the end of 1931 to over six millions at the beginning of 1933. At the same time Brüning supported German agriculture by high tariffs and by the *Osthilfe* (Eastern Help Fund), which subsidized the agrarians of East Prussia, and which some of them shame-lessly abused. Brüning also supported industrial concerns in difficulties by buying up their shares for the state at inflated prices or, as in the case of the Danat (*Darmstädter und National Bank*), by taking over their assets and merging them with other institutions.

Hitler and the crisis. But though, during 1931–2, the reparations question was at last solving itself through the increasingly obvious inability of Germany to pay, and though the economic crisis was at least as severe in the United States as in Germany, Hitler continued a raging propaganda against the Versailles treaty and the Weimar system as the cause of all German miseries. The youth of Germany, unemployed, without hope of employment and without the parental savings, lost in the inflation, to fall back on, streamed into the *S.A.* which at least gave them a uniform, drilling, street fighting and processions as outlets for their energy, and a minimum of pay on which to live. But Hitler also gave them new hope. Out of the chaos of this defeated, economically broken Germany, he promised in tones of fierce confidence to lead them into a promised land, greater, more powerful than the Germany of their fathers. *Ein Volk, ein Reich, ein Führer* —the defeat of all their enemies internal and external, the reunion of all Germans in one great state, the destruction of Jews, capitalists, Marxists, the enemies of the German folk. He set before them the picture of a great united society of all patriotic Germans working together in harmony for the glory and prosperity of the Fatherland. It was this ideal to which German youth responded and for which, in fanatical devotion to its Führer, it was prepared to sacrifice its very life.

Neither Brüning, nor the Social Democrats, nor the German Nationalists themselves, bound to the old system of military-economic dominance, could compete with this appeal. The membership of the Nazi party rose rapidly (120,000, 1929; 200,000, 1930; 800,000, 1931), and its private army, which Röhm was recalled to command, consisting of fit and vigorous young men, numbered 600,000 by the beginning of 1932, and was an aggressive force as compared with the middle-aged, defensively minded, members of the Nationalist *Stahlhelm* or the Republican *Reichsbanner*. Street fights between young Nazis and Communists became a daily occurrence, and the tension inside Germany grew as the social misery deepened. Early in 1932 Hitler was given the opportunity of showing his strength to his opponents. Hindenburg's term of office was at an end and a new election had to be held. With some hesitation Hitler decided to oppose the old President, and the Communist leader Thälmann also stood. The final vote (10 April 1932) gave Hindenburg 19 million votes, Hitler 13 million and Thälmann less than 4 million. Since Centre and Social Democrats as well as sections of the Right stood behind Hindenburg it was evident that many of the supporters of Hugenberg, as well as millions of those who had not voted before, and some who had voted Communist, must have voted for Hitler.

By this time Hitler was enjoying support from German heavy industry. In 1931 Kirdorf and some of his business associates had begun to subsidize him, and, in January 1932, a meeting of the Düsseldorf Industrial Club, at which Thyssen, Vögler, Röchling and other coal, iron and steel magnates were present, decided, after a masterly speech by Hitler, that they had common interests with the Nazis in rearmament, social reorganization (by which they meant the destruction of the trade unions) and economic imperialism. Such relations with big industry were not known to Hitler's rank and file, or if known, were regarded as evidence of his skill in duping the old bourgeoisie. And the size of his poll at the presidential election served only to whet his own followers' appetite for power.

THE 'PRESIDENTIAL' EXPERIMENT AND THE NATIONAL 'REVOLUTION'

Hindenburg's re-election as President, largely by Centre and Social Democrat votes, might have been expected to ensure his support for Brüning's government which he had himself called to office. But in May 1932 he refused his assent to decrees prepared by Brüning which would have reduced the *Osthilfe* subsidies and have provided for state acquisition of bankrupt estates for small holdings. And when Brüning and his cabinet were driven out of office by the intrigues of Schleicher, Hindenburg embarked on a new, dangerous and definitely unconstitutional experiment by appointing a non-party 'presidential' cabinet of nobles—at once dubbed the 'Barons'—which had no basis in the Reichstag at all, for it excluded even Hugenberg and the German Nationalist party. The leader of this government, Papen, was a Catholic noble allied by marriage with the Ruhr heavy industry, a born intriguer, a dilettante politician, and a man of great personal charm. But Papen's hope that his presidential cabinet would be tolerated by the Reichstag was at once shattered by the vehement refusal of all the Reichstag parties, including his own—the Centre—to give him any support.

Papen reaped the benefit of Brüning's work by the final settlement of the reparations problem at the Lausanne Conference (10 July), and some slight signs of an industrial revival were given the assistance of government credits for industry. Yet mass unemployment and the social tension it created did not materially diminish. On 20 July he ejected the Social Democrat-Centre Coalition government in Prussia and made himself *Reichskommissar* for Prussia by presidential decree, thus gaining control, by wholly unconstitutional means, of the machinery of government in three-fifths of Germany. The failure of the Social Democrats to resist Papen's attack revealed their weakness, and the alarm aroused in the southern states, especially in Bavaria, was allayed by Papen's assurances that no similar steps would be taken against states (*Länder*) with 'national' governments.

Papen's action against Prussia was a conservative revolution, and its roots may be found in the ideas current in 1895 (p. 120). Yet Papen and Hindenburg were not ready to overthrow the constitution by force, and therefore a general election was necessary to secure tolerance for the ministry and to provide it with a legal basis. On 31 July 84% of the German electorate went to the polls. The main parties returned with the following strength:

National Socialists	230
Nationalists	37
Centre (including Bavarians)... ...	97
Social Democrats	133
Communists	89
All other parties together	22
	608

The Nazis had more than doubled their poll and their mandates, and had seduced many of Hugenberg's former supporters. The parties which were anti-democratic on principle (Nazis, Nationalists, Communists) together commanded more than half the votes of the Reichstag (356 out of 608), a fact which, in itself, showed the weakness of the democratic idea. But, though Papen's government could count on no support at all in the

Reichstag, to which, under the constitution, it was responsible, the divisions between the parties made the formation of any other government commanding a majority impossible.

Under the practice of the constitution, which he rejected in principle, Hitler, as leader of the largest party, could claim to form a government. His Storm-troopers, engaged in daily, and often fatal, affrays with Communists and Social Democrats, were growing impatient for power and the spoils of office. Yet, when Hindenburg gave him an audience on 13 August, and Hitler demanded the position which Mussolini had received from Victor Emmanuel after the march on Rome, he received a sharp reprimand and a curt dismissal from the old President. Neither Hindenburg, nor General Schleicher and the Reichswehr, nor Papen himself, whose taste for power was growing, were ready to hand over the control of Germany to Corporal Hitler and his party. They would tame him and his followers before granting them even a share in the government.

Divisions in the governing class. But the small group of the governing class had no clear plan for solving the constitutional dilemma, and they were divided amongst themselves. Schleicher had grandiose dreams of indefinitely proroguing the Reichstag and allowing the country to be governed by the President and the Reichswehr, with a Cabinet of Hindenburg's friends. In one sense this was not quite so fantastic as it seemed, for as soon as the new Reichstag met it had to be dissolved and the situation became still more strained. The Nazis went into violent opposition and the magnates of heavy industry withdrew their subsidies from them. In the second elections of this year (November 1932) the Nazis lost thirty-four seats, and the party was faced with financial bankruptcy. Its reply was to join with the Communists in a tramway strike in Berlin in order to increase the alarm of the ruling and middle classes lest it should go to the Left. The ostentatious alliance of the Nazis with the Communists was not wholly convincing, but it had its effect upon Schleicher, to whom Gregor Strasser persistently pointed out the danger of the Nazi *S.A.* getting out of hand.

In this situation the divisions amongst the governing group

played a decisive role in saving the situation for Hitler. In December Schleicher forced Papen to resign and on 2 December took over the Chancellorship himself—reluctantly, because, although he loved power, he preferred to work behind the scenes. He aimed at forming an inter-party coalition by splitting the Nazis, and by bringing in the Centre, the trade unions, and the more moderate members of the Right. He proclaimed himself in broadcasts as a 'social general' and offered a programme of state aid to finance employment and of land settlement in the eastern provinces. This raised the very issue of *Osthilfe* which had led to Brüning's fall, and Hindenburg was soon roused by his advisers, Papen among them, against Schleicher's proposals. Moreover, Papen had an alternative plan. Hitler was now in a more humble mood. Had not the time come to make him Chancellor, but a Chancellor in chains? A Nazi-Nationalist cabinet, of which Hitler would be the figure-head but the ministers mainly Nationalists, would have the advantage of popular appeal and the possibility, by gaining the tolerance of the Centre, of a Reichstag majority, whilst still resting on the President's authority. For this plan Papen gained the support of the agrarians and industrialists, to whom Schleicher's social policy seemed 'Bolshevik', and he also secured Hitler's assent at a meeting with him at Cologne. Under pressure from his son, a friend of Papen; from Meissner, his trusted secretary; from most of his personal friends, Hindenburg at last overcame his repugnance to the Austrian corporal. On 30 January 1933 Hitler entered the President's palace in Berlin and accepted office as 'presidential' Chancellor of a government, every post in which had to receive Hindenburg's approval. In the list of Ministers there appeared the names of only two Nazis beside his own— Frick, Minister of the Interior for the Reich, and Göring, Minister without Portfolio in the Reich, but also, under Papen, Minister of the Interior in Prussia. Papen became Vice-Chancellor and remained *Reichskommissar* for Prussia, Hugenberg was Minister of Economics, Seldte—the *Stahlhelm* leader— Minister of Labour, whilst five of Papen's 'Cabinet of Barons' figured in the list, with Neurath at the Foreign Office and

General Blomberg as Reichswehr Minister. Hitler had at last attained power but, so the Nationalists thought, only as the servant of the conservative forces which had created and sustained the Reich.

The beginning of the Nazi terror. The Nationalist illusion was swiftly shattered. The long columns of Nazi Storm-troopers bearing torches, who marched, cheering and singing, through the streets of Berlin and other German cities on the night of 30 January, were the heralds of a revolution. A mounting wave of terror began to spread over Germany and the Reichstag fire (28 February) let loose the flood. In command of the Prussian police, Göring authorized them to shoot without fear of consequences and enlisted thousands of young Nazis as *Hilfspolizei* (assistant police) to take what action they pleased against Communists and Socialists. On 2 March Frick instituted *Schutzhaft* (protective custody)—imprisonment without trial in concentration camps. In the 'Brown Houses' of the Nazi parties in Berlin and other great cities Jews, Communists, Social Democrats, were beaten with rubber truncheons, and political murders grew in number. The last elections under the Weimar Constitution were carried through under this terror, and without the protection of the vital clauses of the constitution, which guaranteed freedom of speech, of the press, of public meeting, and freedom from arrest, but were suspended by Hindenburg on the night of the Reichstag fire.[1] Though the Social Democrats and Communists returned 201 members to the Reichstag between them, the Communist deputies were excluded from taking part in its proceedings. When, on 23 March 1933, the German Reichstag passed an 'Enabling Act', which gave the Cabinet power to legislate on its own authority and, in effect, suspended the constitution, only the Social Democrat party voted against it.

---

[1] The Reichstag fire was one of the most successful frauds ever committed. Not only were the National Socialists and not the wretched van der Lubbe or the Communists responsible for the outbreak, but the impression they intended to create that the Reichstag building was seriously damaged has been widely accepted. This is certainly not true of the main fabric of the building nor of the ground floor rooms and the debating hall which was seen in 1937 to be intact, except for slight signs of fire in one of the back rows of benches in the debating hall.

Amidst many weaknesses and failures, both in political courage and judgment, that vote stands as the final witness of a great party against the destruction of the basis of legality in the German state.

The Nationalists in the government thought to safeguard their position by the clause declaring that the Enabling Act would be 'considered as annulled if the present government is replaced by another'. Yet, by the end of June, the Nazis had suppressed all political parties but their own; on 27 June Hugenberg resigned, and on 14 July a Cabinet decree-law declared 'there is only one political party in Germany, the National-Socialist German Workers' party'. The one-party state on the Russian or Italian model was now fully established. The 'national revolution' was, in principle, complete.

WHY DID THE REPUBLIC FAIL?

In view of the future of Germany the reasons for the failure of the democratic Republic present a problem of great importance, which, for reasons of space, can only be dealt with inadequately here. Yet a brief examination reveals certain results. There has never been a successful revolutionary movement in Germany based on the desire for political and social liberty. The revolution of 1848 cost few lives and failed for lack of unity of aim and strength of purpose. That of November 1918 was, it has already been said, largely the result of defeat and war weariness and, when it occurred, the republican parties were more concerned to secure internal order than to break the power of the ruling classes of Imperial Germany. The sense of reverence for the army, as the one great instrument of national unity, transcending all their social, religious and political differences, of which the Germans were acutely aware, survived the revolution and carried with it the acceptance of a hierarchical society in which leadership was the function of an 'officer' class, whether in the army or the civil service, in agriculture or in industry.

Before 1918 this ordered society had always directed its personal loyalties to the established ruler—the emperor, the kings (of Bavaria, etc.), the grand-dukes, the army leaders. Even for men of the Left the transference of their emotional loyalty to the drab politicians of a bourgeois Republic was not easy. For the men of the Right it was, in many cases, impossible. The unfamiliar process of parliamentary government by parties, which the Bismarck system had perforce turned into interest groups, was repugnant to all those who, under a strictly organized and largely military regime, had been accustomed to strong and decisive government and had been content to have their minds made up for them, in political matters, by their 'natural' leaders. They did not desire political responsibility for themselves and profoundly doubted the capacity of their new parliamentary leaders to exercise it for the nation.

The parliamentary system, too, intensified and brought to the surface the disunity of the German people. The religious cleavage between Protestants and Catholics, the historical tribal cleavages between Prussian, Bavarian and Saxon, the deep social cleavages between the classes, most fatal of all from the republican point of view, the political cleavage between Social Democrats, Minority Socialists and Communists in the working class, were all brought to the surface by the nature of a free political system. Under the regime of proportional representation adopted at Weimar the existing parties, which represented these internal differences, were guaranteed fair representation, but, for that very reason, no homogeneous government was at all likely to emerge from the Reichstag. As a result all parties alike lived in a condition of frustration. The Protestant-Nationalist-Monarch-ists of the Right who, bitterly resentful of the Republic, partici-pated only in two of the nineteen parliamentary Cabinets be-tween 1919 and 1930, could no more hope for the realization of their ideals than could the Social Democrats or Communists of theirs. The Centre Catholics became the hinge of the parlia-mentary machine, and the differences in social outlook between the various sections of their party rendered any clear policy, apart from the defence of Catholic interests—the very principle which made them obnoxious to the rest of the nation—impossible for them. Thus, within the Weimar system, there developed that condition of *stasis*, of party strife, which ruined the democracies of so many Greek states. Hence, all the great political parties organized their private armies—German Nationalists had the *Stahlhelm*, the Social Democrats the *Reichsbanner*, the Nazis the *S.S.* and *S.A.*, the Communists the *Rotfrontkämpfer* (Red Front Fighters). As a result the 'non-political' Reichswehr, deeply conservative in character, especially in the higher ranks, stood out—until Schleicher dragged it into politics—as the one armed force which represented the state above the parties, and was relied on by many, even among the members of the parties themselves, as the only safeguard against civil war.

Meanwhile, for both economic and political reasons, Germany needed that strong and decisive government which could only proceed from national unity. On the economic side the Versailles settlement, by the limitation of German armaments, and by the 'Balkanization' of Europe, deprived the essentially expansionist German industry of many outlets and stimulated the desire for treaty revision. And, after the period of sham prosperity between 1924 and 1929 based on foreign loans, the sharp antagonism between the interests of the industrialists and the working class in Germany became more evident than ever. The owners desired state subsidies, an expansionist policy of rearmament, the reduction of wages and the destruction of trade unionism. The workers clung to the concessions won under the Republic. But the Republic itself could satisfy neither. Brüning's policy of financial orthodoxy, combined with limited bribes to the agrarians and big industry, as well as drastic cuts in the social services, neither gave the owners the opportunity of profits nor saved the unemployed workers from bitter distress and semi-starvation.

Nor, on the political side, could the Republic provide satisfaction in the all-important field of foreign affairs. The pressure applied by the Allies to secure reparations after 1918 was natural enough, but was fatal to the hope that the German Republic would strike roots deep among the people, for it was followed by the inflation which the masses could not fail to attribute to it.

But the territorial settlement, and the 'war-guilt' clause were also profound sources of weakness to the Republic. Even if the return of Alsace-Lorraine to France could be accepted, the separation of East Prussia from the Reich, the division of Upper Silesia, the prohibition of union with Austria, the loss of the fleet and the colonies, the one-sided disarmament provisions and other clauses of the treaty were difficult for any patriotic German to accept. And the attribution of the whole responsibility for the war of 1914–18 to Germany and her Allies was an invitation and an opportunity unlikely to be missed by German nationalist propaganda. In so far as the Republic stood for the policy of fulfilment it stood condemned from the first in the minds of large sections of the German people.

Distribution of members of the Reichstag in 1930 by age-groups

	Social Democrats	Centre	Nationalists	Communists	Nazis
Over 70	1	3	1	1	—
50–70	73	36	27	1	12
40–50	49	22	10	20	21
30–40	20	7	2	47	63
Under 30	—	—	1	8	9

Source: S. Neumann, *Die deutschen Parteien* (Berlin, 1932) p. 134.

Thus, lack of training and aptitude for responsible government; traditional adherence to an authoritarian system; the sense of internal disunity enhanced by the party system in the Reich and in the states; economic difficulties and social distress; a sense of injustice at the treatment of 'democratic' Germany— all these things contributed to the downfall of the Republic and to the growing popularity of Hitler and his movement. And it was amongst the younger generation, who could not be accused of any responsibility for the war of 1914–18 but had to suffer its consequences, and to whom patriotic propaganda to throw off the yoke of the victors of 1918 had its strongest appeal, that the Nazi movement made its most rapid progress. Some idea of the relation of the parties to youth can be obtained from the above table. But only those who saw those energetic young *S.A.* and *S.S.* men in the thirties, burning for action to restore the glories of Germany, and convinced beyond reason that the 'system' of Weimar in its weakness and division was responsible for all their country's woes, can fully understand the dynamic force which converted Hitler's nomination to the Chancellorship from a mere change of government into the German National Revolution with all its dangerous implications for the world.

2. NATIONAL-SOCIALIST GERMANY

THE MEANING OF HITLERISM

The deepest significance of the National-Socialist movement, then, is that it aimed at securing at long last the complete unification of the German people—in outward institutions and in inner spiritual belief. For that very reason it insisted increasingly that it, and it alone, was a great movement of the mind and soul of the German people (*Volksbewegung*) and not merely a new political party amongst many rival parties. It sought to transcend all the deep divisions of tribe and class, of religious and political creeds, amongst Germans, and to unite them in fanatical trust both in the mission and future of their country and in the God-given infallible personality of the leader, Hitler.

Since the movement aimed at action based on emotional faith, it was essentially anti-intellectual, for reasoning involved divisions of opinion fatal to unity. Since its purpose was German greatness in the sense of military and economic power, it was indifferent to objective truth and would only admit as 'true' such facts, or ideas, as assisted its aim. Moreover, the useful lie, which, as Hitler explained in *Mein Kampf*, is usually the Great Lie, was justified, as were all other means—brutal cruelty, breach of faith, bribery or blackmail or terror—which would assist in attaining the supreme political aim.

Since, too, this aim necessarily involved the disruption of the European order imposed by the Versailles *Diktat* and, therefore, one or more wars, and since these wars, themselves the inevitable product of the underlying law of struggle (*Kampf*) from which only the weak amongst mankind seek to escape, would certainly be 'total' wars, the German *Volk* and all its resources must be organized as a single vast politico-military army. In every sphere the 'fundamental principle that, in its day, made the Prussian army the most wonderful instrument of the German people... must become the basis of our whole conception of the state: Authority of every leader over those below him. Responsibility to those above him' (*Mein Kampf*).

It is in the light of these principles that Nazi doctrine and practice become intelligible. The doctrine of purity of race served as a stimulus to national pride (the *Herrenrasse*—race of Masters), to physical fitness, and the desire for children to replenish the chosen stock. The anti-Jewish campaign represented the obverse of this—hatred of mixed marriage—but, not only did it serve as a measure to preserve German 'racial' purity, it also provided a divided people with that great aid to unity—a common object of hate, a scapegoat, upon whom the responsibility for all the woes of Germany could be heaped.[1] The religious question presented greater difficulties to national unity, which Hitler was never able to solve satisfactorily, but in education the process of capturing the mind of the younger generation for the Nazi faith was pursued with the greatest energy.

THE POLICY OF CO-ORDINATION

In the wide field of political, economic and social policy and institutions, the creation of national unity and the organization of the centralized politico-military state were carried through, between 1933 and 1939, with ruthless vigour and a high degree of completeness. The process was described as *Gleichschaltung* (co-ordination) and the sanction behind it was terror. The Gestapo (*Geheime Staatspolizei*) created by Göring (April–November 1933) was organized with German thoroughness, and no one who dared to oppose the regime even on grounds of religion or conscience could rely on immunity.

With the aid of the great outburst of genuine national patriotism that accompanied his accession to power, combined with the terror that threatened all opponents, Hitler was able to master

---

[1] A special session of the Reichstag was held at Nuremberg in 1935 at which the Nuremberg laws depriving German Jews of citizenship and forbidding intermarriage with Germans were passed.

the old Nationalists, who had thought to use him as their servant, and to carry through, in a few months, measures for the unification of Germany such as Bismarck, in face of the loyalties existing in his day to the local dynasties, and the constitution-makers of Weimar, with their liberal principles, had neither desired nor dared to attempt.

The abolition of all political parties has already been mentioned. In addition, the states (*Länder*), without being formally abolished, were 'co-ordinated' with the Reich by the appointment of governors (*Reichsstatthalter*), and the elective system was abolished throughout the whole of state, provincial and municipal government. In place of the traditionally 'federal' Germany, with its many competing sovereignties, which Bismarck had preserved from reasons of conservative inclination and policy, Hitler had, by 1935, created a single, centralized German state after the model of Napoleonic France. In itself this political centralization of Germany was a profound revolution, fully in accordance with the needs of modern capitalist organization, and unlikely to be willingly undone by any future German government.

The trade union movement, which presented another possible focus of resistance and danger to unity, was at once broken up (2 May 1933), its offices occupied, its funds confiscated, its leaders portrayed by Goebbels's propaganda machine as embezzlers of the workers' payments. In its place was set an all-embracing German Labour Front (Law for Organization of National Labour, 20 January 1934), with which was later associated the 'Strength through Joy' organization of the workers' leisure to provide them with 'circuses' as well as 'bread'. Within two years of the *Machtübernahme* ('taking over of power') in 1933, the whole life of the German people, with the most important exception of religion, had been *gleichgeschaltet*—co-ordinated—under Nazi control. Agriculture and industry, the 'free' professions—lawyers and doctors—were organized on Nazi lines. All makers of public opinion were under official control. Professors in the universities, who had been used to pride themselves on 'academic freedom' and 'objectivity'; teachers in schools; journalists, authors, musicians and artists—these last under Goebbels's Reich

Chamber of Culture—had been forced, or induced, or had, in many cases gladly, volunteered to join in unison to sing the praises of the Third Reich and of its leader, Adolf Hitler. The Propaganda Ministry controlled the press and radio, issued directives to the newspapers and moulded public opinion through broadcasting. In the hands of Goebbels it was a powerful and flexible instrument for securing the acceptance of the Nazi views on all subjects of importance.

Hitler's tactics. Yet it must not be supposed that this co-ordination was either complete or accomplished without difficulty, and Hitler's tactics and method internally deserve study, for they were used with the greatest effect also in foreign policy. They were based on a completely opportunist combination of persuasion, deception (in an organized form for the masses) and terror. And, however rigidly fanatical in his ultimate aims, he was ready to make any necessary temporary compromise to gain his end.

At home his purpose was to gain as large a volume of support in all classes as possible. Even in the elections of March 1933, held under the terror, Nazis and Nationalists combined had only just gained an absolute majority of the votes polled (52·3 %, of which the Nazis obtained 44·1 %). To secure the maximum of support it was necessary to provide jobs for as many of the unemployed as possible and at the same time to provide profits for industrialists and agrarians. It was equally necessary to avoid at all costs another currency inflation which, if it came, would rob the regime of popularity overnight.

By strict control of foreign exchange, and by Dr Schacht's skilful manipulation of it, this last danger was avoided. At the same time the erection of a vast party bureaucracy, side by side with that of the state; a purge of anti-Nazis in the civil service; the expulsion and imprisonment of Jews; the organization of labour service; the subsequent reintroduction of conscription (1935) and, finally, the initiation of a vast rearmament programme, combined with road-making, land drainage and other schemes of public works, reduced the figures of unemployment rapidly. From a total of over 6 million unemployed in January 1933 the figure dropped to less than 2 million in July 1935 and, at the outbreak of war in 1939, Germany was already suffering from a shortage of labour. As a result of this policy the working class, though the skilled artisan in the trade unions had lost his privileged position and received lower wages for longer hours, had received from Hitler what the sad processions of Social Democrat and Communist unemployed demanded on their banners in 1932, *Arbeit und Brot* (work and bread). And, at the same time, the powerful body of great industrialists not only received back at a low figure the shares they had sold to the state in the bad times, but, unhampered by trade union restrictions, were called into position of leadership in their factories, were given vast orders at profitable rates, and provided by law with further powers of concentrating and cartellizing their industries (Act for the Formation of Compulsory Cartels, July 1933). Any fears they may have had of socialization soon passed, and, though they were compelled to accept the competition of Nazi party enterprises (the Hermann Göring Works, Bank of German Labour, many party newspapers, etc.), the very existence of these was further evidence of the community of interest between the party and big business. Their subventions to the Nazi funds had secured a highly expansionist regime with the congenial prospect of satisfying their interest and patriotism alike in a future war for Germany's *Lebensraum*, and they were well content with their bargain.

To the agrarian nobility of Prussia the regime was, perhaps, less wholly acceptable. Their rigid sense of caste was offended by the presence of upstarts of lowly origin exercising high authority in the state. Yet the agricultural policy of the Nazi government brought them great advantages, since the prices of their products were fixed high above costs and they received credit from the state on easy terms; and, though the controlling machinery of the Reich Food Organization (*Reichsnährstand*) worked clumsily, they were soon relieved from fears of expropriation. Whilst land settlement continued to figure during 1933–4 in some Nazi speeches (e.g. those of Koch, the Gauleiter of East Prussia), the actual figures of settlement declined from 9000 new farms and 225,000 acres in 1932 to approximately 5000 farms and 155,000 acres in each of the two following years. At the same time Hitler not only recognized the principle of entail (*Fideikommisse*) for the greater estates, but introduced an analogous system by the Hereditary Farm Act (*Erbhofgesetz*) for the larger peasant holdings.

Even more than their increased sense of security and their greater profits it was the satisfaction of their desire for a strong foreign policy, for which a great army officered by their sons would be necessary, which reconciled the landowning nobility to the Nazi régime. And Hitler's supreme skill in handling the Reichswehr was the greatest factor in establishing his regime on a firm basis.

HITLER AND THE REICHSWEHR

The special prestige enjoyed by the Reichswehr in Weimar Germany was not merely due to its position above, or apart from, the contending political parties. It had inherited the respect paid to the Prussian army in the German Empire, earned by the victories of Frederick the Great, of Blücher and of Moltke. Under the Empire the Minister of War was always a Prussian General and, with the fall of Gessler (20 January 1928) and with a Prussian Field Marshal as President, the practice was resumed. General Groener and General Schleicher were succeeded at the Reichswehr Ministry, when Hitler took office, by General Blomberg. Upon his ability to handle the army Hitler's régime depended.

He was wise enough to proceed cautiously. The influence of Nazi ideas was, he knew, bound to increase amongst both officers and men, more especially as the members of the Hitler Youth came forward to do their military service. In Blomberg he found a collaborator increasingly sympathetic to Nazi ideas. And his determination to break through the restrictions imposed at Versailles and to recreate the German army at its full strength was, in itself, sufficient to win him the sympathy of the Officers' Corps. Had he not written in *Mein Kampf*, 'the recovery of lost provinces is not achieved by solemn invocations of the Beloved Lord or through pious hopes in a League of Nations, but only through armed violence'—a striking echo of Bismarck's famous words? (see p. 46). With such views all German officers were in agreement, and, even without any effort at direct propaganda for Nazi ideas in the Reichswehr, Hitler could be sure of a gradual increase of Nazi influence. To this policy, Röhm, head of the *S.A.*, was opposed. Instead of gradual infiltration he wanted organic incorporation of his *S.A.* formations in the Reichswehr—a Nazi army under his command to stand beside the regular army. Whether there were also serious plans in Röhm's circle in 1934 for a second, social, revolution is not clear, but the massacre of 30 June 1934 was Hitler's answer to all Röhm's plans, to the discontent of his followers—and to other discontents.

The meaning of 30 June 1934. On that day, by Hitler's orders, the *S.A.* leaders, Röhm, Ernst, Heines and many of the most prominent Nazis of the 'old Guard' were put to death without trial in Munich and the neighbourhood, whilst Göring conducted an even more extensive massacre in Prussia. But, at the same time, a large number of others, who had at one time or another opposed Hitler, suffered the same fate. General Schleicher, the greatest of the Reichswehr intriguers, and his wife; Kahr, the Bavarian ex-Minister, now 72, who had failed or 'betrayed' Hitler in 1923; Colonel Bredow, formerly ministerial chief under Schleicher; Klausener, one of the political leaders of Rhineland Catholicism; Bose and Jung, Papen's secretaries—killed at their work in the Vice-Chancellor's office—and very many others, some of them, indeed, by mistake but most of them by careful selection.

The massacre of 30 June 1934 is of deep interest as an illustration of Hitler's methods and of great importance in the establishment of his system. It satisfied the Reichswehr in that it ended the threat from Röhm's *S.A.*, but the murder of Schleicher and Bredow was a warning from Hitler that not even the German Officer Corps was beyond his reach. The names of many of the other highly respected Nationalists and Centrists were equally a warning to all opponents, however far to the Right or highly placed in society, that he would brook no opposition, that his memory was long, and his vengeance deadly. At the same time he improved the occasion by telling the Reichstag 'at that hour

I was responsible for the fate of the German nation and supreme judge of the German people'. By giving their approval to a law of 3 July, which described the murders as 'legitimate self-defence by the state', the Nationalists in the Cabinet made themselves accessories after the fact. And, when Hindenburg died within a month, Adolf Hitler became both Reich President and Chancellor, and 38 million Germans voted their approval, or were declared officially to have done so, at a plebiscite. The Reichswehr took the oath of allegiance to the Führer and the fullness of power was now concentrated in Hitler's hands. The German *Rechtstaat*, with its not unworthy record of impartial justice, disappeared. The old ruling class—officers, nobles, bureaucrats, agrarians and industrialists alike—had accepted the dictatorship, with its methods of terror, and the consequent abolition of the rule of law. In doing so they placed themselves and the fate of the German people in the hands of a political adventurer of genius—but of a genius diseased. Any resistance of a political kind became impossible, and, within a few years, a general (Fritzsch) or an industrialist (Thyssen) was little more safe from Himmler's Gestapo than the most proletarian communist. Yet Hitler's immense successes in foreign policy provided them with compensation and, so long as those successes lasted, they were intoxicated by their Führer's apparently infallible powers of judgment.

HITLER'S FOREIGN POLICY

Hitler's aims in foreign affairs were drastically clear, to himself and his inner circle, from the outset, and as carefully masked from the outside world by a series of speeches, pathetic, patriotic and pacific by turns, carefully calculated to enlist all possible sympathy for Germany abroad and to exploit the differences between the foreign states which might interfere with his designs.

The first main objective was to create the great German Reich which should bring within its fold all the provinces of the Prusso-German empire lost at Versailles, with their German minorities and, in addition, should incorporate German Austria and the

German minorities of the old Austrian empire in Czechoslovakia, Yugoslavia or elsewhere. The Pan-German dream, rendered more fluid and dynamic by the conception of *Lebensraum* (living space), was to be realized at the earliest possible moment. That, once realized, the strong arm of the new Great Germany would stretch out to cover *Auslandsdeutschtum* (Germans living abroad), wherever they found themselves; that it would seek to recover the lost colonies and insist on a share of Africa corresponding to its needs; that it would challenge and overthrow the 'Jewish-Bolshevik tyranny' of Russia and recreate the situation embodied in the terms of Brest-Litovsk were later stages of the dream. First the Treaty of Versailles must be torn to shreds, the rearmament of Germany completed, the Rhineland and the Saar recovered, Austria brought within the Reich and then, with or without war, the rest would follow.

In six years (1933–8) Hitler carried through his minimum programme. Before he came to power the League of Nations had revealed its weakness by the failure to check Japanese aggression in Manchukuo (1932–3), and the Japanese withdrawal from the League and from the Disarmament Conference (March 1933) was followed by that of Germany (October 1933). That action Hitler had already foreshadowed in an article in the *Völkische Beobachter* a year earlier. He covered it now by a barrage of pacific words and by his Ten-Year Pact with Poland (January 1934), interpreted not only by the Poles, but in England and France, as evidence of his good intentions, rather than as a temporary measure to safeguard his rear whilst he faced the Western Powers. 'Our boundless love for and loyalty to our own national traditions', he said in a great speech (17 May 1933), 'make us respect the national claims of others. . . . The mentality of the past century which made people believe that they could make Germans out of Poles and Frenchmen is completely foreign to us.' It is easy to understand the welcome given to such words by the statesmen of all Germany's neighbours, still staggering under the great economic depression, half-disarmed, deeply affected by the pacific ideals embodied in the League, and incredulous that any German government, however fierce in its treatment of its own nationals, could have the 'folly' to repeat the mistakes of Bülow and Wilhelm II, of Berchtold and Francis Joseph.

Of all these factors favourable to his policy Hitler was fully aware, as he was also of the distrust felt in England of French policy and political instability, of the hostility in powerful circles in both England and France towards Soviet Russia, and of the ambitions of Mussolini, which were to bring him into conflict with the Western Powers. And he took every chance of deepening and exploiting the cleavages between his opponents.

The premature Nazi *Putsch* (July 1934), in which the Austrian Chancellor, Dollfuss, was brutally murdered, was at once disavowed by Hitler, but it was a setback to his policy, for it brought Italian troops to the Brenner; whilst the entry of Soviet Russia into the League of Nations (September 1934) seemed to promise a new guarantee against German aggressiveness. Yet, with the Saar safely in his hands after a plebiscite conducted under heavy Nazi pressure (January 1935), Hitler felt strong enough in March openly to defy the Treaty of Versailles by reintroducing conscription and announcing the creation of an air force. This, in turn, was followed by the Stresa Conference at which France secured Italian and British agreement to a joint condemnation of German action. But, so strongly was the feeling of the British government in favour of giving Germany 'fair play' that he was able, in June 1935, to secure the signature of an Anglo-German Naval Agreement, which was unquestionably open to the accusation that it amounted to a violation of the Versailles treaty by two of the parties without general assent, thus constituting a serious derogation from international law and opening the way to further invasion of the treaty of 1919.

The beginnings of the Axis. After the Anglo-German Naval Agreement common action by Britain and France against further German violations of the Treaty of Versailles was clearly impossible for a long time. Moreover, it encouraged Mussolini to proceed with his attack on Abyssinia and when, after the repudiation by British opinion of the Hoare-Laval pact, the League applied half-hearted sanctions against Italy, Hitler was able to take advantage of the break-up of the Stresa front to reoccupy and remilitarize the Rhineland (March 1936) and to begin his preparations for war. In April 1936 Göring was appointed Commissioner for Raw Material and Foreign Exchange, and in September, Plenipotentiary for the Four-Year Plan. In this capacity he read to a Ministerial Council on 4 September 1936 a memorandum prepared by Hitler[1] which, pleading the peril of Bolshevism as its justification, ordered the German economy and armed forces to be made ready for war within the next four years. At the same time Hitler renewed his courtship of Mussolini, which had been broken off after the failure of the Nazi *Putsch* in Austria. In order to forward friendship with Italy, on 11 July 1936, he recognized 'the full sovereignty of the Federal State in Austria', and undertook not to exert influence either direct or indirect on her affairs.

When Britain and France hoped to use the ending of sanctions against Mussolini to regain the Stresa position, Mussolini's support for Franco's revolt against the Spanish republican government, which threatened France on her Pyrennean frontiers, made their efforts useless. Hitler used his own support for Franco as an added inducement to win Mussolini over to his side while resisting himself the attempts of Britain and France to get him to sign a new pact guaranteeing the western frontiers. In October 1936 Ciano, the Italian Foreign Minister, visited Hitler at Berchtesgaden. In November Hitler signed the Anti-Comintern Pact with Japan, continuing his policy of posing as the crusader against Bolshevism and of playing on social discords among the Western Powers to gain sympathy for his aims. In 1937 the process of winning over Italy continued. In the first six months, Göring, Neurath and Blomberg all visited Rome. In September Mussolini visited Berlin, and Italian adherence to the Anti-Comintern Pact followed in November. The Axis was firmly established and Italy, even though she had not yet realized it, was on the way to becoming a German vassal.

The Hossbach Protocol. On 5 November 1937 Hitler at last

---

[1] This document may be found in translation in *Trials of War Criminals before the Nuremberg Military Tribunals* (Nuremberg, n.d.), vol. XII, pp. 430–8.

revealed his plans to his chosen confederates in a conference, the minutes of which are known after his military adjutant, Major Hossbach, who kept them, as the Hossbach Protocol.[1] Hitler told his associates that, in order to preserve and enlarge the German racial community, it was necessary to secure increased living-space in Europe, whatever the risk. In this Germany would have to reckon with the enemies, Britain and France. The immediate objectives, to be seized whenever the political situation allowed, were Austria and Czechoslovakia. The problem of living-space could only be solved by force.

The disclosure of his plans alarmed the German army leaders and Baron von Neurath, who were well aware of the disparity between German strength at that time and Hitler's objectives, and who had not judged the internal weakness of the western powers so shrewdly as had Hitler. The winter of 1937–8 saw them repeating their objections backed by Schacht, anxious at the strain rearmament was placing on Germany's economic recovery. In December 1937 Hitler removed Schacht from his position of Minister of Economics. In January 1938 Göring and Himmler moved against the Army leaders, using Blomberg's unwise marriage to force his resignation and 'framing' Fritzsch, the Army Commander-in-Chief, on moral charges. In their place, Hitler, whose part in these machinations remains obscure, jumped at the chance of usurping Blomberg's position as Commander-in-Chief of the Armed forces, creating a separate High Command of the Armed Forces to take on the routine duties of the War Ministry (now abolished) and filling it with his own creatures. At the same time, Ribbentrop replaced Neurath as Foreign Minister and Funk, another Nazi, took over the Ministry of Economics.

Hitler as War Lord. With these changes Hitler removed from his cabinet the leading nationalists imposed on him in 1933, and put himself at the head of the German war machine. In March 1938 his attempt to bully Schuschnigg, the Austrian Chancellor, into filling his government with Austrian Nazis backfired.

[1] This important document may be found translated in *Documents on German Foreign Policy 1918–1939, Series D* (London, H.M.S.O.), vol. I, no. 19.

Schuschnigg, although aware that Italy would no longer aid him to resist German pressure, called for a plebiscite in Austria and forced Hitler into a military invasion, justified to Mussolini in a letter saying 'Do not see in this anything but an act of legitimate national defence.... Whatever may be the result of coming events I have fixed a definite German frontier towards France, and now I fix another, equally definite, towards Italy, the Brenner.'

Neither Mussolini nor the Western Powers were in any position to resist. The death of the League as an instrument for controlling aggression was recognized by Mr Neville Chamberlain's statement that 'We were under no commitment to take action *vis-à-vis* Austria'—despite the fact that Great Britain and Austria were both members of the League and both were signatories, as was also the German Government, of treaties which provided that the independence of Austria was inalienable except with the consent of the Council of the League of Nations. Protests by the British and French governments were sent to the German government, but it was considered inadvisable to set the machinery of the League in motion.

The Munich crisis. Fired by his success Hitler turned on Czechoslovakia. On 28 March 1938 he saw Henlein, leader of the German minority in Czechoslovakia, who had been in German pay since 1935 and instructed him to put forward demands for the German minority which would be unacceptable to the Czech government. In April the Army's new leaders were instructed to prepare plans for an attack on the Czech fortifications. His preparations frightened the Czechs into a partial mobilization during the week-end of 20–21 May, which was backed by British and French diplomatic protests, and Hitler was forced to assure the Czechs that he had no aggressive plans towards them. This humiliation determined him in revenge to smash Czechoslovakia by military action as soon as possible. The directive for this operation, 'Case Green' (*Fall Grün*), was issued on 28 May.

The summer was occupied in military and diplomatic preparations. The Poles and Hungarians were encouraged to press the demands of their minorities in Czechoslovakia, and the Sudeten

Germans under Henlein increased their own agitation against the Czechs. At the same time the opposition in German military and bureaucratic circles was driven by fear of war to the point of conspiracy against Hitler. But their attempts both to strengthen the will of the leaders of the western democracies to resist Hitler, and to drive the new army leaders to overthrow him were unavailing, Hitler proving an accurate judge both of the fear of war among western statesmen and of the complaisance of the men with whom he had replaced Blomberg and Fritsch. By September Hitler was making public threats of war against Czechoslovakia and Chamberlain's flights to Berchtesgaden, Godesberg and Munich only produced the basis of a plan by which, whilst war was temporarily averted, the Czech frontier areas inhabited by substantial German minorities and the main Czech fortifications against a German attack were to be handed over to Germany. British and French pressure on the Czech government forced them to accept it. Mussolini's intervention to secure the Munich conference had convinced Hitler that it was better to forgo for the moment the war he desired to revenge his humiliation of May, and to take the remainder of Czechoslovakia at a later date.

The results of Munich. The results of Munich left Czechoslovakia defenceless, but did not appease Hitler's lust for destruction. During the winter of 1938 there was much speculation as to his next move. For a time he seemed to have designs on the Ukraine, or Holland. Behind the cover of these speculations German diplomacy was moving to split opinion in the west, to isolate Britain and to distract the United States by supporting Japan in the Far East. Negotiations for a tripartite military pact with Japan and Italy began at Munich and continued until August 1939. In December 1938 a German-French Declaration seemed to secure French disinterest in Central Europe. In January 1939 great efforts were made to persuade Poland to abandon the Polish Corridor and Danzig to Germany and to seek compensation at Russia's expense in the Ukraine. On 15 March Hitler seized the opportunity of a crisis between the Czechs and the autonomous Slovak regime set up after the

Munich conference, to march into Prague and absorb the remainder of the Czech state, making Slovakia a separate state,
nominally independent, but in fact a German puppet. A week
later (22 March) the German navy forced Lithuania to cede the
port of Memel.

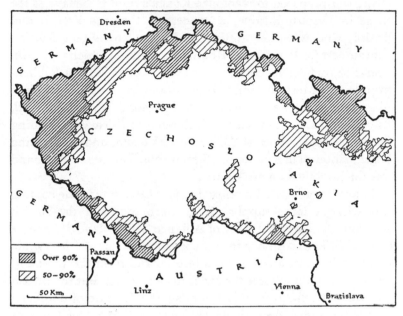

Map 21. The Sudetenland. The percentages in the key are of the
German-speaking population.

The final crisis. Having settled the fate of Czechoslovakia,
Hitler at once renewed his pressure on Poland but was given
a final and definite refusal to consider his plans, whilst his
action frightened Britain belatedly into guaranteeing Poland,
Roumania and Greece against Axis aggression. Hitler reacted
as in May 1938. The first directive for the attack on Poland—the
so-called 'Case White' (*Fall Weiss*)—was issued on 3 April. After
pressure on the Japanese had failed to break down their determination to confine the proposed pact to war against Russia,
Hitler lost patience and concluded an alliance, the 'Pact of Steel'
with Italy on 22 May. The next day he announced to his generals

his intention of attacking Poland at the first possible opportunity. At the same time, acting on hints dropped by the Russians, he reopened trade conversations with Russia, suspended after Ribbentrop's visit to Warsaw, and these, after hesitations on both sides, were to pass from the economic to the political sphere. Hitler was prepared to recognize Russia's right to behave as she chose in Eastern Europe, a concession that the French and British, who were negotiating in Moscow to obtain Russian guaranteees for Poland and Roumania, without which their own would be ineffective, could never offer. On 22 August Ribbentrop flew to Moscow, and two days later the Nazi-Soviet Non-Aggression Pact was signed, with a protocol leaving Finland, Estonia and Latvia to Russia, Lithuania to Germany, dividing Poland along the lines of the San and Vistula, and recognizing Russian interest in Roumanian Bessarabia. The attack on Poland was due to follow on 26 August.

At this stage Mussolini refused to join Germany in the coming war without large supplies from Germany, and the British government signed a Treaty of Alliance with Poland. The news caused Hitler to postpone the attack on Poland for five days while he made one last attempt to isolate Poland from the West and persuade Britain to force the Poles to capitulate. But the British government refused to play Hitler's game in spite of unofficial mediation and a deceptively moderate statement of German demands. On September 3 German forces attacked Poland. The British ultimatum and a declaration of war followed one day later.

Similar action was taken by France. Hitler at last had his war before he was fifty and the great German gamble *Weltmacht oder Niedergang* (World Power or National Downfall) had begun.

CHAPTER IV

GERMANY AT WAR, 1939–45

HITLER'S WAR AIMS

WITH the attack on Poland, Hitler was at last able to attempt in action the realization of his plans to create the Greater Germany of his dreams. Early in his career, in *Mein Kampf*, he had expressed the aim of finally settling Germany's position in the West by the conquest of France, as a preliminary condition for the achievement of German domination of Russia west of the Urals, with its wealth of corn, oil and raw materials. The Nazi-Soviet Pact had secured his eastern front, while he dealt with France and Britain. In *Mein Kampf* he had envisaged using Britain as an ally against France. But by the end of 1937 he had realized that Britain would be as bitter an enemy as France of the Greater Germany he planned to create, and had determined to isolate Britain from Europe. The actual conquest of Britain does not seem to have entered his plans at this time, as the break-up of the British Empire would only have benefited the maritime Powers, the United States and Japan. Germany's empire, he determined, was to be continental not maritime, Eurasian rather than oceanic.

The strains and stresses of war modified rather than altered his plans. Territorially he came very near to achieving his goal, but his failure to concentrate his resources proved disastrous, and his utter absorption in the conduct of the war left him little time for the organization of the conquered territories. The 'New Order' in Europe was built by his followers according to their interpretation of Nazi ideology and as part of their struggle for power and for his favour. As the war advanced, this struggle became more intense and the balance inside the Nazi party shifted in favour of the extremists. At the end, the Nazi leaders returned to their original nihilism; their aim of world power being frustrated, they exulted in its alternative, national catastrophe. In their fall, the Nazi leadership could still however destroy the ill-organized attempts of the Army malcontents and of the survivors of Christian, civilized Germany to overthrow them. Their destruction of every German institution that could provide an alternative political leadership for Germany, and their Nazification of the administrative structure left Germany helpless and in chaos when defeat finally removed them.

THE PERIOD OF GERMAN VICTORIES, 1939–42

The German attack on Poland began at dawn, 1 September 1939. Three weeks later German and Russian forces had met at Brest Litovsk. The Poles fought gallantly, but their army was weak in everything but courage, and their air force had ceased to exist after the first three days of the campaign. Warsaw alone held out for a few days longer, but its surrender was inevitable. On 27 September Ribbentrop left for Moscow to discuss the future of the occupied territories with Stalin.

The price Hitler was prepared to pay to secure his eastern frontier was a very high one. Stalin demanded the abandonment of the German plan for a rump Polish state under German protection. He also demanded that Germany should disinterest herself in the fate of the three Baltic states and Finland. The settlement which emerged from the Moscow conversations brought Russian power to the borders of Hungary. In return, far-reaching economic agreements, signed on 24 October 1939 and 11 February 1940, largely defeating the effect of the Allied blockade, secured for Germany oil, timber, iron ore, grain and chemicals. Even here the Russians drove an extremely hard bargain, insisting on payment in war materials to such an extent that for a short time deliveries to Russia had to be given priority over those to the German armed forces. But for the rest of 1939 and for the vital first six months of 1940, the defence of Germany's eastern frontier occupied only seven German divisions.

The price he paid makes it obvious that Hitler was determined to settle accounts with the West as quickly as possible. The much advertised peace offer made in his speech of 6 October 1939 was for propaganda purposes only. Without even waiting for the British and French reactions, he ordered his army to prepare for an attack against Holland, Belgium and France. The order met with strong opposition from the German High Command and once again the civilian opposition to Hitler attempted to get the army leadership to carry its resistance to the point of a *coup d'état*. Once again, as in 1938, their hopes were vain. Hitler browbeat his generals into silence and only continuous bad weather frustrated his plans for a winter offensive in the west.

In the east the unholy alliance between Germany and Russia held good. Joint pressure was brought to bear on Turkey and the Balkan states to maintain their neutrality, and when Russia decided to improve the defences of Leningrad by the absorption of Finnish border territories, Hitler went to great lengths to demonstrate German indifference. The possibility of Allied aid to Finland through Norway and Sweden, however, turned Hitler to consideration of plans prepared by the German Naval High Command for the occupation of the Norwegian coast. Norwegian and Swedish iron ores were vital to German war production. The German Admiralty and Rosenberg, head of the Nazi Party Foreign Policy Bureau, were in touch with the small Norwegian Nazi party led by Quisling, who visited Germany and had audience of Hitler in December 1939. In the new year Hitler abandoned temporarily his plans for an attack in the west, and set the Army and Navy staffs to planning an attack on Norway and Denmark. The Soviet-Finnish armistice of 12 March 1940 removed the danger of an Allied landing in Norway, but Hitler continued his designs. On 1 April 1940 the attack was ordered for nine days later. On the diplomatic front the early months of 1940 were devoted to repelling an American peace offensive. On 9 February 1940 it was announced that Sumner Welles, Under-Secretary of State, was to visit Rome, Berlin, Paris and London. His aim was to learn from the belligerents the terms on which they would make peace. The reception he met with in Rome stirred the Germans sufficiently for Ribbentrop, the German Foreign Minister, to visit Rome himself with a letter from Hitler. He urged Italy to come to an agreement with the Soviets, and thus end the main strain on German-Italian relations and promised large-scale coal deliveries. On 18 March, eight days later, Hitler met Mussolini on the Brenner Pass. Mussolini gave him assurances of Italian entry into the war, and with this the Sumner Welles mission became hopeless.

At the same time as Hitler had been developing his plans for an attack on Norway, the Allies had reached the decision to cut off the Norwegian iron ores from Germany by mining Norwegian territorial waters south of Narvik. British and French forces were embarked to forestall any German counter-action. The Allied mine-laying actually preceded the German attack by a day. But the German attack was much better conceived. Quisling's *coup d'état*, it is true, was a failure and the Norwegian king and his government escaped the trap that had been laid for them; but the whole of southern Norway was swiftly occupied together with the two vital ports of Trondheim and Narvik. The Allied plans proved ineffective and the Allied forces insufficient and inadequately equipped. In six weeks all Norway was under German control and Germany had unhindered access to the Atlantic. She had, however, paid a heavy price, in the disproportionately heavy losses suffered by the German navy.

Before the Norwegian campaign had ended, Hitler had launched his main attack in the west. The original plan of campaign had envisaged a drive through Belgium on the lines of the Schlieffen plan which had come so near to success in 1914; and the Allied forces had been disposed to meet this threat. In February 1940, however, Hitler was convinced by Rundstedt, Commander in Chief, Army Group A and his Chief of Staff, Manstein, that the main weight of the German thrust should be placed at the centre of the long front, aiming through the wooded Ardennes, to Sedan and on to the Channel ports and the Somme. It was brilliantly successful. Ten days after the German attack had been launched on 10 May 1940, German forces had reached the mouth of the Somme. The Allied forces advancing into Belgium were trapped between two German army groups and the sea. The Dutch army, overwhelmed by airborne attack which rendered the obstacle provided by the dykes and inundations unavailing, surrendered within a few days of the attack being opened. On 28 May the Belgian army followed suit.

The speed of von Rundstedt's advance towards the Channel led to Hitler's first error in the direction of the war. On 23 May Rundstedt halted his armoured forces south of the trapped Allied forces, to allow for regrouping. The following day Hitler confirmed this order over the opposition of the German Army High Command. He intended apparently that the German forces advancing through Belgium should drive the Allied forces, as beaters drive game, on to the very strong line of canals on which von Rundstedt's panzers had been halted. He appears to have been influenced in his refusal to commit the panzers north of these canals, as was Rundstedt, by the need to preserve them for the task of finishing off the main French armies, now regrouping on the Somme, south of Rundstedt's break through, by the conviction that the battle in Flanders was already won, by Göring's exaggerated claims for the Luftwaffe, and perhaps also by fears of losing tanks, needed elsewhere, in fighting in the Flanders mud. The order was not rescinded for three vital days. By 26 May when he reversed his decision, the British southern flank was sufficiently secure to permit the Dunkirk evacuation. At the time his error seemed a venial one, except in British eyes. On 5 June German troops crossed the Somme. By 14 June they were in Paris. At midnight on 16 June the newly formed Pétain government sued for an armistice. On 10 June in response to a succession of letters from Hitler and in great fear lest he be left out of the peace settlement he expected to follow, Mussolini also declared war on France and Britain. His hopes of far-reaching territorial accessions were in vain, as Hitler was determined to avoid driving the French possessions overseas into the arms of the British. As finally signed on 21 June 1940, the armistice terms provided for German occupation of northern and Atlantic France, but they left a French government in control of the remainder, and the French fleet and France's colonies remained untouched.

Germany, and Hitler, now waited for the British to sue for peace. They waited for very nearly a month. Soundings were made through neutral capitals, and Hitler launched a final peace appeal in a speech to the Reichstag on 19 July 1940. Characteristically, the order to plan for an invasion of Britain had already been issued on 2 July and the preliminary directive signed on 16 July. It is clear that until May Hitler had never

Map 22. The Armistice line in France, 1940

thought in terms of an invasion of Britain and still contemplated the project with the gravest of misgivings. Moreover, a break-up of the British Empire which would have primarily benefited the United States and Japan was far from his mind. But he now hoped that an air assault backed by the threat of a full-scale invasion might lead to the overthrow of the Churchill government by a peace party, and the preparations for invasion at least constituted a threat to British morale.

There followed a month of confused debate between the planning staffs of the German army and navy, while both waited for the Luftwaffe to achieve the command of England's skies without which invasion was impossible. Göring seems again, as at Dunkirk, to have overestimated the strength and potentialities of his air force. By early August the German naval authorities were protesting that he was not directing air attacks with the aim of facilitating the invasion but rather fighting a total war in the air. On 15 September 1940 the biggest daylight attack of the campaign ended with the loss of fifty German planes. British air attacks had damaged one in eight of the barges and pontoons assembled to ferry the German troops across the Channel. On 12 October the invasion was postponed until the spring of 1941. Hitler's mind had already turned east.

The British refusal to sue for peace after the fall of France had aroused in Hitler the suspicion that Britain was relying on the hope of Russian and American aid, perhaps with Russian encouragement. Morcover, by mid-1940, Russian advances in eastern Europe had brought Russian control across all Germany's main supply routes. Through Finland, the vital nickel ores of Petsamo, as well as the iron of Sweden were threatened. The Russian occupation of the Baltic States in June 1940 deprived Germany of large supplies of foodstuffs and oil shale. The Russian annexation of the Bukovina and Bessarabia, also in June, put Russian troops astride the Carpathians and brought the oil-wells of Ploesti from which Germany drew 50 % of her oil supplies within easy reach of Russian bombers. From Russia herself Germany drew a further 25 % of her oil, 60 % of her grain, as well as phosphates, iron, chrome, manganese, timber and cotton. Through Russia lay Germany's only link with the Far Eastern supplies of tin, rubber, and soya beans. For these reasons alone German control of Russian Europe seemed essential. Only in the limitless steppes of Russian Europe could Hitler find the living-space for the immense increases in German population that he wished to see. He anticipated no difficulty in defeating the Red Army.

Nevertheless the decision to invade Russia was clearly taken, when taken, on military grounds, as a means of breaking England. The parallel with Napoleon's career is very striking. With Russia gone, so Hitler reasoned, fear of Japan would restrain the United States from intervening; and Britain, deprived of the two countries in whom she placed her hopes, would have to surrender. Hitler announced his decision to attack Russia to his generals on 31 July 1940, and preliminary planning began immediately. Preparations for the invasion of Britain continued simultaneously. It was Hitler's practice to hesitate between alternative courses of action, and to postpone his final decision until the moment at which his intuition and sense of timing dictated it. He was in fact also considering a third course of action at this time, and throughout the latter six months of 1940 —one strongly supported by Göring and Admiral Raeder, the Commander in Chief of the German navy. This was the plan to bring Spain into the war, to attack Gibraltar, and to occupy the Canary Islands and the Azores as a prelude to clearing British power from the Mediterranean. It was thought of as an operation which would require few German troops, as the main brunt would be borne by the Spanish army. Diplomatic preparations for these plans occupied the remainder of 1940.

The project for an attack on Gibraltar and the Mediterranean broke down for three reasons: Hitler's inability to choose between Vichy France and Franco Spain, his consequent failure to persuade Franco to enter the war, and the Italian defeats at Taranto and in North Africa. The visit made by Serano Suñer to Berlin in September showed that Spain's terms would be very high, including French Morocco, Oran, the enlargement at French expense of Spanish West Africa, together with far-reaching economic and military assistance. Hitler found himself unable to concede French territory for fear of losing control of French North Africa, with its army, to the Free French. Moreover, he appears at one time to have hoped to induce these forces in North Africa to attack the British. A prolonged interview between Hitler and Franco on 23 October, at Hendaye in the Pyrenees, failed to win Franco to intervention. The following day Hitler met Pétain at Montoire, and agreed to compensate

France for any loss of French territory in North Africa at the expense of Britain, in return for French support against Britain. Four days later, Mussolini, angered by the dispatch of a German military mission to Roumania, launched his troops against Greece with the minimum of prior notice to and without consultation with Hitler. The attack failed disastrously. That Hitler still hoped to win Franco over is shown by the issue of orders to German troops on 4 and 12 November, to co-operate in attacks on Gibraltar and the Azores. On 11 November British torpedo planes crippled the Italian battle fleet as it lay at anchor in Taranto. On 7 December a renewed attempt to induce Spain to attack Gibraltar failed and Hitler cancelled the operation ten days later. Diplomatic pressure on Franco continued until well into February 1941, and with no success.

In the meantime there had occurred two very curious episodes: the signature in Berlin on 27 September 1940 of the Tripartite Pact between Germany, Italy and Japan, and Molotov's visit to Berlin in November. The first followed on a Japanese initiative in August, one received very coldly in Berlin until the increasing American support for Britain (lease of British bases in the West Indies in return for fifty over-age destroyers, the U.S.-Canadian Agreement of 17 August 1940) made it desirable for some restraint to be put on the U.S.A. The text of the treaty, besides the usual recognition of separate spheres of influence, was very clearly directed against the United States. But its effect was weakened in practice by the Japanese reserving to themselves the right to say what constituted a *casus belli*. During the negotiations Germany offered her good offices in smoothing Russo-Japanese relations, and the text of the pact specifically excluded Soviet Russia from its operations.

German relations with Russia were deteriorating at this time as a result of the German diplomatic preparations for the attack on Russia. Signs that the Russians were considering a second war with Finland in the summer of 1940 brought a very different reaction from the strict neutrality Germany had observed in the winter of 1939. Large-scale Finnish purchases of arms were authorized in Germany and negotiations opened for a political agreement, signed on 22 September. German troops were transported across Finland to northern Norway. At the same time a frontier dispute between Hungary and Roumania, which threatened to result in war, forced German intervention, as a result of which Hungary was awarded most of Roumanian Transylvania in a conference at Vienna. The resulting disturbances in Roumania drove King Carol to abdicate and brought the pro-German General Antonescu to power. On 23 September Roumania adhered to the Axis pact, and on 7 October German armoured troops, disguised as a military mission, entered Roumania to protect the oil fields. On 13 October Ribbentrop invited Molotov to Berlin. The invitation was accepted and Molotov arrived in Berlin on 12 November. The military plans for the attack on Russia were continued, notwithstanding.

In the course of the talks with Molotov, both Hitler and Ribbentrop made very strong efforts to divert Russian attention from Eastern Europe to the Middle East and Persia, where a conflict with Britain would be certain. Whether Hitler would have abandoned his plans for the attack on Russia had he succeeded in embroiling Russia and Britain is arguable. But he did not succeed and was forced to submit to prolonged interrogation from Molotov on German intentions in Roumania and Finland. The Russian price for following Hitler's plans was set out, on Molotov's return to Moscow, as the withdrawal of German troops from Finland and the signature of a Russian-Bulgarian pact of assistance. The Russian memorandum embodying these requests was not answered by the Germans. On 18 December preparations for the attack on Russia were ordered to be ready by 15 May 1941.

The period between the Molotov visit and the attack on Russia was occupied in further preparations and in rectifying the position in the Balkans, which had been badly upset by the complete defeat of the Italian attack on Greece and the arrival of British troops in Greece. In November Hitler reinforced the German troops in Roumania, demanded Hungarian participation in the attack on Russia, and summoned King Boris of Bulgaria to Berlin where he was persuaded to invite a German military mission into Bulgaria. In December Hitler ordered German Luftwaffe units to Sicily and panzer troops to North Africa. The same month staff talks in Berlin arranged for Hungarian and Finnish contributions to the attack on Russia. In February 1941 similar talks arranged for Bulgarian participation in the attack on Greece, designed to clear the flank for the Russian adventure, and German troops entered Bulgaria. Economic pressure was also brought to bear on Yugoslavia. On 22 March 1941 Yugoslav envoys signed a Protocol of adherence to the Tripartite Pact at Vienna.

On 23 March King Peter, relying mainly on the support of the pro-British army leaders, dismissed the pro-German Yugoslav government, and on 5 April an assistance pact was signed between Yugoslavia and Russia. The next day Hitler's forces, under an order of 27 March, attacked the Yugoslav and Greek frontiers. On 17 April the Yugoslav army capitulated and on 27 April German forces entered Athens. At the same time Rommel's first offensive in the western desert regained all the ground lost in January and February by the Italians to Wavell. On 20 May German forces parachuted into Crete, and German arms were flown through Vichy-controlled Syria to support native revolts in Iraq. The entire British position in the Middle East seemed about to collapse. But Hitler's eyes were now firmly fixed on Russia, whose defeat would, he estimated, take about three months. Only in the autumn of 1941, with this achieved, would he turn back to the Mediterranean. On 22 June German and satellite troops attacked along the whole length of Russia's European frontier.

At first the German offensives were attended with their usual success. By the middle of July the German forces had entered Smolensk, two hundred miles from Moscow and four hundred and fifty from their starting-points. Disagreement between Hitler and the German army leadership whether to press for Leningrad and the Ukraine, or whether to continue the drive on Moscow halted the advance for nearly two months. Very considerable Russian forces were destroyed in the battles for the Ukraine, but each advance further dispersed the German forces,

and lengthened dangerously their lines of supply and communi-
cation. In October and November Hitler renewed the offensive
on Moscow and came very near to its capture, but stubborn
Russian resistance and the onset of the Russian winter thwarted

Map 23. The German advance into the U.S.S.R., 1941–3

Stages in the advance are shown by the lines numbered as follows: 1. Start
line, 22 June 1941; 2. End of August 1941; 3. End of November 1941; 4. Start
line of the summer campaign, 28 June 1942; 5. End of October 1942.

him. On 6 December the first great Russian winter offensive
opened.

On 7 December the Japanese fleet attacked Pearl Harbour
and moved against the British and Dutch possessions in East
Asia. Ribbentrop had long urged Japan to attack Singapore,

as an added distraction to Britain, but the attack on Pearl Harbour came as a complete surprise to the German leaders. Hitler who had long chafed against American aid to Britain and Russia, and America's increasing intervention in the Atlantic

Map 24. The German retreat from the U.S.S.R., 1943–4

Stages in the retreat are shown by the lines numbered as follows: 1. Limit of German advance, November 1942; 2. Line on 5 July 1943; 3. Line on 1 January 1944.

struggle, welcomed the opportunity of declaring war. He seems grossly to have underestimated American military potentialities, as he also underestimated her industrial strength. The first consequence of the German declaration of war on the U.S.A. was the opening to the German U-boat fleet of new areas of operation off the American Atlantic and Caribbean coasts, thus further dispersing the hard-pressed Allied escort forces. Had Germany possessed at this time the U-boat fleet which Hitler now began building, the consequences might well have been disastrous. As it was, their shipping losses in 1942 and the spring of 1943 taxed the Allies to the limit. Possibly anticipating an Allied attempt to bottle the German submarine fleet into the North Sea, or to link hands with Russia, Hitler now became obsessed with the idea of an Allied landing in Norway, and the remaining German warships were concentrated there at great risk, leaving the southern sea-lanes free for the Allied armada which was to invade North Africa.

Meanwhile, in Russia Hitler was faced with the first major crisis of the war. The severity of the Russian winter, against which his own folly had left his troops unprotected, combined with the Russian offensives to threaten a complete debacle. In this crisis Hitler's nerve remained unshaken. Rejecting the advice of his generals to retreat to a shorter line, he announced his personal assumption of command (17 December 1941) and ordered the German troops to stand firm at all costs. His firmness prevented the collapse of German morale, haunted by memories of 1812. But it only confirmed him in his already exaggerated estimate of his own abilities. From the winter of 1941 onwards his subordinates could no longer obtain a hearing for advice or information which ran contrary to his wishes. The crisis had, in fact, resulted from his own failure to concentrate his forces properly in the early months of the German offensives. But his success in surmounting it seemed to him proof that his intuition was infallible.

Hitler was to repeat his error in the summer of 1942. The Japanese victories in the East Indies enabled Raeder to interest Hitler again in the plan for an attack on the British position in the Middle East, presented as part of a 'Great Plan', to link forces with Japan in the Indian Ocean. In accordance with this Rommel launched his greatest desert offensive in June 1942 and drove the British forces right back to El Alamein, the last defensive position in front of the Nile delta. But Hitler again refused to follow this up with an attack on Malta, and the German supply lines across the Mediterranean remained under attack. As the northern wing of the plan, the German summer offensive in Russia was launched in the south. Once more its initial success deluded Hitler into splitting his forces. His original plan had been to drive on Stalingrad. But the apparent collapse of the Russian front led him to divide his forces in September, when he could easily have taken the city, and to drive for the Caucasian oil-fields. In the event he achieved neither objective, and by the time he had regrouped his forces to attack Stalingrad the Russians had recovered sufficiently to be able to hold the city, while building up their forces on the long exposed northern flank of the German advances, a flank held mainly by satellite and second-grade German divisions.

This moment, the moment of Hitler's greatest advances, the moment when his forces were stretched to the uttermost limits of geographical dispersion was the moment of German defeat. On 23 October the Eighth Army attacked the German line at El Alamein and, after twelve days' fighting, broke out into the desert. On 7 November American and British forces, which had sailed in separate convoys from the United States and Britain landed on both the Atlantic and Mediterranean coasts of French North Africa, and within a few days occupied the whole area up to the Tunisian border. On 19 November three Russian Army Corps, reports of whose existence Hitler had characterized as 'idiotic twaddle', attacked north and south of Stalingrad and encircled twenty-two German divisions. The German attack on the Caucasus came to an immediate end, and frantic and unsuccessful attempts were made to relieve the encircled troops whose retreat Hitler refused to countenance. In each case Hitler's reaction was the same; no retreat and no surrender. The remainder of France was occupied. German and Italian troops were poured into Tunisia. The surrounded forces in Stalingrad were ordered to fight to the last man. Their surrender in January 1943 did not mark the end of the second Russian winter offensive, and the German line in South Russia was not stabilized until the end of February 1943.

HITLER'S EUROPE IN THEORY AND PRACTICE

At this point, when Hitler's dominions in Europe had reached their furthest point of territorial expansion and were beginning again to contract, it is worth pausing to examine the structure of Hitler's Europe and the opposition within Germany that it aroused. For Hitler the concept of a 'New Order' was a useful propaganda phrase with which to answer the Atlantic Charter advanced by his enemies. Any attempt to translate it into reality he regarded with suspicion and hostility. His aim was German domination of Europe, not German hegemony within Europe. But his absorption in the conduct of the war, especially after the winter of 1941, left him little opportunity to do more than set up the individual administrations in the various captured territories, and to intervene wherever flagrant departures from his ideas caught his eyes. The concept of a 'New Order', a reorganization of Europe on more centralized and logical economic lines, a community of peoples politically self-contained and economically self-sufficient, was far more the work of lesser Nazi figures and of the Propaganda Ministry.

The major Nazi theorists who at times backed these plans were Alfred Rosenberg and Himmler's planning staff in the *S.S.* The aim for which they worked was the 'germanization' of the non-German races of Northern Europe, Norwegians, Danes, English, Walloons, Dutch and Bretons, and their employment in the colonization of European Russia. Rosenberg's plans laid the main emphasis on colonization of the Baltic States, Himmler's on the Crimea. The foundation of the Dutch Niederlandsche Oestcompagnie in 1942 reflected these plans. Himmler was simultaneously engaged, in his capacity as 'Commissioner for the strengthening of the race', in a plan for the resettlement in Germany of all the German minorities in Eastern Europe and elsewhere. Whether this collection of all of German origin into a compact mass in Central Europe was to be the prelude to a new German Diaspora, or whether he was unable to decide between the virtues of a compact national mass or a diffusion of colonies of the master-race is uncertain. But the conflict between the two plans resulted in the withdrawal of the German minorities from Eastern Poland and the Baltic States at the same time as efforts were being made to promote the German colonization of these areas. Indeed, some unfortunates were no sooner brought back to Germany than they were sent out anew to colonize the land they had come from. In general, however, the large mass of these evacuees got no further than the *S.S.* transit camps, where they were overtaken by the German defeat.

The Nazi administration of Europe is best classified according to the Nazis' own theories of race and resettlement. First, there were the areas of 'pure' German racial structure. These received two types of administration according to the degree to which the areas had been dominated by pan-German organizations before their capture. Those where such organizations had been strong, the Saarland, Austria, the Sudetenland, Eupen-Malmedy and pre-1914 German Poland, were directly annexed. Those where pan-German sympathies had been weak or countered by other loyalties were attached to the German province (*Gau*) on which they bordered and placed under a German 'Chief of Civil Administration', who was usually the neighbouring Gauleiter. These included Alsace-Lorraine, Luxemburg and Slovenia (divided into two areas, Carniola, attached to Carinthia, and Lower Styria, to Styria). After the German attack on Russia, the Polish province of Bialystok, allotted to Russia in the 1939 partition of Poland, was similarly attached to East Prussia.

A second type of organization was used for those areas of definitely 'Aryan' racial composition, but whose national cohesion made them unsuitable for direct annexation. These comprised Holland, Norway and Denmark. Holland and Norway were both placed under high-ranking Nazis as 'Reich Commissioners', Seyss-Inquart in Holland and Terboven in Norway. Their administrative structure was unaltered though the political direction was naturally removed. Power remained in the hands of the higher posts in the civil services of the two countries, whose occupants were chosen where possible for their Nazi sympathies. Not until the attack on Russia, with the consequent shortage of German man-power and an accompanying swing towards radicalism within the Nazi leadership (see below p. 226), were the small Nazi-type parties of Mussert in Holland and Quisling in Norway allowed to form cabinets. Even then they acted mainly as vehicles for German directives and had little authority of their own.

Denmark occupied a special position as a kind of model protectorate. Although she was placed under German occupation, her king and government were allowed great freedom, and the German Reich Plenipotentiary was a diplomat, enjoined to use diplomacy not force. North Schleswig, with its large and nationalist German minority remained Danish. Only the persistent Danish opposition to Nazi measures, culminating in the great Copenhagen strikes of August 1943, forced Hitler to reduce Denmark to the level of Norway and Holland, to extend German police and S.S. jurisdiction across her borders and to place her under a Reich Commissioner. Economically all these countries were integrated as much as possible into Germany through the Four-Year Plan organization. With Holland there was a mutual obligation to accept each other's currency, growing later to the gradual removal of all currency control and of economic control on the common border. In return for co-operation with the occupying authorities, Dutch citizens were granted dual citizenship. In all three countries the Reich Commissioners shared jurisdiction with the commanders of the German occupation forces but held precedence over them as the Führer's representatives.

For strategic reasons, others of the 'non-incorporated' areas were placed under military government. These included Belgium and northern France (until July 1944, when they were placed under civilian commissioners), occupied France,[1] Greece and the Serbian rump-state. After the Italian collapse, northern Italy and the areas previously under Italian occupation were added, as so-called 'Zones of Operations'. For administrative purposes these were divided into the 'Adriatic Littoral' (on both sides of the Adriatic), and the 'Alpine Foreland'.

In south-east Europe the Germans relied on a chain of puppet

[1] Both northern France and the remainder of France were still formally under the Vichy Government.

and satellite states. Their role in Nazi theory was to provide security for the flank of Germany's drive to the east, not to fall victim to it. Relations with these states were handled through diplomatic channels, and German intervention restricted to insistence on far-reaching privileges for their German minorities, and pressure for co-operation in Germany's policy of Jewish deportation. The German Protectorate of Bohemia-Moravia filled a somewhat similar role. Certain branches of its administration passed directly under the control of the appropriate Ministry in Berlin. A Czech administration was allowed to exist and function and a Czech diplomatic representation was maintained in Berlin (though nowhere else); but it was controlled and paralleled at every administrative level by a German administration under the German overlord, the Reich Protector.

If the regime established in the west was one of forced co-operation, that in the east was one of despoliation. The role of the Slavic east in Nazi theory was to provide land for colonization and raw materials for German industry. Its inhabitants were to be reduced to the status of the helot in ancient Sparta. The first administration to reflect this was the 'General Government' set up in 1939 to administer those areas of Poland which had not been directly incorporated into the Reich. Its administration, with Governor-General, State-Secretary and twelve departments, was entirely German except at the very lowest levels, though its elaboration reflected in part the empire-building proclivities of its Governor-General, Frank. It was separated from the Reich by customs and monetary boundaries and used as a dumping ground (and a killing ground) for racial undesirables.

The German administration of the areas conquered in Russia reflected the divisions within the German leadership. Rosenberg, whom Hitler appointed head of the *Ostministerium* (Ministry for the East), created to control and supervise this administration, planned to encircle ethnic Russia by a chain of independent states under German protection. In the north, as already mentioned, the Baltic States were to become a German colony (Rosenberg himself was a German Balt). In the south independent Ukrainian and Don Cossack states were to be set up, the Caucasian republics placed under German protection and a Mohammedan republic erected in Turkestan.

Accordingly, the conquered areas were divided into two Reich Commissariats, one for the 'Ostland', covering the Baltic republics and White Russia, the other for the Ukraine. Within the Reich Commissariat Ostland, each Baltic republic became a General Commissariat, with White Russia making up a fourth. In the Baltic States attempts were made to recreate the native administrations destroyed in the Russian occupation, on the lines of the administrations of Norway and Holland. White Russia on the other hand, thought to be much more corrupted with Bolshevism, was treated on the same lines as the General Government.

Economically these organizations were administered by Göring's Four-Year Plan organization. This found the Russian system of state ownership of factories and farms far too useful an instrument of exploitation to allow these to pass back into private ownership, and apart from some farmland, organized on a co-operative basis, merely replaced the Russian organizations by German monopoly companies. Labour recruitment for work in Germany and the operation of Himmler's *Einsatzkommandos* (see p. 232 below) laid large areas waste and deserted, brought the local economy to a standstill, and stultified Rosenberg's hopes of winning over the local population.

In the Ukraine Rosenberg had to deal not only with the independent activities of Göring and Himmler, but also with calculated disobedience on the part of Koch, the Reich Commissar, his nominal subordinate, who flatly refused to allow any Ukrainian nationalism or native administration. In this there is little doubt that he had Hitler's backing, as Hitler had no sympathy for Rosenberg's plans for a remodelled Russia. His policy was despoliation, enslavement and eventual German colonization. The setting up of new states would merely obstruct the realization of this policy. In the same way he refused to make use of the Vlassow movement, with its Free Russian army, for any except propaganda purposes. In these countries he said, 'we shall act as if we wanted to exercise a mandate only. But at the same time we must know that we shall never leave them.'

CHANGES IN THE NAZI LEADERSHIP DURING THE WAR

The Nazi political leadership cannot be discussed except in terms of the struggle for personal power, a struggle which was encouraged by Hitler as a means of preventing any challenge to his own position. By 1939 there were three main organizations in competition with each other within Germany, the state administration, under the various ministries, the Party organization, and the S.S. under Himmler, on whose loyalty Hitler relied completely. A similar struggle for power took place within each organization. In 1939 the position seemed fairly stable. Göring's position was unassailable in view of his position as Hitler's successor and the confidence he enjoyed among the non-Nazi sections of the German people. Neither Himmler nor Hess, the head of the Party organization, could extend his own empire much further, although Himmler still hoped to take over the German administration of justice.

By 1941 this position had changed considerably. The palpable failure of the Luftwaffe and his own withdrawal into a private life of sybaritic luxury had irretrievably damaged Göring's standing and prestige, except with Hitler, whilst Hess had removed himself from the scene by his flight to Scotland. He had been succeeded by his deputy, Bormann, who proceeded to build up his position on his control of access to Hitler (a step welcomed by Hitler in his absorption in the conduct of the war), and by the extension of Party control over the members and functions of the state administration. The supervision of civil service appointments, the direction of labour recruitment and economic administration, and the organization of civil defence were all made the responsibility of the regional party leaders, the Gauleiters, during 1942.

This year was also taken up with the final subordination of the German legal machinery to the Nazi demands that the judiciary should merely be a branch of the administration. Hitler himself directly intervened in this struggle, first by his speech to the Reichstag, of 26 April 1942, threatening those judges who failed to co-operate in the purposes of the Nazi leadership with dismissal, and then to resolve the conflict that arose within the Nazi leadership itself. For Hans Frank, the Governor-General of Poland, and head of the Party's Legal Bureau, regarded these attacks on the judiciary as dangerous to his own position and embarked on a series of speeches to the main German universities denouncing them as attempts to suppress the old German respect for law in favour of police state ideals. Hitler settled the conflict, in which Goebbels, Himmler and the entire party and *S.S.* press was opposed to Frank, by dismissing him from all Party offices, forbidding him to make any more speeches in public, dissolving the Party's Legal Bureau and promoting Thierack, the Nazi President of the People's Court and one of Frank's bitterest assailants, to be Minister of Justice. But even Thierack proved too legally minded for the extreme Nazi radicals such as Goebbels.

The defeats of December 1942 increased the swing to the radical wing of the Nazi party symbolized by Bormann's rise and Frank's defeat. A radical, Sauckel, was promoted to lead an all-out programme of labour conscription in January 1943. In April Ribbentrop 'purged' the Foreign Ministry, replacing most of the senior civil servants with his own nominees, and appointing a number of *S.A.* men, survivors of the 1934 *Putsch*, to diplomatic posts. In July 1943 Himmler took over the Ministry of the Interior, with full control of the German police. The process continued through 1944, as German defeat drew nearer. Goebbels, already administrator of Berlin, became plenipotentiary for total war in July 1944, and in September the organization, control and leadership of Germany's last reserves of manpower into the Volksturm was handed over entirely to the Gauleiters and the Party.

As defeat closed inexorably around Germany, the Nazi leaders returned to their original nihilism, the revolutionary destructiveness of those who had been without power or possessions, or the hope of obtaining them. In their years of success, the urge to pull down the fabric of a society which denied them the power they desired had lain dormant, satisfied only by occasional outbursts of brutality, such as the Röhm *Putsch* or the anti-semitic riots of November 1938. But now that defeat seemed about to reduce them to the impotence from which they had arisen, this nihilism reawoke. Goebbels used his powers to introduce a regime of puritanism into Germany. Theatres, cabarets, music-halls were closed, orchestras disbanded, institutes of learning suppressed. The entire Nazi press exulted in the destruction brought by the ceaseless Allied bombing. And Hitler ordered the widespread application of the 'scorched earth' policy to all areas which had to be abandoned to the Allies. Only the machinations of Speer, the Nazi economic dictator, a technocrat, who kept his head, frustrated this.

At the same time, Bormann moved against his last rival, Himmler, himself under pressure from his *S.S.* subordinates to overthrow Hitler and sue for peace. He succeeded in getting Himmler appointed to command on the eastern front against the Russians and began systematically to poison Hitler's mind against him. In the last days of Nazi Germany he used the news of Himmler's peace approaches to the Swede, Count Bernadotte, to secure his overthrow as he also secured that of Göring. His own power ended with Hitler's suicide two days later. Bormann's rise and fall illustrates the nature and degree of Hitler's domination of Germany. While Hitler lived, there was one source of power, and one alone, in all Germany, and his leading associates contended against each other only for his favour from which alone that power flowed.

GERMAN OPPOSITION TO HITLER

Opposition to Hitler during the war came largely from two groups, those who were driven by Nazi invasion of their prerogatives and privileges into moral resistance to Nazism and opposition to its doctrines, and those whose dissatisfaction with Hitler's leadership and methods led them to positive conspiracy to overthrow him. In the first category came the organized institutions of the universities, the legal profession and the churches. With the legal profession we have already dealt (see above, p. 226). The universities contributed many martyrs to Nazism, both among teachers and students, most notably the 'White Rose' group at Munich University, hanged in April 1943. But these were individuals. As institutions the universities remained silent. With the churches much the same picture prevailed. Resistance was strongest among the German Confessional Church and among the Catholics. But the withdrawal of concessions to the churches in 1941, inspired by Bormann and the radicals, provoked considerable protest, which found public expression. Here again, protest and condemnation of Nazi practices as such were more the work of individual church leaders: their importance lay in their being the only means of public expression in Germany not under Nazi control, working as they did through the annual church conferences, notably that of Fulda in 1942, and the machinery of sermons and pastoral letters.

The second category whose members came eventually together to organize the conspiracy to murder Hitler, which failed on 20 July 1944, and the government to replace him once his removal had been accomplished, falls into roughly three divisions: the nationalist soldiers and civil servants who had collaborated in the overthrow of the Weimar regime, but who could not stomach Nazi methods; a large group of middle- and lower-ranking staff officers (including the directorate of the Armed Forces Intelligence Agency, the Abwehr), whose opposition came from a mixture of motives, part class hostility, part fear of defeat, part religious antipathy; and finally a larger group of diverse sympathies linked in the so-called 'Kreisau circle'. Its leaders came from the East Prussian aristocracy, but its main bond was a kind of Christian Socialism which could unite both Catholic and Protestant intellectuals with the underground Social Democrat and trade union leadership.

The problem of overthrowing Hitler presented itself to the German opposition in three aspects. First, there was the problem of force, of gaining control either of the Army or of the S.S. and police. Secondly, there was the problem of deciding what was to replace Nazism. Thirdly, there was the problem of making the change of government acceptable to Germany's enemies, so that the war might be ended without a degradation of Germany which would discredit the conspirators and make the way easy for a recrudescence of Nazism under another name. All of these presented considerable difficulties.

The Army leadership presented three particular types of obstacle to the arguments of the conspirators. Their power would suffer most in the event of an Allied victory. They used their oath of loyalty to Hitler as a cloak for their indecision. And, purged of Beck, Fritsch and Hammerstein, they proved easy victims to the force of Hitler's personality. Thus they only really listened to opposition spokesmen during 1939 when Hitler's plans to attack in the west seemed militarily impossible, and after the defeats of December 1942 which made it plain that the war was lost. And their protests in November 1939 were easily silenced by Hitler.

The problem of approach to the Allies was equally difficult. In 1939 prospects seemed best before battle had really been joined; though the terms demanded from the Allies would probably have proved unacceptable to Allied opinion, as they included the retention of the Sudetenland and western Poland. After 1939 the overwhelming German victories stood in the way, as when contact was made in 1942, when the Bishop of Chichester visited Sweden. Once the tide of victory had turned, the Allied insistence that surrender must be unconditional made contact doubly difficult, since the purpose of contact was to extract some assurance from the Allies which might be used to induce the German army leadership to take action, and make the overthrow of Hitler's regime acceptable to German public opinion. Russian use of the Free German Committee (founded July 1943), and the League of German Officers (September 1943), formed from German prisoners of war, complicated matters further by seeming to offer a quite unreal choice between contact with the Western Allies or with Russia. Dispute about this choice was responsible for the vacancy in the post of Foreign Minister in the 'shadow cabinet' drawn up by the opposition in June 1944.

Agreement on the second of the three problems, that of the

state which was to replace Nazism, was only reached during 1943 in a series of meetings held at Kreisau. The older conspirators had at first leaned towards a monarchical restoration. The majority of them accepted the swing towards social democracy embodied in the agreements finally reached. Some of the more right-wing members were sufficiently opposed, however, to attempt to stir Himmler into resistance to Hitler since they despaired of ever moving the army to action, hoping to win for their purposes the only other repository of armed power in Germany, the *S.S.* The attempt ended as they might have foreseen in their arrest. The main note of the Kreisau agreements, besides the social flavour of many of their pronouncements, was that of return to a state based on the rule of law, the *Rechtstaat*, as opposed to the arbitrary will of the ruling party leadership. As the conspiracy moved from the expression of discontent to the organization of a *coup d'état*, so the Gestapo closed in on it. In February 1944 the *S.S.* succeeded in taking over the Abwehr. The last stages before the *coup* were marked by the gradual whittling away of the leadership of the conspiracy by arrest, and were taken under the impact of the advances of the Allied armies in the east and west. The conspiracy actually failed on 20 July 1944 because its technical details went awry. Hitler was not killed by the bomb left at his staff conference, nor were his radio connections with the rest of Germany severed. But the failure was not merely technical. The conspiracy foundered on the vacillations of the Army leadership without whose co-operation the defeat of the Nazi system's own armed forces, the *S.S.*, was impossible, and on the almost unattainable conditions the army leaders imposed on the conspirators before they would grant them their support. The ease with which Hitler could cow and dominate the army leaders made failure to kill or silence him disastrous to the conspiracy.

Once the conspiracy had failed and its members been hunted to their deaths by *S.S.* and Gestapo, no other opposition to Hitler was possible, even in the blackest days of German defeat. To organize opposition to a dictator and secure his overthrow, there must be some traditional or constitutional symbol which the opponents can use to rally opposition and around which they can organize an alternative government. In Italy this was provided by the Italian crown. But Hitler had concentrated in his own person all the powers, functions and traditions of the German state including to a large extent those embodied in the Army. The failure of the 1944 *Putsch* removed even this, the only remaining alternative to the Party, and made the entire destruction of Germany's governmental system down to the lowest levels of local administration an unavoidable corollary of defeat.

THE ELIMINATION OF EUROPEAN JEWRY

In 1939 the areas of Europe which fell under Nazi domination held about nine million Jews, over six million of them in Poland and western Russia. By May 1945 the particular sub-office within Himmler's Reich Security Office (*Reichssicherheitshauptamt*), responsible for the Jewish question, had succeeded in organizing the killing of between four and four and a half million of them, mainly, though not entirely, through the concentration camps and special units of the *S.S.*

Their main effort was directed against the Jews of east Europe, but in the perpetual battle for new jurisdiction which followed each new Nazi conquest they extended their activities into western Europe and brought considerable pressure to bear on each of Germany's satellites and allies to co-operate with them. In these areas the Jews escaped only where foreign pressure could protect them, where there was a tradition of assimilation or where the country's own administration could resist or obstruct the Nazi plans effectively. Swedish pressure saved all but a few of the small Norwegian Jewish colony. The king of Denmark prevented the introduction of anti-semitic laws into Denmark for most of the war. But in Holland, occupied and under German administration, five out of every seven Jews were killed.

The procedure followed in each new territory was fairly standardized. First, the Jews were compelled to register separately, usually under their own organizations. Economic discrimination and the Nuremberg racial laws (see p. 190, n.) were introduced. Next came enforced concentration into ghettos or similar areas within the bigger cities. Lastly came deportation to the concentration camps of Eastern Germany or Poland where death through overwork, starvation or the gas-oven awaited them.

The passage from deportation to mass murder did not finally take place until the invasion of Russia. Previous efforts resulted from individual initiative rather than from a general directive, though the policy of deportation to Poland began soon after the Polish capitulation in September 1939. During 1940 world opinion was misled with talk of deportation to Madagascar, an utterly impracticable proposition. In March 1941 Himmler was given independent powers for police actions in the occupied territories in Russia, and in May 1941 special S.S. extermination units, the *Einsatzkommandos*, were organized to follow the invading armies into Russia and eliminate the Russian Jews wherever they were found. These units did in fact carry out large-scale massacres of Russian Jews behind the German army lines with the knowledge and in some cases the co-operation of the German army commanders, who regarded their hands as tied by the special powers given to Himmler.

The first plans for the setting up of extermination camps in Poland took shape in October 1941, though an experimental gassing station was set up at Oswiecim (Auschwitz) a month earlier. The first permanent gassing camp opened at Chelmno in Posen in December 1941. On 20 January 1942 a conference of representatives of all German ministries, under Himmler's deputy Heydrich, met at Gross Wannsee in Berlin, and discussed and settled all the necessary measures for this 'final solution' of the Jewish problem in Europe. The machinery they set up worked without cessation until the Russians overran the extermination camps in Poland in October 1944, and the retreating S.S. units in many cases took their potential victims with them. The last massacres took place within two weeks of the German capitulation.

It is beyond dispute that the facts of the deportations and the massacres in Russia at least were known widely in Germany.

But the men responsible remained unknown, and, even within the non-Nazi hierarchy, fear closed the eyes and sealed the lips of those who might have protested. This extermination of the Jews was one of Hitler's dearest ideals. Many of those responsible within the Reich Security Office escaped at the end of the war. They failed to achieve the final elimination of European Jewry; but only through their own inefficiency, through bureaucratic delays and the obstruction practised in the occupied countries and through the German collapse.

THE END OF HITLER'S GERMANY

From the defeats of December 1942 the pendulum swung slowly at first but with increasing violence against Germany. On the eastern front the year was marked by the first Russian defeat of a German summer offensive, and, in spite of victories in the early part of 1943, by December the Germans were very definitely in retreat. In spite, too, of the replacement of Raeder, the Commander in Chief of the Navy, by Doenitz, the submarine expert, the battle of the Atlantic had been definitely won by the Allies by the end of the year. And in the air Germany lay open to the attacks of the American bombers by day, and of the R.A.F. by night. Hamburg was devastated by fire in July with 60,000 casualties.

But the most dramatic German defeats of this year came in the Mediterranean. The German riposte to the Allied invasion of North Africa had only placed a second large German army in an impossible position, and their surrender was inevitable. In July Allied forces landed in Sicily and rapidly overran the island. Major German concessions to Italy in February and two Hitler-Mussolini meetings, at Salzburg in April and at Feltre on 19 July, failed to save the Italian position. Mass strikes in Italian industry preceded revolt in the Fascist Grand Council. On Mussolini's return from Feltre the Grand Council rebelled against his leadership. The Italian king arrested him and appointed Marshal Badoglio as Premier. Two months later the Italian government signed an armistice with the Allies. Hitler's reaction, the seizure of Rome by German troops, the disarming of the Italian army in North Italy and the Balkans, and the rescue of Mussolini was brilliantly planned and deprived the Allied landings on the European mainland of most of their immediate effect, but only served to delay, and not to avert, his ultimate defeat.

In March 1944, with the Soviet advances into Rumania and Poland, Hitler took similar steps to prevent the defection of Hungary where Kallay had been appointed Premier to take Hungary out of the war early in 1943. Horthy was summoned for interview to Salzburg and bullied into dismissing Kallay and accepting a German commissioner and German *S.S.* and police forces in Hungary. Hitler had proved that he could still act with decision where he held the preponderance of force. But over the major German war-fronts without such preponderance he could only fall back on a senseless and wasteful refusal to abandon any position. In 1941 such a policy had prevented the repulse before Moscow from becoming a rout and had saved the German front in Russia. In 1944 it only cost Hitler manpower he could ill afford to lose.

Under the impact of defeat he gradually abandoned contact with the German people, isolating himself more and more in his headquarters. He retreated into dreams of splits between the Allies, plans for fantastic secret weapons that might magically turn defeat into victory. The imminence of defeat, the gradual exhaustion of Germany's material resources, the destruction of her factories, the invasion of her frontiers could not penetrate the veils of fancy behind which he had taken refuge. As defeat advanced he lost contact more and more with reality, at the end issuing impossible orders to non-existent armies. But no one in command in Germany dared oppose him.

The full weight of disaster struck Germany in the summer of 1944. The Russian summer offensive almost obliterated the German line in the east, and reached the Vistula, cutting off a large German army group in the Baltic states. Halted on the Vistula they swept into south-east Europe. In August 1944 Horthy dismissed the government imposed on him in March and sued for an armistice. In September King Michael of Rumania arrested his pro-German Premier, Antonescu, and signed an armistice with the Russians. A second German *coup d'état* cut short the Hungarian attempt to follow suit, and the slender German reserves on the eastern front were thrown into Budapest where they held out until February 1945. But by October Russia had forced Bulgaria and Finland out of the war and had linked forces with Tito's partisans in Belgrade.

Before then, and immediately after the fall of Rome (4 June), the Anglo-American forces had landed in Normandy on 6 June, consolidated their bridgehead against all German attacks, and had broken out two months later. Hitler's last orders for a German counter-attack secured the destruction of the only German army between them and the German frontier. By September the Allies had liberated Paris and Brussels, eliminated the launching bases of Hitler's first 'secret weapon', the flying bomb, and had reached the German frontier. Division of counsel and difficulties of supply prevented the full exploitation of their victories and their attempt to outflank the Rhine barrier by airborne landings followed up by ground forces failed at Arnhem.

Hitler now began to rally all remaining German resources for one last throw. Germany's oil supplies were at their minimum with the loss of the Rumanian oil wells and the Allied bombing of the synthetic oil plants. Germany's last reserves of manpower were being rallied by the Party in the Volksturm. But German opinion, deprived of all hope by the failure of the July conspiracy, driven desperate by American discussion of the Morgenthau plan to reduce Germany to a purely agricultural state, benumbed by the Allied bombing and the reiteration of the slogan of 'unconditional surrender', remained solidly behind him.

Hitler's final offensive was planned in the west. Estimating that the Americans could not move without air cover, and that they and the British were held back by shortage of supplies, Hitler planned to strike at the hinge of the Allied armies and drive through for Antwerp. At best he might force the British forces to a second more difficult Dunkirk. Eighteen out of twenty-five Volksturm divisions, two-thirds of the Luftwaffe's remaining fighter strength and most of the remaining tank and assault gun reserves were used. The attack was launched in the Ardennes region on 16 December 1944. Initially it achieved a certain success, but the Allied strength and resources doomed it to failure. In January 1945, 180 Russian divisions attacked on the Vistula and the German defences went down like matchwood. In March the western Allies crossed the Rhine and encircled an Army Group in the Ruhr. There was to be no pause in the Allied offensives in the east and west until the German surrender.

In his last days Hitler wavered for a time between plans to withdraw to the Alpine areas of southern Germany and Austria and to continue resistance. But he finally decided to remain in Berlin and immolate himself amid the ruins of the city. His scorched earth orders were frustrated by Speer, the economic controller. He discussed the massacre of all prisoners of war, and the use of new and terrible poison gases. He hoped that Roosevelt's death on 12 April would save him from defeat as the death of the Czarina Elizabeth had saved Frederick the Great. It was not until 22 April that he appeared to realize his defeat, abdicating all his powers and responsibilities in a fit of temper, only to resume them the following day. The end came on 30 April in the air-raid shelter of the Reich Chancellery. Hitler nominated Admiral Doenitz to be his successor, and shot himself. Goebbels followed his example, and Bormann was most probably killed trying to escape from the ruins of Berlin.

On 7 May the German forces surrendered unconditionally. Their country was without administration, their towns and factories in ruins, their transport system paralysed, their fate in the hands of the victorious Allies. Weakness, ambition and fear had led them to follow Hitler and enabled him to present them with a situation where their only alternative to his rule was anarchy. Opposition became only a small voice heard in privacy and in fear. At the last their leader failed and abandoned them, suicide giving him a way of escape from the consequences of failure. Germany remained, leaderless, divided, the riches of five years domination of Europe lost in defeat.

BIBLIOGRAPHICAL NOTE

Whole libraries have been written about the history of Germany, and this bibliographical note does nothing more than indicate the books which might provide a stimulus and a guide to further reading. The main emphasis is given to works in English, and only a relatively small number of the most outstanding books in German are included.

GENERAL

1. Many good general histories of Germany have appeared since the Second World War, amongst the most stimulating of which is A. J. P. Taylor, *The Course of German History, A Survey of the Development of Germany since 1815* (London, 1945). Other useful surveys are Ralph Flenley, *Modern German History* (London, 1953), which emphasizes the social, economic and intellectual factors which have been of importance in modern German history; Koppel S. Pinson, *Modern Germany, Its History and Civilization* (New York, 1954), which deals with the interplay of nineteenth-century cultural, intellectual and economic forces; and John A. Hawgood, *The Evolution of Germany* (London, 1955), a topical study of Germany and its past, which provides a valuable introduction to the study of German life and culture generally.

2. For more detailed study the relevant chapters of the *Cambridge Medieval History* (Cambridge, 1911–36), the *Cambridge Modern History* (Cambridge, 1902–12), and the *New Cambridge Modern History* (1957–) provide authoritative surveys.

3. The more important undercurrents of modern German history are examined in Hans Kohn (ed.), *German History. Some New German Views* (London, 1954), to which Friedrich Meinecke, Walther Hofer and other distinguished scholars contribute; in Friedrich Meinecke, *The German Catastrophe*, translated by Sidney B. Fay (Harvard, 1950), in which this great historian reflects upon the events of his own long lifetime; in the essays on Napoleon, 1848 and Bismarck in A. J. P. Taylor, *From Napoleon to Stalin: Comments on European History* (London, 1950); and in L. L. Snyder, *German Nationalism. The Tragedy of a People* (Harrisburg, 1952), an erudite study of German nationalism which gives particular emphasis to its cultural roots.

4. There are some excellent German historical atlases which naturally pay a great deal of attention to Germany: von Spruner-Menke, *Hand-Atlas für die Geschichte des Mittelalters und der Neueren Zeit*

(Gotha, 1880); Droysen, *Allgemeiner Historischer Atlas* (Bielefeld and Leipzig, 1920); F. W. Putzger, *Historischer Schul-Atlas* (57th ed. Bielefeld and Leipzig, 1939). The following English atlases are also very useful: R. L. Poole, *Historical Atlas of Modern Europe* (Oxford, 1902); W. R. Shepherd, *Historical Atlas* (7th ed. London, 1930); *The Cambridge Modern History Atlas* (2nd ed. Cambridge, 1924); *The Cambridge Medieval History: Volume of Maps* (Cambridge, 1936).

5. For a comprehensive and readable account of the geography of Germany, contained within a relatively small compass, it is not necessary to go further than Robert E. Dickinson, *The Regions of Germany* (London, 1945), although the same author's *Germany. A General Regional Geography* (London, 1953) provides the basis for more advanced study.

GERMANY BEFORE 1815

1. Despite the increase in our knowledge since it was first published in 1864 James Bryce, *The Holy Roman Empire*, not only makes delightful reading, but still remains the best introduction to a study of this great political era. The student of the transition from medieval to modern Germany can now read Bryce in conjunction with H. A. L. Fisher, *The Medieval Empire* (2 vols., London, 1898), and G. Barraclough, *Origins of Modern Germany* (Oxford, 1947), with the latter author's *Factors in German History* (Oxford, 1946) as a useful supplement.

2. An outline of the rise of Brandenburg-Prussia is to be found in J. A. R. Marriott and C. G. Robertson, *The Evolution of Prussia* (2nd ed. Oxford, 1937), the earlier chapters of which should be read in conjunction with F. L. Carsten, *The Origins of Prussia* (Oxford, 1954) which incorporates more recent research on the period 1000–1700. For the eighteenth century the full and scholarly study by G. P. Gooch, *Frederick the Great, the Ruler, the Writer, the Man* (London, 1947) is invaluable, while the progress of Prussian militarism during the same period is dealt with authoritatively in the first volume of Gerhard Ritter, *Staatskunst und Kriegshandwerk. Das Problem des Militarismus in Deutschland* (Munich and Oldenburg, 1954), especially chs. 1 to 4. For the later period of Prussian history, Sir J. Seeley's classic *Life and Times of Stein* (London, 1875) still affords a full and readable basis of study.

3. The best book in the English language on German social history in the eighteenth century is W. H. Bruford, *Germany in the*

Eighteenth Century: The Social Background of the Literary Revival (Cambridge, 1935).

4. The evolution of German political thought in the last decades of the eighteenth century is dealt with in chs. 1 and 2 of R. D'O. Butler, *The Roots of National Socialism* (London, 1941), and more fully in G. P. Gooch, *Germany and the French Revolution* (London, 1920). H. A. L. Fisher, *Napoleonic Statesmanship: Germany* (London, 1905) contains a scholarly and judicious account of Napoleon's 'New Order' in Germany. G. H. Turnbull, *The Educational Theory of J. G. Fichte* (London, 1926), is one of the few works in English to deal adequately with Fichte's political writings, although chapter 6 of Friedrich Meinecke, *Weltbürgertum und Nationalstaat* (1st ed. Munich and Berlin, 1907), covers the subject brilliantly in German. The latter book as a whole is still the most scholarly introduction to the historical study of German nationalism, and should be read in conjunction with its author's earlier work, *Das Zeitalter der Deutschen Erhebung* (Bielefeld, 1906).

5. An excellent account of the obstacles to German unity in the period before 1815 is to be found in Erich Brandenburg, *Die Reichsgründung* (2 vols. Leipzig, 1916), vol. 1, ch. 2.

1815–71

1. A. J. P. Taylor, *The Course of German History*, to which reference has already been made above, may be read in conjunction with two earlier standard works: A. W. Ward, *Germany* (3 vols, Cambridge, 1916–18), and H. von Treitschke, *History of Germany in the 19th Century*, translated by E. and C. Paul (7 vols., London, 1915–19). The relevant chapters of the *Cambridge Modern History* (vol. x, ch. 11; vol. xi, chs. 3, 6, 7, 15, 16, 21) should also be consulted.

2. Of the great mass of German works, two of the most important are: H. von Sybel, *Die Begründung des deutschen Reiches durch Wilhelm I* (7 vols. Munich and Berlin, 1901–8), and E. Marcks, *Der Aufstieg des Reiches* (2 vols., Stuttgart, 1936).

3. A work written from the Austrian point of view is H. von Srbik, *Deutsche Einheit* (2 vols. Munich, 1935), and for the Austrian history of the period generally one of the best works is A. J. P. Taylor, *The Habsburg Monarchy, 1815–1918* (London, 1941).

4. For the revolutions of 1848 and their antecedents the English reader is fortunate to have V. Valentin, *1848, Chapters in German History* (London, 1940), which is an abbreviated translation of the

same author's famous two-volume history, *Geschichte der deutschen Revolution, 1848–9* (Berlin, 1930–1). In a lighter, but no less erudite vein there is L. B. Namier, *1848: The Revolution of the Intellectuals* (Oxford, 1944).

5. The diplomatic history of the seventy years following the outbreak of the revolutions is dealt with lucidly in A. J. P. Taylor, *The Struggle for Mastery in Europe, 1848–1918* (Oxford, 1954).

6. Part of a classic study of the last stages in the Austro-Prussian struggle for hegemony in Germany is to be found in H. Friedjung, *The Struggle for Supremacy in Germany, 1859–1866*, translated by A. J. P. Taylor and W. L. McElwee (London, 1935).

7. On Bismarck one of the best introductory studies in English is E. Eyck, *Bismarck and the German Empire* (London, 1950), which summarizes the salient points of the same author's great three-volume study of Bismarck published at Zurich between 1941 and 1944. Other excellent biographical works are A. J. P. Taylor, *Bismarck, The Man and the Statesman* (London, 1955), C. G. Robertson, *Bismarck* (London, 1918) and Sir J. W. Headlam-Morley, *Bismarck* (New York, 1900).

8. In German a brief but valuable study for the reader requiring something less comprehensive than Eyck's major biography is E. Marcks, *Otto von Bismarck* (Stuttgart and Berlin, 1915), while, on the military side, the four-part chapter 8 ('Moltke und Bismarck—Strategie und Politik') of G. Ritter, *Staatskunst und Kriegshandwerk*, to which reference is made above, is extremely useful.

9. Bismarck's speeches are a source of first-class importance and were edited by H. Kohl in *Die politischen Reden des Fürsten Bismarcks* (17 vols. Stuttgart, 1892–1904). The first two volumes of Bismarck's *Gedanken und Erinnerungen* are available in English in *Bismarck, his Reflections and Reminiscences*, translated by A. J. Butler (2 vols. London, 1898); the third volume has been translated by A. B. Miall (London, 1920).

10. Surveys of German economic development include: Sir J. H. Clapham, *The Economic Development of France and Germany* (3rd ed. Cambridge, 1928), and A. S. von Waltershausen, *Deutsche Wirtschaftsgeschichte, 1815–1914* (Jena, 1923). For special economic topics the following may be consulted: W. O. Henderson, *The Zollverein* (Cambridge, 1939); P. Benaerts, *Les Origines de la Grande Industrie Allemande* (Paris, 1933); M. E. Hirst, *Life of Friedrich List* (London, 1909); and H. C. M. Wendel, *The Evolution of Industrial Freedom in Prussia, 1845–9* (New York, 1921).

1871–1918

1. Bismarck's *Reminiscences* and *Speeches* have already been referred to, as have the biographies of Eyck, Taylor and others, which are equally useful for the later period. The memoirs of two of Bismarck's successors have also been published in English: Hohenlohe, *Memoirs*, translated by G. W. Crystal (2 vols. London, 1906); Bülow, *Memoirs*, translated by F. A. Voigt (London, 1931). Even more informative are the volumes of *Holstein Papers*, containing the memoirs, diaries and correspondence of Friedrich von Holstein, *Vortragender Rat* in the Political Department of the German Foreign Ministry from 1878–1906, edited by Norman Rich and M. H. Fisher (Cambridge, 1955, 1957).

2. For the diplomatic history of the period A. J. P. Taylor's *The Struggle for Mastery in Europe* (see above) is invaluable.

3. A useful general sketch of modern Germany is to be found in G.P. Gooch, *Germany* (London, 1926). W. H. Dawson's *The German Empire* (2 vols. London, 1919) remains a standard work.

4. The role of Wilhelm II is dealt with biographically in Joachim von Kürenberg, *The Kaiser: a Life of Wilhelm II, last Emperor of Germany*, translated by H. T. Russell and Herta Hagen (London, 1954). A full scholarly account of the period following the fall of Bismarck is to be found in Erich Eyck, *Das Persönliche Regiment Wilhelms II, Politische Geschichte des deutschen Kaiserreiches von 1890 bis 1914* (Zurich, 1948).

5. For German foreign policy from 1871 to 1914 E. Brandenburg's *From Bismarck to the World War*, translated by A. E. Adams (Oxford, 1927) is still very useful. Another good survey, with emphasis on domestic history, is Johannes Ziekursch, *Politische Geschichte des neuen deutschen Kaiserreiches* (3 vols. Frankfurt, 1927–32), while for the development of the political parties L. Bergsträsser, *Geschichte der politischen Parteien* (9th ed. Munich, 1955) has yet to be surpassed.

6. In addition to the larger official histories of the War of 1914–18 a good outline is that by C. R. M. F. Cruttwell, *A History of the Great War, 1914–18* (Oxford, 1936). The inner development of Germany during the war is dealt with by A. Rosenberg, *The Birth of the German Republic*, translated by I. F. D. Morrow (London, 1931).

7. The economic history of Germany after 1871 is dealt with in the following works: Thorstein Veblen, *Imperial Germany and the Industrial Revolution* (New York, 1939), Sir J. H. Clapham, *The Economic Development of France and Germany* (3rd ed. Cambridge, 1928), W. H. Dawson, *The Evolution of Modern Germany* (London, 1911);

BIBLIOGRAPHICAL NOTE

W. F. Bruck, *Social and Economic History of Germany from Wilhelm II to Hitler* (Cardiff, 1938).
The following works deal with more specialized topics: M. E. Townsend, *The Rise and Fall of Germany's Colonial Empire, 1884–1918* (New York, 1930); A. J. P. Taylor, *Germany's First Bid for Colonies, 1884–1885* (London, 1938); W. A. Aydelotte, *Bismarck and British Colonial Policy, the Problem of South West Africa* (Philadelphia, 1937).

1918–39

A. 1918–33

1. A. Rosenberg, *History of the German Republic*, translated by I. F. D. Morrow and L. M. Sieveking (London, 1936) can usefully be compared and contrasted with the able analysis, from a different angle, by R. T. Clark, *The Fall of the German Republic* (London, 1935).

2. Godfrey Scheele, *The Weimar Republic. Overture to the Third Reich* (London, 1944), a sound general study with good chapters on economic problems and development, may be supplemented by the more detailed and up-to-date *Geschichte der Weimarer Republik* by Erich Eyck (2 vols. Zurich and Stuttgart, 1956) which uses source material which has come to light since the Second World War. For the later years of the Weimar Republic, beginning with the election of Hindenburg to the Presidency, chs. 6 to 8 of Walter Görlitz, *Hindenburg: Ein Lebensbild* (Bonn, 1953) are particularly useful, as are the latter chapers of J. W. Wheeler-Bennett, *Hindenburg, the Wooden Titan* (London, 1936).

3. An authoritative and detailed account of German secret rearmament during the Weimar period is to be found in J. W. Wheeler-Bennett, *The Nemesis of Power, The German Army in Politics* (London, 1953), Part 1, which may be supplemented by the valuable documentary material in O. E. Schüddekopf, *Das Heer und Die Republik, Quellen zur Politik der Reichswehrführung, 1918 bis 1933* (Hanover, 1955). Seeckt's role is dealt with in chs. ix and x of Walter Görlitz, *The German General Staff, Its History and Structure, 1657–1945* (London, 1953), and there is much new information about Stresemann's attitude in Hans W. Gatzke, *Stresemann and the Rearmament of Germany* (Baltimore, 1954).

4. J. W. Wheeler-Bennett, *The Nemesis of Power* (see above) also covers collaboration between the Weimar Republic and the Soviet Union, an autobiographical account of which, by a former official of the German Embassy in Moscow, is also to be found in Gustav Hilger and Alfred G. Meyer, *The Incompatible Allies, A Memoir-History of*

242

German-Soviet Relations, 1918–1941 (New York, 1953). Another survey, based upon published Russian sources, as well as on official German records, is Lionel Kochan, *Russia and the Weimar Republic* (London, 1954).

B. 1933–9

1. For Hitler and National Socialism the best study in English is A. Bullock, *Hitler, A Study in Tyranny* (London, 1952), which may be supplemented by Hitler's *Mein Kampf*, translated by J. Murphy (London, 1939) and *Hitler's Speeches*, translated and annotated by N. H. Baynes (London and Oxford, 1942). *The Third Reich* (London, 1955), an international symposium on Fascism and Nazism prepared with the assistance of U.N.E.S.C.O., is particularly useful on the intellectual origins of National Socialism.

2. Earlier works on National Socialist Germany which are still of value include S. H. Roberts, *The House that Hitler Built* (London, 1937), F. Neumann, *Behemoth* (London, 1942) and W. E. Dodd, *Ambassador Dodd's Diaries, 1933–38* (London, 1941).

1939–45

1. While the definitive history of the Second World War has still to be written, mention should be made of three short histories Cyril Falls, *The Second World War* (London, 1948), Major-General J. F. C. Fuller, *The Second World War, 1939–45* (London, 1948), and 'Strategicus' (H. C. O'Neill), *A Short History of the Second World War* (London, 1950). Though mainly military histories, these three works cover in part the diplomatic background to the war.

2. The best account of Hitler's development during the war is to be found in A. Bullock, *Hitler, A Study in Tyranny*, to which reference has been made above. There is as yet no complete study of Hitler's direction of the war. General Halder's *Hitler as War Lord* (London, 1950), though based upon personal knowledge acquired while acting as Army Chief of Staff, is strongly influenced by Hitler's dismissal of the author in 1942. F. H. Hinsley, *Hitler's Strategy* (Cambridge, 1951) gives a good picture of Hitler's Atlantic and Mediterranean strategy, and is based on the German Admiralty archives, but hardly touches the war in the east. Most of the surviving German military leaders have published their memoirs, which should be read with caution. Mention should also be made of the captured records of Hitler's military conferences, published in Felix Gilbert (ed.), *Hitler Directs his War* (New York, 1951). A valuable study of how far

treachery played a part in promoting early German military successes, and a useful corrective of many popular misconceptions, is L. de Jong, *The German Fifth Column in the Second World War*, translated from the Dutch by C. M. Geyl (London, 1956).

3. Useful individual studies of aspects of German foreign policy during the war are contained in E. Wiskemann, *The Rome-Berlin Axis* (London, 1949), G. L. Weinberg, *German-Soviet Relations, 1939–1941* (Leyden, 1954), H. L. Trefousse, *Germany and American Neutrality* (New York, 1952). F. C. Jones, *Japan's New Order in Asia* (London, 1954) contains valuable chapters on German policy in the Far East from 1937 onwards. See also W. L. Langer and F. C. Gleeson, *The Struggle for Isolation, 1937–1940* (New York, 1952), and the *Undeclared War, 1940–41* (New York, 1953). German relations with Spain are covered in H. Feis, *The Spanish Story* (New York, 1948).

4. A useful account of internal developments in Germany is to be found in C. J. Child, 'The Political Structure of Hitler's Europe' in The Royal Institute of International Affairs, *Survey of International Affairs, 1939–46, Hitler's Europe* (London, 1954). Works on the German opposition to Hitler are already legion. Gerhard Ritter, *Carl Goerdeler und die deutsche Widerstandsbewegung* (Stuttgart, 1955) gives a particularly well balanced, yet sympathetic, account.

5. On the German administration of occupied Europe see also R. Lemkin, *Axis Rule in Occupied Europe* (Washington, 1944), and A. Dallin, *German Rule in Russia, 1941–1945: A Study of Occupation Policy* (London, 1957).

6. The role of the Army in German wartime politics and its connection with the opposition to Hitler is authoritatively considered in the later chapters of J. W. Wheeler-Bennett, *The Nemesis of Power*, to which reference has been made above.

7. On the German treatment of the Jews see Gerald Reitlinger, *The Final Solution* (London, 1953). The same author's *The S.S.: Alibi of a Nation, 1922–1945* (London, 1956) provides an authoritative account of the macabre instrument of Hitler's extermination policies. On the concentration camps see also Eugen Kogon, *The Theory and Practice of Hell* (London, 1950) and A. Mitscherlich and F. M. Mielke, *Doctors of Infamy* (New York, 1949).

8. The years of German defeat are best studied in Chester Wilmot, *The Struggle for Europe* (London, 1952). One of the best accounts of the disintegration of the Nazi leadership under the impact of defeat is H. R. Trevor Roper, *The Last Days of Hitler* (London, 1950).

INDEX

INDEX